Christian Understandings of Christ

The Historical Trajectory

David H. Jensen

CHRISTIAN UNDERSTANDINGS OF CHRIST

The Historical Trajectory

Cover image: © iStock / enjoynz; Textured Paint background

Cover design: Alisha Lofgren

Paperback ISBN: 978-1-4514-8276-8

eBook ISBN: 978-1-5064-5398-9

The paper used in this publication meets the minimum requirements of American National Standard for Information Sciences — Permanence of Paper for Printed Library Materials, ANSI Z329.48-1984.

Manufactured in the U.S.A.

This book was produced using Pressbooks.com, and PDF rendering was done by PrinceXML.

Christian Understandings of Christ

For Peter Hodgson and Sallie McFague

Contents

Preface: Jesus, Two Thousand Years Later

Jesus Christ stands at the center of Christian faith. Without him, there would be no Christian faith. A little more than two thousand years ago, a man who apprenticed as a carpenter became an itinerant preacher, proclaimed the reign of God, healed persons racked by various ailments, spent much time breaking bread, and taught in parables. He gathered a band of disciples who followed him from place to place, mostly insignificant locales in Galilee. The last days of his ministry brought him to Jerusalem and its environs, where he was perceived as a threat. There he was arrested, placed on a hastily arranged trial, and condemned to death by the Roman authorities. By the time of his crucifixion, his followers—with the notable exception of a few women—had abandoned him. After this ignominious death, his body was placed in a tomb. The women who had not abandoned him visit the tomb a few days later to tend to his body. When they arrived at the grave, they were told that their teacher had risen from the dead. Confronted with this news, they fled the tomb in fear and amazement. Others eventually experienced visions and encounters with the risen Christ. Such is the skeleton of events surrounding Jesus as presented in the New Testament, a mixture of the ordinary and extraordinary. If the events surrounding the life of this itinerant preacher initially attracted a few, mostly from the house of Israel, succeeding centuries yielded phenomenal growth, such that now those who profess to follow Jesus number more than two billion.

The church looks to Jesus as its foundation. Its existence is continuous with the ministry that began with a carpenter from Galilee. Interpreting Jesus, then, is fundamental to Christian faith. Nearly everything that Christians say, do, and believe in some way needs to reflect the memory of who Jesus was and what he did. Over the centuries, millions upon millions have reflected, in their lives and their words, on the life of this One who lived two thousand years ago. And these interpretations have varied. Indeed, the life of Jesus has proved so significant to history that not only Christians have developed portrayals and interpretations of him. This book offers one attempt at surveying the centuries of interpretation of Jesus and how that interpretation matters for remembering Jesus today. In theological terms, this book offers a survey of the church's Christology (its understanding of Jesus's person and work) and its soteriology (its understanding of salvation in Christ). Because it is a survey, the volume is incomplete. It would be nearly impossible to offer a comprehensive survey of the varied portrayals of Jesus, especially in a readable space. Because of these limitations, I have had to make choices. I have identified highlights within that history, marking major movements and significant shifts in the church's interpretation of Jesus over time. I have tried to offer snapshots of different eras and different regions of the globe. But I easily could have included four times as many voices. Some things fell to the cutting room floor, and there are significant gaps (such as contemporary Orthodox theology). The result is a survey that invariably reflects some of my own ecclesial and social location as a white, male, mainline Protestant. But I have also tried, especially in the concluding chapters, to give some attention to the increasingly global phenomenon that is the ongoing interpretation of Jesus. Clearly, the story of Jesus belongs to no one tradition alone. That story doesn't even belong to the church.

The intent of this survey, moreover, is not simply to record history, or to state what others have said *about* Jesus. Throughout the book, I offer reflections, as words of appreciation and critique, about how the witness of the past informs our portrayal of Jesus today. The book concludes with some sketches on how this work might continue. I remain more convinced than ever that no interpretation of Jesus emerges in a vacuum. Even the portraits of Jesus that criticize earlier versions rely on previous history. They stand on the shoulders of those who have gone before them. In order to interpret Jesus faithfully today, we rely on others, most of whom are long dead. This is part of what it means to be a part of a living tradition, a great cloud of witnesses. And so we learn from, absorb, criticize, and laugh at those who have preceded us, knowing that our progeny will no doubt do the same. Each generation needs to listen to the voices that have preceded it in order to interpret Jesus on its own terms; in the process even those "own terms" will change. Our interpretations of Jesus are invariably affected by our contexts, cultures, and interests; but at the same time Jesus shakes up and transforms those contexts, cultures, and interests. We shape portraits of Jesus as they also shape us.

I began writing this book at almost the same time I began my tenure as academic dean at Austin Seminary. I quickly learned that the life of an administrator is usually not conducive to a book project. Months went by when nothing happened on the project. Summers were better, but still often occupied with many other tasks that were foreign to me before serving as dean. Over four years, I owe many people thanks: to Alison Riemersma for amazing proofreading and editing under very tight deadlines; to Denis Janz, for inviting me to be a part of this series and for his keen editorial eye; to Fortress Press, for almost endless patience as I completed the book; to Ted Wardlaw, Austin Seminary president, and my faculty colleagues for understanding my need to almost cloister myself during the last month of the project; to all my students, who have responded to many of these reflections in classroom contexts; and, above all, to Molly, Grace, and Finn: they know the countless reasons why.

Throughout my life, I have been blessed with outstanding teachers. Two stand out in my theological education: Peter Hodgson and Sallie McFague. Over the course of this project, I found myself turning to notes I had written in their courses more than two decades ago. The words of these two teachers have stayed with me over many, many years. They have doubtless shaped my interpretation of the history of Christology, the portrayal of the One whose disciples called him "teacher." I dedicate this book to two theologians who will always remain my teachers.

1

New Testament Portrayals of Jesus

Scripture is the foundational resource for the church's understandings of Jesus. The reasons for this foundation are many: First, outside of the writings that eventually became the New Testament, there are hardly any first-century (or early second-century) writings that mention Jesus. Those that do, moreover, are almost exclusively Christian writings. If Jesus of Nazareth generated attention, it was chiefly among those who were captivated by the movement that gathered around him. The church's Christology, accordingly, looks to Scripture because it contains the most ancient witness about Jesus. Second, the church has turned to Scripture because much of the remainder of early writing about Jesus was eventually deemed deficient. Though this chapter explores some of the noncanonical or apocryphal portrayals of Jesus, the interpretations of Jesus that have had the most enduring impact come from the New Testament. Third, the church has turned to Scripture because among its varied traditions, the Bible constitutes some degree of authority. Throughout much of its history, the church has judged whether a Christology is sufficient or insufficient, in part, in regard to how it corresponds with a strand (or strands) of the New Testament. It is therefore not an exaggeration to say that for most Christian communities, Christology begins with Scripture.

Yet when we turn to the New Testament, we encounter not a singular portrayal of Jesus, but astonishing diversity. There is not merely one Christology in Scripture against which all others are judged, but multiple Christologies. From the outset, Jesus has evoked multiple interpretations. This is witnessed in the fact that there are four Gospels, not one: a Gospel "according to" Mark, Luke, and so on. But it is also witnessed in the texture of the literature that composes the New Testament: letters, sermons, and an apocalypse. Jesus appears on nearly every page of this diverse collection of writings; as the writers of the New Testament address different themes, the Jesus who appears on these pages gets refracted in different ways. Each writing stresses different emphases that get amplified throughout the centuries that follow. Amid this diversity, however, are some (mostly) common chords: (1) a figure who reflects, reinterprets, argues with, and advocates for various Jewish traditions; (2) a figure whose death represents a culminating sacrifice; (3) a figure who is not only a prophet to his people at a certain time but also a cosmic, resurrected redeemer who offers salvation to the world, for all time. Not all of these themes are present in each layer of New Testament writing, but together they constitute some of the foundation of subsequent christological reflection.

In this chapter, I reflect on these themes (and others) by considering how varied New Testament authors portray Jesus.

The chapter proceeds somewhat chronologically rather than thematically. In what follows, I will examine: (1) Paul; (2) the Synoptic Gospels; (3) the Gospel according to John; (4) some of the other letters of the New Testament; (5) Revelation; and, (6) selected noncanonical treatments of Jesus. The chapter concludes by considering some issues that this early witness to Jesus does *not* address in much fullness. This survey of the earliest witness to Jesus thus reveals much about the early church's attention and what it considered most significant in confessing Jesus as Lord.

Paul's Jesus

Most biblical scholars agree that the earliest writings in the New Testament come from the hand of Paul, with 1 Thessalonians constituting the oldest of Paul's authentic letters. Ancient as these letters are, it is important to note that they come from the hand of a person who, presumably, never met Jesus of Nazareth (see 1 Cor 15:8). The earliest writings of the New Testament, therefore, come not from an eyewitness, but from one who is heir to various traditions surrounding Jesus, and who most certainly propagated many of those traditions in a new vein, as evangelist to the gentiles. If the earliest followers of Jesus (such as Paul) were all Jews, the earliest writings of the New Testament contain the impetus to make the Jesus movement known in the gentile world. In Paul, therefore, we see a Jew arguing for the need for non-Jews to come and follow Jesus without becoming Jewish themselves. From the outset, this presents significant challenges for subsequent interpretation of Jesus: Does Paul's articulation of Jesus to non-Jews effectively distance Jesus from his own context? Or does it open that context to those who are not formed by it? The way that the church has wrestled with Paul's legacy reveals much: from voices that argue for supersession, or the replacement of God's covenant with Israel with a new covenant meant for the whole world in Jesus Christ; to others who consider what happens in Jesus to be an expansion of the one covenant with Israel, in whom the nations are included; to others who argue for two distinct covenants, one for Israel, another for the nations. From the outset, the question of how to interpret Jesus, and how the church is to interpret Israel, are bound closely together.[1]

Who is Jesus for Paul? In answering that question, it is surprising what Paul does *not* stress. Most contemporary approaches to understanding a person's character or legacy resort to *biography*: the events and details of a person's life help reveal who that person was. But Paul almost never refers to Jesus's life. Nowhere in his letters do readers encounter a teaching of Jesus; nowhere do we glimpse a healing; nowhere an excerpt of Jesus's itinerant preaching. Paul talks extensively of Jesus, of course, but does not resort to biographical detail. This lack of traditions surrounding the life of Jesus might be due to several factors: (1) Paul does not have access to many of the traditions about Jesus's life; (2) he had access to those traditions but did not consider them important enough to enumerate in his letters; or (3) he assumes his audience knows these traditions as background for his interpretations of Jesus to the gentiles. Any of these factors is possible, but it is important to note that Paul does not have much to say about Jesus's life, with one exception: Jesus's words and actions in the Last Supper (1 Cor 11:23–25). Here Paul refers to things that Jesus did, in words that have echoed throughout the church's celebration of the Eucharist. This recognition, in itself, is significant. When Paul refers to this tradition about the life of Jesus, he connects it directly to liturgical actions in the Christian church: "For as often as you eat this bread and drink the cup, you proclaim the Lord's death until he comes" (v. 26).

1 Thessalonians

Paul's earliest writing presents a fairly sparse, yet rich, presentation of Jesus. He is the one who died, was raised from the dead, and will come again. This affirmation, too, is redolent with the church's liturgical practice, a phrase that echoes down to the present whenever churches celebrate the Lord's Supper. "For since we believe that Jesus died and rose again, even so, through Jesus, God will bring with him those who have died" (1 Thess 4:14). Much of this letter contains exhortation and encouragement to the congregation in Thessalonica: leading a life worthy of God, honoring and loving each other, maintaining standards of holiness. These moral standards are essential for Paul because the return of Christ is imminent. The portrayal of Christ throughout the letter is therefore eschatological: focused on the cosmic Christ who comes from the heavens. Here is perhaps the most memorable of these portrayals: "For the Lord himself, with a cry of command, with the archangel's call and with the sound of God's trumpet, will descend from heaven, and the dead in Christ will rise first. Then we who are alive, who are left, will be caught up in the clouds together with them to meet the Lord in the air; and so we will be with the Lord forever" (4:16–17). Here, in one of the oldest strands of writing about Jesus, is not a memory of some aspect of Jesus's earthly ministry, but anticipation of his triumphal return, raising the dead, and gathering the faithful to himself. In vivid imagery, touching sight and sound, the oldest portrayal of Jesus in Scripture presents a *future* Jesus. Such imagery has given birth to centuries of art and music: from Handel's *Messiah* to William Blake's apocalyptic paintings and Johnny Cash's "The Man Comes Around."

This future return is imminent, however. Those who are still alive are to remain awake and prepared, since the "day of the Lord will come like a thief in the night" (5:2). Paul assumes the significance of Jesus's death for salvation ("For God has destined us not for wrath but for obtaining salvation through our Lord Jesus Christ, who died for us," 5:9–10), but does not explain *how* that death is significant. Unlike later letters, where the cross plays a significant role, in 1 Thessalonians, the cross is not even mentioned. Hope in Christ lies not primarily in something that happened in the past, but in the advent of Christ that will happen swiftly and surely. Paul's earliest Christology, therefore, is thoroughly eschatological. There are more details about what is yet to come than what has already occurred in Christ.

Philippians

The crucifixion becomes more prominent in subsequent letters. In Philippians (a letter that is unique in Paul's correspondence, since it addresses not a controversy, but friendship between Paul and the congregation), the cross appears at the center of the letter, in what is likely an early (pre-Pauline) piece of Christian liturgy. This Christ hymn, which Paul quotes in the context of exhorting the congregation, has become one of the most familiar strands of Paul's corpus. The hymn offers a short confession of faith, using the pattern of Christ's humiliation and exaltation. Jesus's life, death, and resurrection follow a pattern of descent and ascent. Though the hymn does not claim Christ's preexistence, it does name him as being "in the form of God." Christ is the One equal with God, who relinquished whatever status or privilege that might entail, and

> emptied himself,
> taking the form of a slave,
> being born in human likeness. (Phil 2:6)

In comparatively few words, this hymn interprets the incarnation as an act of divine self-giving. God's descent in Christ begins with incarnation, and continues in death. This language underscores the gulf, or the distance, between humanity and divinity that is bridged in Jesus. It is both cosmic in depicting Christ's descent from heaven into human flesh, and it is ethical in depicting the pattern of Jesus's earthly life, which culminates in the cross. The descent is not simply from one realm into another, but in the pattern of Jesus' obedience

> to the point of death—
> even death on a cross. (v. 8)

The hymn employs the jarring language of slavery, and thereby offers a distinct vision of God, who is revealed not initially in glory, but in humility, obedience, and death. In the incarnation, God chooses what is lowliest—a slave—to reveal the fullness of God's life for the world. The cross, therefore, stands at the center of the hymn. It is the "lowest" point of descent, a particularly humiliating death (since it is displayed publicly as a spectacle) reserved for criminals and the dregs of society. And it is because of this lowliness that God exalts Christ.

From this nadir, the exaltation begins. Christ's resurrection is interpreted as giving Christ a "name that is above every name" (v. 9). The self-emptying of God in Christ is followed by fullness. The humiliation is not an end in itself, but a means to fuller life. This is what differentiates this interpretation of incarnation and death from sheer masochism. The story does not end in a suffering death, but in vindication by God, and the fullness of the world's life. The hymn ends with a resounding chorus, echoed in heaven, on earth, and under the earth, where all confess Christ as Lord (vv. 10–11). What began "in heaven" now echoes throughout the cosmos. There is triumph in this exaltation, but it is not the triumph of a crusade. Christ is the one who is exalted because of his humiliation. The power at the center of the incarnation is not power over others, but the willingness to relinquish status, privilege, and even life for the sake of others.

The primary thrust of this Christ hymn, then, is not an atonement theory. The hymn does not describe why Christ's death was necessary, how it addresses sin, or even spell out the benefits of Christ's crucifixion and resurrection. The incarnation is not a puzzle to be solved, but a model for the Christian life. This early Christology, in other words, is intensely practical. The preface to the hymn gives the appropriate context: "Let each of you look not to your own interests, but to the interests of others. Let the same mind be in you that was in Christ Jesus" (vv. 4–5). In this pattern of humiliation and exaltation, Jesus reveals the character of God. In his pattern of life, death, and resurrection is impetus for living for and with others. Many subsequent Christologies in the tradition might be labeled triumphalist in that they argue for the superiority of Christ over others. The stunning thing about this Philippian vision of triumph is that it is predicated on self-giving, for the sake of others. Jesus, the man for others, the divine self-giver, invites those who follow him into an analogous way of life. This Christology, in the end, is primarily focused on discipleship: In his descent and ascent, Christ shows us the way to live fully. These are undoubtedly good questions to ask nearly every Christology that follows: How does our confession of Christ promote the fullness of life in Christ? How does it turn our attention to others? How does it indicate sacrifice and fullness? Though this early Christology is not exhaustive, it offers tantalizing clues for how one might keep all of these questions in mind. Confession of Christ and regard of others, in short, are always bound together.

Galatians

Paul is pivotal in supplying the church with some of its most significant christological language in connection with salvation. Though he is hardly systematic in laying out a soteriology, the echoes of his language have reverberated in the centuries since, as the church has interpreted Jesus as Savior. With Paul, the church begins to reflect on *how* Christ saves humanity. As missionary to the gentiles, Paul devotes much of his attention to the connections between Jesus, the people Israel, and the (gentile) church. For him, the language of "justification" or "reckoned as righteous" holds center stage in these relationships. In Galatians, Paul argues that gentile converts to the Christian church must not be required to observe Jewish law. This is the case, for Paul, because "a person is justified not by the works of the law but through faith in Jesus Christ" (Gal 2:16). The language here is notoriously tricky. Paul can be read in two ways here: We are counted as righteous by faith *in* Christ; or, alternatively, by the faith *of* Christ. In the first reading, the believer is counted as righteous because of some act of trust that the believer makes; in the second reading, the believer is counted as righteous (or justified) because of Christ's faithfulness to God. Both readings, however, emphasize a transfer of something that was previously alien to us (righteousness) that is tied directly to the effects of Christ's life, death, and resurrection. The language is explicitly judicial or forensic, evoking a process whereby the guilty is pronounced *as* righteous. If sin is what makes the person guilty, the faith of Christ (or faith in Christ) is what causes us to be *counted* as righteous. Centuries of theological reflection and argument have issued forth from this vocabulary. In either reading, however, salvation begins with the work of Christ for humanity.

In this view of justification, Paul emphasizes the believer's participation in Christ. Strains of mystical theologies throughout the centuries have been sustained by Paul's claim, "For through the law I died to the law, so that I might live to God. I have been crucified with Christ; and it is no longer I who live, but it is Christ who lives in me. And the life I now live in the flesh I live by faith in the Son of God, who loved me and gave himself for me" (2:19–20). There is here a personalization of Christology. What happens to Christ also happens to the believer. Crucifixion and resurrection are not once-and-for-all-time events, but ongoing realities to those who are "righteoused" by Christ. Dying and rising with Christ constitute the pattern of discipleship. If the judicial imagery of justification emphasizes an "external" righteousness, this participatory language also speaks to inner transformation, as our life takes a more Christoform shape.

Some interpretations of Paul, particularly in the wake of Luther, but also present in early church figures (such as Marcion), tend to polarize "faith" and "law." In extreme versions, this has led to denigration of the law as something that condemns or traps humanity. Such interpretations feed views of Christian supersessionism: that the laws of Jewish tradition prior to Christ are overturned with the coming of Jesus. In this view, the "new" covenant of Jesus replaces the "old" Jewish laws. Such interpretations overlook the complex and interrelated nature of faith and law in Paul. Paul certainly claims that before faith, "we were imprisoned and guarded under the law" (3:23). His main point in tracing the relationship of faith and law is not to abrogate the law, but to refuse to render law binding for the gentile members of the church. His motivation, at least in part, is to point to the new community that is being built in the church, a community where the hard-and-fast distinctions that divide people begin to wash away. Very soon after he mentions the law as something that imprisons and guards, Paul notes: "There is no longer Jew or Greek, there is no longer slave or free, there is no longer male and female; for all of you are one in Christ Jesus. And if you belong to Christ, then you are Abraham's offspring, heirs according to the promise" (3:28–29). Paul is hardly consistent in his remarks on the law: On the one hand, he upholds keeping the commandments (see 5:14, "For the whole law is summed up in a single commandment, 'You shall love your neighbor as yourself'"). On the other hand, he rejects the law as binding on all members of the new community (such as mandating circumcision, "For in Christ Jesus neither circumcision nor uncircumcision counts for anything; the only thing that counts is faith working through love," 5:6). According to E. P. Sanders, Paul rejects "the aspects of the law which were against his own mission, those which separated Jew from Gentile in the people of God." His approach to the law is somewhat ad hoc, subject to revision and redefinition.[2] But in the end, all are saved through Jesus Christ, salvation that unites Jew and gentile in the community that God is building in the church. But Christ himself brings a kind of "new law" of bearing each other's burdens in community (see 6:2). If one is looking for absolute consistency in Paul's understanding between law and faith, one will not find it. Christologically speaking, however, Paul is clear: Christ is the fulfillment of the law, who does not render all aspects of law irrelevant, but removes the law as a barrier between Jew and gentile in the reconciled people of God.

1 Corinthians

The tensions and interrelationship between law and faith gain further attention in Paul's subsequent letters (particularly Romans and 1 Corinthians). But other christological themes gain greater prominence. In 1 Corinthians, the resurrection emerges as particularly significant. Here is the only portion of Paul's correspondence that offers any biographical detail about Jesus (and witnesses to the risen Christ) that is common to the gospels. In chapter 15, Paul notes Christ's death for sin, his burial, his being raised on the third day "in accordance with the scriptures," and his appearance to the disciples, apostles, and Paul himself (1 Cor 15:7). The resurrection, in Paul's mind, is not something that merely happens to Jesus; it is also something that happens to us, as we participate in the life God gives to the world in Jesus's resurrection. As death comes through one human being, resurrection comes "through a human being; for as all die in Adam, so all will be made alive in Christ" (vv. 21–22). The resurrection is the pivot of Christian hope; without it, the proclamation of Christian faith is "in vain" (v. 14). Christ's resurrection heralds the transformation of all things, where the perishable puts on what is imperishable, mortality puts on immortality (vv. 53–54). Indeed, there are hints of cosmic transformation in this understanding of resurrection. Though Paul pays most attention to the nature of the human resurrected body, the resurrection of Christ also touches the glory of sun, moon, and stars (v. 41). Though it would be an exaggeration to deem this an ecological view of the resurrection, it is clear that Paul's understanding of resurrection in Christ is also a renewal of all creation. The risen Christ brings new life to the cosmos. Like Paul's earlier writings in 1 Thessalonians, this passage steers Christology toward eschatology. Indeed, the end times are not merely something that the cosmos awaits in the days ahead; these times have already begun in the resurrection: an event that touches the life of every person, bird, fish, and star.

Romans

Paul's lengthiest New Testament correspondence contains germs of christological material already discussed: eschatology (Rom 8:18–30), the relationship between faith and law (7:7–13), and the resurrection (6:5–11). But it also amplifies themes of Christ's reconciling death, a note that has resounded throughout the centuries. For Paul, Jesus's death accomplishes a reuniting of God and humanity, effectively healing a relationship that sin had broken. Paul's use of "reconcile" (*katallasso*) is analogous to "justify" (his more common term for describing the relation between Christ and the work of salvation), but it carries more relational freight. If justification describes salvation in forensic terms, reconciliation captures the healing that is brought about because of the righteousness of Christ. For Paul, this healing is possible through Christ's death. Again, Paul is hardly systematic and the terms are fluid:

> But God proves his love for us in that while we still were sinners Christ died for us. Much more surely then, now that we have been justified by his blood, will we be saved through him from the wrath of God. For if while we were enemies, we were

> reconciled to God through the death of his Son, much more surely, having been reconciled, will we be saved by his life. But more than that, we even boast in God through our Lord Jesus Christ, through whom we have now received reconciliation. (5:8–11)

Here reconciliation, salvation, and justification blur together: not as distinct "stages," as much later theology develops it, but as different images capturing the same dynamic: what Christ accomplishes in his death. Paul lays the foundational vocabulary for multiple theologies that emerge in his wake. Yet because of Paul, there is no escaping the atoning significance of the cross. The death of this One makes all the difference. His language, of course, draws on prior notions of sacrifice within Jewish tradition. Sacrifice, in Jewish tradition, as the Hebrew word suggests (*qārbān*) means to "draw near." Sacrifice is done not primarily to appease a distant deity, but so that we might enter into closer relationship with the living God. In Christ's sacrifice for us, even enemies are drawn near.

As in other areas of his correspondence (1 Cor 15), Paul makes use of an Adam/Christ typology to describe this reconciliation: through Adam came sin and death; through Christ's death came justification and life. "For if the many died through the one man's trespass, much more surely have the grace of God and the free gift in the grace of the one man, Jesus Christ, abounded for the many" (Rom 5:15). Later, Paul states a contrast between Adam, whose trespass leads to "condemnation for all" and Christ, whose "act of righteousness leads to justification and life for all" (v. 18). Two things are implicit here: (1) Adam and Christ stand as archetypes for sin and reconciliation; (2) both inaugurate, through their actions, effects that those who stand in their wake partake in. In other words, humanity is rendered sinful through Adam and reconciled through Christ.

If this typology tends to externalize sin and salvation, by making both the consequence of actions that precede the initiative of each person who stands in Adam and Christ's wake, the subsequent section of Romans internalizes the working of salvation in Christ. Here Paul makes use of baptism imagery. Reconciliation doesn't simply happen to us; rather, we participate in reconciliation through baptism, which is immersion in the death and resurrection of Christ. Paul merges crucifixion and resurrection imagery with the life of the believer: "We know that our old self was crucified with him so that the body of sin might be destroyed" (6:6). The resurrection, likewise, does not simply happen to Jesus, but to us as well: "Just as Christ was raised from the dead by the glory of the Father, so we too might walk in newness of life" (v. 4). To underscore that this is not a passive reception, Paul also exhorts his readers to "present yourselves to God as those who have been brought from death to life, and present your members to God as instruments of righteousness" (v. 13). Those who participate in the resurrection of Christ live out of a new reality, where sin no longer has dominion. Resurrection life is the way of discipleship.

In Paul's proto-Christology, we have the strands of many of the most significant themes that animate the life and piety of the later church: justification, reconciliation, crucifixion, resurrection, salvation. Though none of these themes receives elaborate treatment, the images that Paul bequeaths the church are foundational for what follows. What Paul misses, of course, are threads that depict the life and teachings of Jesus. For those strands, we turn to the Gospels.

Jesus in the Synoptic Gospels

The first three books that occur in the New Testament are commonly referred to as the Synoptic Gospels. Most scholars of the New Testament claim that each draws from a common pool of Jesus traditions. From these pages (and from the Gospel of John) appear the most familiar chords in the collective memory of Jesus. Even people who have never read the Gospels are probably aware of at least some of these stories (such as Jesus's birth, his Sermon on the Mount, or his crucifixion). Though Mark, Matthew, and Luke employ slightly different emphases in their portrayals of Jesus, they are consistent in their depiction of Jesus: (1) proclaiming the kingdom of God, (2) healing the sick, (3) teaching in parables, and (4) dying and rising from the dead. The Gospels are finite in content but almost inexhaustible in provoking reflection on that content. Indeed, the "biography" of Jesus presented in these pages is rather compact (especially in comparison with other figures from the Roman Empire), but this brevity leads to nearly infinite commentary.

One way of capturing some of the difference among these three Synoptic portrayals of Jesus is in how each Gospel ends. For Mark, the story of Jesus ends with witnesses to the empty tomb running away afraid, indicating the mysterious and abrupt nature of this Son of God. For Matthew, the story of Jesus ends with his telling the disciples to go out into the world and baptize disciples from all nations, indicating an evangelistic reach. And, for Luke, the story of Jesus ends with the disciples in the temple in Jerusalem, blessing God, indicating a Savior who comes first to his own people.

Mark

Most contemporary New Testament scholars claim that Mark is the earliest Gospel. It is also the briefest, and the Jesus who emerges within these pages is somewhat enigmatic. He confounds as often as (if not more than) he comforts; he moves rather quickly from place to place; he says rather little about himself; and he is apocalyptic. This Gospel is fast-paced; the word "immediately" occurs twenty-seven times. Jesus emerges on the scene quickly (without the benefit of a birth narrative) and departs (at least in the oldest manuscripts) without the resolution of a resurrection appearance. If this is the oldest Gospel, it can also seem the strangest to readers who want a tidy or "nice" Jesus. Mark's Jesus is an apocalyptic prophet, a teacher who embodies what he teaches, who suffers and dies as a result of that teaching. The beginning is stark. The first words out of Jesus's mouth are these: "The time is fulfilled, and the kingdom of God has come near; repent, and believe in the good news" (Mark 1:15). Jesus appears on the scene to be baptized by John, and then is "immediately" driven into the wilderness to be tempted. In neither of these occasions does Jesus speak. When he does return, he preaches repentance and the imminent arrival of God's kingdom.

If this message sounds stark and unattractive to modern ears, Jesus the messenger quickly gains a following. The first chapter of Mark is filled with examples of people who hear Jesus's proclamation, are affected by it, and follow him. Jesus calls and people follow "immediately." Within the span of a few verses, Jesus gains four disciples who follow him without question, leaving their previous companions (including a father) behind (vv. 16–20). By the end of this first chapter, Mark claims that Jesus "could no longer go into a town openly," hinting that his message had become both controversial and popular. Yet people "came to him from every quarter" (v. 45). This momentum of an increased following accompanied by increasing controversy carries through until the Gospel's conclusion. Yet by the time Jesus is crucified, nearly all of his followers have fled.

The Jesus who calls is also the Jesus who heals. This first chapter of Mark also contains examples of Jesus as physician and exorcist. He commands an unclean spirit to come out of a man (vv. 25–26); he alleviates the fever of a disciple's mother-in-law (v. 31); he cures diseases and casts out demons (v. 34); he touches a leper and makes him clean (vv. 41–42). Jesus calls, heals, and preaches. These three verbs capture much of the movement of the rest of the Gospel. Moving from place to place, Jesus touches those whom he meets with his words, with his hands, changing their lives and changing their status in society. This Jesus is also a boundary-crosser, touching those who are unclean (and hence making them clean); welcoming the outcast (and rendering them no longer outcast); calling them from one place in life to another. He speaks relatively few words—and those he does speak are often jarring—but people take notice and become reoriented because of his words.

His most memorable words come in the form of parables. Jesus the teacher speaks in words that expand and multiply meanings rather than restrict them. He teaches in parables that illustrate, reorient, and expand questions. The parables of Jesus do not so much answer questions as much as they reorient the asking of questions. Here is how theologian Sallie McFague describes it: "A parable is an extended metaphor. A parable is not an allegory, where the meaning is extrinsic to the story, nor is it an example of story where, as in the story of the Good Samaritan, the total meaning is within the story. Rather, as an extended metaphor, the meaning is found only *within* the story itself although it is not exhausted *by* that story." For McFague, these parables of Jesus carry "shock," "surprise," and "revelatory aspect."[3] Sometimes Jesus offers explanations of his parables, as in the case of the sower, where a sower is compared to the word (4:14). In other cases, Jesus offers little interpretation of his parables, as in the case of the mustard seed (vv. 30–32). Indeed, Jesus seems to expect that many of his hearers will be confused by his teaching:

> For those outside, everything comes in parables; in order that
> they may indeed look, but not perceive,
> and may indeed listen, but not understand. (vv. 11–12)

These parables, however, become clear to those close to him, since Jesus "explained everything in private to his disciples" (v. 34). These parables create something of an insider-outsider distinction, for the same words that are explained to disciples also cause confusion in other hearers. Often in Christian imagination, the disruptive nature of the parables gets underemphasized, as if the parables offered straightforward teaching. But a close read of the Gospels reveals that they are anything but transparent in meaning (as in the parable of the growing seed, vv. 26–29). One way of considering these parables is that they show Jesus as the teacher of God's wisdom: wisdom that can be approached and addressed in words, but that never can be exhausted by words. These parables of Jesus the teacher, in other words, invite continual interpretation, much as the Jesus of Mark invites interpretation of himself.

This Jesus who teaches is ultimately rejected. Mark locates the first rejection of Jesus in his hometown, Nazareth. Here, Jesus comes to teach in the synagogue, and astounds some while offending others (6:1–3). Some of his powers appear ineffective in this context, which causes Jesus to be "amazed at their unbelief" (vv. 5–6). Those who are not claimed by his words take offense at them: words that cause some to follow him cause others to reject him. It makes all the difference how his words are heard. The momentum of Mark's Gospel builds the case for further rejection: the longer the story goes on, the more people take offense at his words. Before the Gospel reaches its midpoint, the stage seems set for his final rejection in the crucifixion. Indeed, Jesus foretells his death several times (8:31; 9:31; 10:33–34). This orientation toward Golgotha led Martin Kähler to claim Mark's Gospel along with the Synoptics as "passion narratives with extended introductions."[4] Jesus the teacher must also prepare his disciples for his death.

Before he is arrested, tried, and killed, however, Jesus indicates the earth-shattering nature of his ministry and teaching. This one who comes to proclaim is also one who orients his hearers to the end of days. Jesus's teaching here is hardly comforting: the temple will be destroyed, persecution will follow, sacrilege will be committed, and false messiahs will appear (13:1–22). Jesus the teacher is apocalyptic, who foresees a day when sun will be darkened, moon will be extinguished, and stars fall from heaven (vv. 24–25). His followers must "keep awake" in anticipation for the day that will surely come. By the time Jesus is arrested, it seems like these days are already here.

Just before that arrest, Jesus shares a meal with those who remain: a Passover celebration that also connects his coming death with his own impending sacrifice: "Take; this is my body . . . This is my blood of the covenant, which is poured out for many" (14:22–24). The meal is these disciples' memory of him: though some accompany him after the meal, by the end of the evening all have abandoned him. Jesus's arrest, trial, and crucifixion are recorded without much adornment. He appears before a council and affirmatively answers a question about whether he is the Messiah. This is enough for the council to send him to the Roman governor Pilate, who after a brief examination and a roar of the assembled crowd hands Jesus over to be crucified (14:53–15:15). Jesus's death comes over the course of the day: He is nailed to the cross at nine in the morning and dead by three in the afternoon. His last words, "My God, my God, why have you forsaken me?" evoke desperation.[5] At the foot of the cross, he is alone, except for three women who remain at a distance and a centurion, a representative of Roman occupation, who proclaims him God's son (15:39–40). As Luke Timothy Johnson notes, "With consummate irony Mark chooses this moment to have the ultimate outsider, Jesus' executioner, become the only human character in the narrative to identify Jesus properly."[6]

Yet this is not the end of the story. Mark concludes with the briefest of Gospel resurrection stories. The same women who were present at the crucifixion—Mary, Mary Magdalene, and Salome—come to Jesus's tomb to anoint his body. But the one whom they would anoint is no longer there. A man who is present at the tomb tells them Jesus is risen and has gone on ahead of them to Galilee. The oldest manuscripts of Mark conclude with these women running away in fear, saying nothing to anyone (16:1–8), a jarring ending to a jarring Gospel. It ends with good news of resurrection, but no appearance of the risen Christ. The three who have remained faithful until the end say nothing to anyone. But the readers of the Gospel know in hindsight that they have said something, for the story has continued to be told. This enigmatic Gospel ends with an invitation back to the beginning—to encounter the risen Christ in Galilee, where the ministry of Jesus commenced: the place of his healings, preaching, and rejection. Readers of this story are invited to begin again in their encounter with Jesus. And thus the interpretation of Jesus begins anew.

Matthew

The Gospel of Matthew draws on many of Mark's themes—Jesus's preaching, healing, and rejection—while expanding on them with emphases unique to Matthew. In some cases, for Matthew, the disputes with the Pharisees are sharper. This Jesus who preaches is also one who argues with a distinct branch of first-century Judaism. At the same time that this Gospel renders the differences between Jesus and the Pharisees stark, Matthew also takes pains to anchor the Jesus story in the story of Israel. This happens on the opening page, where readers encounter a genealogy of "Jesus the Messiah, the son of David, the son of Abraham" (Matt 1:1). Three sets of fourteen generations span the period between Abraham and Jesus, an ordered pattern that sets the birth of Jesus within a cycle of generations both noble and common. To know Jesus is to know where he came from: a people Israel to whom God has made irrevocable promises.

One of the most memorable of all vignettes in Scripture is Matthew's rendition of the Sermon on the Mount. In Matthew, like Mark, Jesus moves from place to place, teaching and healing. But the Sermon on the Mount encapsulates the teaching of Jesus distinctly. It begins with the Beatitudes, where Jesus proclaims blessing on those from the underside ("the poor in spirit," "those who mourn," "the meek," "those who hunger and thirst for righteousness"). Here Jesus employs inversion, where the poor in spirit inherit the kingdom of heaven and the meek inherit the earth. If Jesus here is proclaiming the kingdom, it resembles an upside-down realm, where the lowly are lifted up and those who mourn are comforted (5:3–6). The sermon proceeds at length and includes his own recasting of the law (vv. 21–48), his teaching of what has come to be known as the Lord's Prayer (6:9–13), various words on conduct, prayer, and warnings of persecution and against false prophets. Whereas Jesus in Mark spoke more abruptly and pithily, here Jesus emerges as a more versed orator, whose words cause others to reconsider words they have previously heard.

The most significant of these reconsiderations are Jesus's words in relation to the law. As we have already seen in our examination of Paul, this gets to some of the thorniest questions in all of Christian history. To what extent does the teaching of Jesus—in the Sermon on the Mount and elsewhere—change, adapt, radicalize, or refute Jewish law? The way one answers this question has obvious implications for Christian understandings of Judaism and Christian-Jewish relations. And the answers have been as varied as the winds. The focus in the Sermon on the Mount, however, is on *radicalizing* the law. Jesus comes not to overturn or supersede, but to get to the heart of the law; to follow not the letter of the law, but to see the intention behind the letter. He makes more demands—not fewer—on his hearers in keeping the law. Hence, he instructs his hearers that it is not only murder that renders one liable to judgment, but anger at a brother or sister as well; not only adultery, but a lustful gaze; not only love of neighbor, but love of enemies as well (5:21–47). This fits with Matthew's depiction of Jesus within his Jewish context. This Messiah comes not to overturn, but to fulfill. If Paul seems to interpret the law at times as constraining, here Jesus interprets the law by adding further constraints on those who would follow him. The kicker comes in the nearly unfathomable command: "Be perfect, therefore, as your heavenly

Father is perfect" (v. 48). It is hard to imagine a more radical and all-encompassing injunction.

The Sermon on the Mount is soaring in its oration, yet the demands that it places on the hearer are strong. Such demands are consistent with Jesus's words elsewhere in the Gospel, where he lists the costs of discipleship: "Those who find their life will lose it, and those who lose their life for my sake will find it" (10:39). This Jesus who calls disciples can cause disruption in the ordinary ties that bind. He makes clear that disciples' primary allegiance is not to kith and kin, but to the living God. His words are stark:

> For I have come to set a man against his father,
> and a daughter against her mother,
> and a daughter-in-law against her mother-in-law;
> and one's foes will be members of one's own household.
>
> Whoever loves father or mother more than me is not worthy of me; and whoever loves son or daughter more than me is not worthy of me. (vv. 35–37)

As Jesus instructs his disciples on the radical implications of discipleship, he also prepares them for the massive disruption caused by his death. In telling them to take up their cross and follow him (v. 38), he foreshadows his own crucifixion.

As much as Matthew situates Jesus amid his Jewish context, stressing fulfillment rather than overturning the law, Matthew also emphasizes the disputes with select religious authorities. Scribes and Pharisees emerge as the most suspect. As one reads these accounts, one is reminded of an intense intrafamilial squabble. Jesus urges his hearers to "do" what the scribes and Pharisees teach, but not to "do as they do" since they "do not practice what they teach" (23:3). He singles out how these leaders seek attention, while those who follow Jesus should "humble themselves" (v. 12). As his discourse against the scribes and Pharisees progresses, his words become increasingly harsh: they are worthy of woe, comparable to "blind guides" (v. 16), "hypocrites" (v. 25), and a "brood of vipers" (v. 33). Jesus implicates them as being concerned with the cleanliness of the "outside" rather than the "inside" (vv. 25–28). Jesus disagrees not with the content of Pharisaic teaching, but with how they carry it out. For him at least, these teachers do not embody their teaching. He calls on his followers to do just that.

Just as in the Gospel of Mark, these disputes contribute to Jesus's death. Matthew's narration of Jesus's passion is lengthier than Mark's, containing more details about Jesus's appearance before Pilate (including how Pilate symbolically washes his hands before the crowd that demands Jesus's crucifixion, proclaiming his own innocence). These details have the effect, whether intentional or not, of exonerating the Roman prefect while casting the impetus for the crucifixion squarely on the rabble-rousing crowd and the authority of the high priest Caiaphas.[7] Jesus's death is narrated in a similar manner to Mark's, with identical last words coming from Jesus's lips (27:46) and a similar account of Jesus's burial (vv. 57–61). But Matthew adds an additional detail: chief priests and Pharisees urge Pilate to secure Jesus's tomb with guards, "otherwise his disciples may go and steal him away, and tell the people, 'He has been raised from the dead,' and the last deception would be worse than the first" (v. 64). Matthew thus records an early counterargument to Christian faith that the resurrection was a hoax. This central affirmation of faith, therefore, seems to have been controversial from the beginning. Thus the ending of Matthew is different from Mark's, containing appearance narratives: first to Mary Magdalene and "the other Mary" (28:1) and finally to the eleven disciples. The Gospel ends with Jesus's words, subsequently known as the Great Commission: "Go therefore and make disciples of all nations, baptizing them in the name of the Father and of the Son and of the Holy Spirit, and teaching them to obey everything that I have commanded you. And remember, I am with you always, to the end of the age" (vv. 19–20). The "end" of the Jesus story, for Matthew, invites readers to carry on the story by gathering new disciples in Jesus's name.

Luke

The third Synoptic Gospel, while gathering themes common to the other two, contains details about Jesus uniquely its own. Like Matthew, it emphasizes Jesus's Jewishness (and the Jewishness of Jesus's followers). Even the Gospel's conclusion, which locates the disciples in the temple blessing God (25:53), directs readers' attention to the faith of Israel. Jesus, for Luke, is the fulfillment of scriptural prophecies concerning a Messiah. The good news of Jesus's life and ministry, moreover, is one of redemption/liberation. Perhaps more than any other Gospel, Luke emphasizes that the salvation found in Christ is liberation from all that constrains the fullness of life in *this world*. It is not surprising, then, that Luke's Gospel has found special favor among various contemporary liberation theologies.

Luke's narrative of what precedes the birth of Jesus is lengthier than any other. Luke takes pains to illustrate the relationship between Jesus's and John the Baptist's births. Both are miraculous. John's mother, Elizabeth, was "barren" (1:7), while Jesus's mother, Mary, was a "virgin" (v. 27). The birth of each child was unexpected. Luke further narrates that Mary and Elizabeth are relatives (v. 36), underscoring connections between the families, and the subsequent ministries of each child. The news of the pregnancy (in Mary's case), and the birth of the child (in the case of John's father, Zechariah), result in the eruption of song. Mary's song captures several of the emphases of Luke's Gospel: The God who has blessed Mary with this child has also "scattered the proud," "brought down the powerful," "lifted up the lowly," and "filled the hungry with good things" (vv. 51–53). The coming birth of Jesus heralds an inversion of social structures that enslave and oppress, for God has remembered Israel

> according to the promise he made to our ancestors,
> to Abraham and to his descendants forever. (v. 55)

Luke's narration of Jesus's birth contains different emphases from Matthew's. Whereas Matthew includes the visitation of the magi, "wise men from the East" (Matt 2:1), Luke focuses on local shepherds, indicating the more humble circumstances of the nativity scene. And whereas Matthew underscores Joseph's action, in leading his family in an escape to Egypt in order to flee Herod (vv. 13–15), Luke emphasizes Mary's reactions to the birth and visitation of an angel and shepherds: "But Mary treasured all these words and pondered them in her heart" (Luke 2:19). Luke also contains the sole scriptural vignette of Jesus's life between birth and the outset of his ministry: an episode of Jesus's childhood in which his family visits Jerusalem for the Passover, and Jesus tarries there while his family leaves. Returning to Jerusalem, his parents find Jesus "in the temple, sitting among the teachers, listening to them and asking them questions" (v. 46). This story reinforces Luke's conviction that Jesus's primary allegiance is not to his birth family, but to the God of Israel: "Did you not know that I must be in my Father's house?" (v. 49). The location of Jesus in the temple, like the

Gospel's conclusion, indicates that Jesus belongs to the God and the people of Israel. Just as at his birth, Jesus's mother "treasured all these things in her heart" (v. 51).

The inauguration of Jesus's ministry, in Luke as in Matthew and Mark, contains a temptation story of Jesus in the wilderness (4:1–13). After this episode, Jesus journeys to Nazareth, his hometown, and reads from the scroll in the synagogue. Luke alone repeats these words from the prophet Isaiah:

> The Spirit of the Lord is upon me,
> because he has anointed me
> to bring good news to the poor.
> He has sent me to proclaim release to the captives
> and recovery of sight to the blind,
> to let the oppressed go free,
> to proclaim the year of the Lord's favor" (vv. 18–19)

Upon reading these words, Jesus says to those gathered, "Today this scripture has been fulfilled in your hearing" (v. 21). Consistent with Luke's understanding of salvation *as* liberation, the beginning of Jesus's ministry signals the inversions of the upside-down kingdom that Jesus proclaims. Good news is good news for the *poor*. If the words of Jesus amaze those gathered in the Nazareth synagogue, they are words that also lead quickly to rejection of him, with even the suggestion that those riled up by his words seek to kill him by hurling him off a cliff outside of town (v. 29). The upside-down kingdom, in other words, soon gathers opponents.

Like Matthew, Luke consistently emphasizes Jesus's itinerant ministry of preaching and healing. Wherever Jesus goes, he proclaims the reign of God, and embodies that reign through healings and cleansings (4:38–41; 5:12–26; 7:1–17). He gathers followers, and preaches a sermon that captures his teaching. But whereas Matthew's Jesus pronounces blessing on the poor "in spirit" (Matt 5:3), Luke's Jesus blesses "the poor" (Luke 6:20). Luke seems even more intent on lifting up the lowly in the ministry of Jesus. Consistent with this emphasis is the prominence of women in Luke's story of Jesus—probably to a greater extent than in any other Gospel. Luke names women who accompany Jesus along with the Twelve (Mary Magdalene, Joanna, Suzanna, and "many others," 8:2–3). Luke also affords attention (alone among the Synoptics) to Martha and Mary, two women who welcome Jesus into their home (10:38–42). As in the other Gospels, Jesus teaches in parables. One of the most significant is unique to Luke, in which a rich man who refuses to aid a poor man, Lazarus, experiences torment in Hades while Lazarus enjoys fellowship with Abraham. Here, the rich experience judgment, while the poor experience communion (16:19–30). Luke's Jesus privileges the poor and oppressed even beyond the grave.

Like in the other Synoptics, the momentum of the Jesus story leads toward his crucifixion. A ministry meant to uplift the outcasts renders Jesus outcast himself. On the road to Golgotha, Luke alone mentions "a great number" of people who follow him, including "women who were beating their breasts and wailing for him" (23:27). In the procession are "two others also, who were criminals" who "were led away to be put to death with him" (v. 32). As these three men are breathing their dying gasps, Luke alone gives one of the criminals a voice: "Jesus, remember me when you come into your kingdom." To whom Jesus responds, "Truly I tell you, today you will be with me in paradise" (vv. 42–43). Even in the last moments of Jesus's life on earth, the outcasts are heard. Jesus's last words in Luke differ from Matthew and Mark. Whereas Jesus's last words in the latter Gospels indicate abandonment by God, in Luke they contain notes of fulfillment: "Father, into your hands I commend my spirit" (v. 46). Jesus's solidarity with the poor is present unto death, and rendered into the life of God.

Resurrection narratives are lengthier in Luke as well, and include the suggestive story of the road to Emmaus. Here, some followers of Jesus are accompanied by a risen Christ, whom they do not recognize, even though he asks them questions, teaches them about the Messiah, and interprets the prophets and Scriptures to them. Only when Jesus is at table with them, taking, blessing, breaking, and giving bread, are their eyes opened (24:13–31). Redolent with Eucharist, this story points to the ongoing presence of the risen Christ in the believing community, whenever the sacrament is celebrated. Indeed, this entire narrative posits a resurrection future that hearkens the past: The risen Christ is present for those who remember him and take part in the actions that he enjoins his followers to do. By ending his Jesus story in Jerusalem, where the disciples "were continually in the temple blessing God" (v. 53), Luke indicates that resurrection faith is rooted in the faith of Israel. The story begins again in the temple.

Jesus in the Gospel of John

John's Gospel contains numerous episodes that echo the Synoptics. The pattern of the Fourth Gospel, in many ways, resembles the others: a prologue followed by teaching of John the Baptist; calling of disciples; an itinerant ministry of preaching, teaching, and healing; disputes with religious leaders; performing of miracles; culminating in crucifixion and resurrection. But the Jesus who embarks on this ministry in many cases *sounds different* from the Synoptics. Whereas Jesus in the Synoptics rarely speaks about himself, in the Gospel of John he often uses the first person. The words "I am" appear frequently on Jesus's lips. The Jesus of John is "the bread of life" (6:35); "light of the world" (8:12); "the gate for the sheep" (10:7); "the good shepherd" (10:11); "God's Son" (10:36); "the resurrection and the life" (11:25); "teacher and Lord" (13:13); "the way, and the truth, and the life" (14:6); and "the true vine" (15:1). If Jesus in the Synoptics points indirectly to his lordship, in John he directly proclaims it.

John is far more concerned than the other Gospels with documenting Jesus's divinity. In several places, John emphasizes the close identity of Jesus with the Father. Jesus is "in" the Father and the Father is "in" him (10:38). Jesus claims that "the Father loves the Son and has placed all things in his hands" (3:35). And perhaps most boldly, Jesus says that "the Father and I are one" (10:30). Jesus participates in intimate communion with the Father; participation in this relationship is part of what constitutes the fullness of life/salvation that Jesus gives to those who follow him: "On that day you will know that I am in my Father, and you in me, and I in you" (14:20). John begins his Gospel with such a promise: "To all who received him, who believed in his name, he gave power to become children of God" (1:12). This "divinity" of Christ, at least as constituted by communion with God, is also imparted to those who follow him. In John, Jesus does not keep divinity to himself, but bestows it on others.

And yet there is something about the divinity of Christ that is set apart from the rest of creation. Whereas other Gospels begin with a genealogy, John begins with an account of the cosmic eternity of Christ. Jesus Christ, the Word, was with God in the beginning: "All things came into being through him, and without him not one thing came into being" (v. 3). The beginning of John's Gospel echoes the opening page of Genesis: The God of all creation, who creates from nothing, is the God found in the Word, who is with God from all eternity. Nearly every subsequent theological interpretation of Christ's preexistence traces roots to this passage. The one who preaches, heals, suffers, and dies is also the One through whom all things came into being. Jesus the Savior is also Christ the Creator.

What is the salvation that Jesus brings? For John, one of the first clues appears in his account of Jesus's meeting with Nicodemus, a Pharisee. In this encounter, Jesus tells Nicodemus that "no one can see the kingdom of God without being born from above" (3:3), a statement that perplexes Nicodemus, who questions whether one can experience a second birth. Jesus then indicates that this second birth is to be born of "water and Spirit" (v. 5), a probable allusion to baptism and the new life given by the Spirit of God that "blows where it chooses" (v. 7). If Jesus is speaking of salvation here, it is clear that salvation is a present reality, not merely a future promise. John's Gospel is permeated by a "realized eschatology," in which the future promises of God bear fruit in the present life. "For God so loved the world that he gave his only Son, so that everyone who believes in him may not perish but may have eternal life" (v. 16). Eternal life here is not something that awaits the believer at the end of time, but a promise in the here and now. Salvation is participation in life in its fullness: "I came that they may have life, and have it abundantly" (10:10).

Like in the Synoptics, John emphasizes Jesus's disputes with religious authorities. But unlike the Synoptics, John's language to describe these disputes does not focus on particular parties (such as scribes and Pharisees), but resorts to rather indiscriminate identification of "Jews." Time and again, John describes resistance to Jesus from the "Jews" (5:10–16; 6:41; 7:11–13; 9:22). Various explanations of this language have been offered: Most prominent among them is that the Gospel was written for early Jewish Christians who had been expelled from the synagogue (and hence reflects the polemics of the time). The language thus lumps together all parties (Pharisees, Sadducees, scribes, and all others) in an effective rhetorical parry. But even if this language was intended for Jews who were grappling with their own expulsion (and hence saw themselves as opposing a majority), the effect of this language has often been negative in subsequent Christology. Very soon after it was written, the Gospel of John also became rooted in gentile contexts, where the language of "Jews" gained different resonances. No longer "insider" speech intended to distinguish a smaller group of Jewish Christians from some of the Jewish religious authorities of the time, John's language served to further a polarity of "insider-outsider" that cast all Jews as "outside" the covenant (because of their "rejection" of Jesus) and cast blame for the crucifixion squarely at Jewish feet: All Jews thus become implicated in the crime of deicide. Subsequent chapters of this book will survey some of this destructive christological legacy, reflected in some of the most influential theologians of Christian history, including John Chrysostom and Martin Luther. In this sense, John's Gospel gave birth to some unexpected and injurious strains of Christology that run against the broad sweep of New Testament witness about Jesus. The Jesus who uplifts outsiders in the Gospels (including John) thus becomes a consummate insider who harshly judges those on the outside.

Throughout the Gospel, John emphasizes Jesus's close relationship with God. "Very truly, I tell you, the Son can do nothing on his own, but only what he sees the Father doing; for whatever the Father does, the Son does likewise" (5:19). Jesus is the One who does the Father's bidding, whose very being and doing is transparent to the work of God. The relationship is so close that Jesus speaks of their fundamental identity: "The Father and I are one" (10:30). Statements such as these have fueled Christology for centuries. If Jesus is prophet and teacher, he is unique from other prophets and teachers in that he reflects the fullness of God's glory. Though it took several generations of the Christian church to arrive at a consensus about what this meant, the orthodox position emerged as one that claimed Jesus's full divinity as well as his full humanity.

John's narration of Jesus's final days also contains unique resonances. His Gospel alone mentions footwashing at the Last Supper. Jesus washes the feet of all gathered at table, and stresses his practice as an example for them: "So if I, your Lord and Teacher, have washed your feet, you also ought to wash one another's feet. For I have set you an example, that you also should do as I have done to you" (13:14–15). Here Jesus the Lord acts as Servant, presenting his servanthood for others to follow. Christologically, the one who is Lord of all is also Servant of all. This juxtaposition of lofty and lowly categories becomes a mark of nearly all Christologies that the church has produced. In washing feet, Jesus also takes on one of the rituals of Israel's priesthood (Exod 30:19–21), signaling that he is both priest and one who extends gestures of that priesthood to all who would follow him.

John's Gospel also narrates an intimacy between Jesus and the Spirit. Telling his disciples that he will not be with them much longer, Jesus promises his followers "the Advocate, the Holy Spirit, whom the Father will send in my name" (John 14:26). This promise becomes a reality at the resurrection, when Jesus appeared to his disciples, "breathed on them and said to them, 'Receive the Holy Spirit'" (20:22). These passages together indicate that the Spirit promised by Jesus is given by the Father and also given by the Son. Though Trinitarian theology took centuries to develop, readers of John's Gospel sense the roots of Trinitarian reflection whenever he speaks of the intimate connections between Father, Son, and Spirit. John's Jesus is thus both inspired by God's Spirit and the One who gives that Spirit to others.

The conclusion to John's passion story resounds with words uniquely John's own. Before he dies, Jesus indicates the creation of a new family for those gathered in his name: "When Jesus saw his mother and the disciple whom he loved standing beside her, he said to his mother, 'Woman, here is your son.' Then he said to the disciple, 'Here is your mother'" (19:26–27). After this, Jesus utters no cry of abandonment, but expresses calm reassurance that his mission is complete: "It is finished" (19:30). Upon Jesus's death, soldiers pierce Jesus's side with a spear; from the wound flow blood and water (v. 34), symbols of the rites that capture so much of his ministry (Last Supper and baptism). John affirms bodily resurrection with details contained in no other Gospel: Here he warns Mary not to touch him because he has not yet ascended (20:17), but invites Thomas to put his hand in his side so that Thomas might believe (v. 27). The resurrection appearances recall gestures of Jesus's ministry, most notably how he takes bread and gives it to others (21:13). John is also more explicit than the other Gospels writers in stating the reasons for his writing: "So that you may come to believe that Jesus is the Messiah, the Son of God, and that through believing you may have life in his name" (20:31). Christology here serves the purposes of soteriology. Whatever Jesus we construct from the details of John's Gospel, the point is to depict One who saves and gives life anew.

Other New Testament Portrayals of Jesus

Paul's undisputed letters and the Gospels constitute a large percentage of the New Testament, yet the portrayal of Jesus is not exhausted by them. Much christological reflection in the history of the church has been sustained by other strands of these foundational resources and express aspects that are absent or understated in Paul and the Gospels.

Hebrews

The Letter to the Hebrews offers no explicit mention of an author. Traditionally referred to as a "letter," it more closely resembles an exhortation or extended sermon. The opening sentences find resonance with much of John, indicating close communion between Jesus and God the creator: "In these last days he has spoken to us by a Son, whom he appointed heir of all things, through whom he also created the worlds. He is the reflection of God's glory and the exact imprint of God's very being, and he sustains all things by his powerful word" (1:2–3). The author devotes much space to demonstrating the Son's superiority to all things in creation, including angels (vv. 5–14). Here are yet further indications of the early church's expression of the divinity of Christ.

Much of the driving force of Hebrews' argument is that Jesus accomplishes something for humanity by atoning for sin. Soteriology fuels Christology. But whereas many other New Testament portrayals of Jesus are content with claiming that Jesus saves, Hebrews offers an account for *how* Jesus saves. The Son is the one who "had to become like his brothers and sisters in every respect, so that he might be a merciful and faithful high priest in the service of God, to make a sacrifice of atonement for the sins of the people. Because he himself was tested by what he suffered, he is able to help those who are being tested" (2:17–18). The problem that humanity finds itself in is that it is bound by sin. Sin requires release. And release comes through the sacrifice of one who comes on behalf of all humanity. Hebrews employs the ancient language of sacrifice as atonement for sin: making an offering, which entails the spilling of blood. This is language with deep roots in Israel's faith. But Hebrews carries this language to a surprising end. Israel's priesthood is effectively being replaced by the coming of "a great high priest who has passed through the heavens, Jesus, the Son of God" (4:14). Jesus, the high priest, inaugurates a new age. Here is how New Testament scholar Lewis Donelson puts it:

> The coming of Jesus does not end the force of blood and sacrifices; it makes those forces eternal. Hebrews assumes that God is holy and that only a holy person can approach God. Hebrews further assumes that properly spilled blood can make a person holy. Christians have a better covenant because they can claim a better sacrifice. Jesus makes for a perfect sacrifice. He is the perfect priest. He spills perfect blood. He spills it in the perfect place. Finally, all this perfection of the sacrifice makes personal perfection, both moral and cultic, possible for Christians.[8]

Jesus becomes like humanity (apart from sin, see 4:15) so that he might offer a perfect sacrifice on our behalf. This is the sacrifice of himself "at the end of the age to remove sin" (9:26). According to the author of Hebrews, the priests of old needed to make sacrifices again and again, "the same sacrifices that can never take away sins" (10:11).[9] Jesus's perfect sacrifice, however, is rendered once and for all time: "For by a single offering he has perfected for all time those who are sanctified" (v. 14). The coming of this high priest represents a new covenant that God is establishing with humanity. The sacrifice of this priest is a death "that redeems them from the transgressions under the first covenant" (9:15). In Hebrews, we have the most extensive rendering of the notion of sacrifice and its connections to Jesus's life and death in the entire New Testament. The subsequent reflection that this letter has spawned has been enormous. Though Hebrews is far from offering an atonement "theory" (in the sense of a formulaic account for how the death of Jesus is salvific), it does present something beyond a bare claim of a sacrificial death, and the beginnings of an account for how that death saves. Jesus's resurrection plays a minimal role here: What finally "saves" for the author of Hebrews is the perfect sacrifice (and suffering) that Jesus's death entails for all creation. As a suffering people, we have hope because Christ has undergone suffering and sacrifice for us.

1 Peter

Similar themes are found in the First Letter of Peter, which amplifies an interpretation of Christ's suffering as a model for those who follow him. This letter does not offer an interpretation of sacrifice as something accomplished on our behalf, but instead instructs its readers to expect suffering as a consequence of discipleship. Christ is an exemplar; disciples are to follow his example. God has "given us a new birth into a living hope through the resurrection of Jesus Christ from the dead, and into an inheritance that is imperishable, undefiled, and unfading, kept in heaven for you" (1:3–4). Believers are to imitate Christ in holiness: "As he who called you is holy, be holy yourselves in all your conduct" (v. 15). Salvation in Christ is not a gift we receive passively; it comes with demands. Nonetheless, Christ's death accomplishes something on our behalf:

"When he was abused, he did not return abuse; when he suffered, he did not threaten; but he entrusted himself to the one who judges justly. He himself bore our sins in his body on the cross, so that, free from sins, we might live for righteousness; by his wounds you have been healed" (2:23–24). First Peter interweaves these themes of healing and suffering, salvation and sin. In Jesus, we have both the balm for what ails us and the example of the people we are called to be. The cross captures both of these themes. Followers can expect suffering in "doing good" (3:17). This is cause for rejoicing "insofar as you are sharing Christ's sufferings" (4:13). Christ stands in solidarity with those who suffer for his sake. It is important to note that this letter was likely composed for a group that was experiencing a tension between the claims of following Christ and their location in Greco-Roman culture. The audience was likely gentiles who had converted to Christianity and experienced some degree of suffering on that account. If this is the case, the letter does not so much valorize suffering but rather offers the consolation of Christ's presence within the community's suffering. In this case, in the experience of the absence of God in anguish, the community could take solace in the confidence that Christ was near, and that their suffering was a part of his suffering. It is belief such as this that has sustained countless communities of persecuted Christians in the generations since: whether in the Roman Empire, American slave churches, underground churches in Nazi Germany, or the barrios of Lima, Peru.

Colossians and 1 John

Most likely coming from the hand of someone other than Paul, the Letter to the Colossians emphasizes resurrection as a present reality in which believers participate. Its Christology is memorable, echoing the Johannine Prologue. Jesus is "the image of the invisible God, the firstborn of all creation . . . all things have been created through him and for him . . . in him all the fullness of God was pleased to dwell" (1:15–19). The letter exemplifies a participatory Christology, whereby Christ's death makes peace "through the blood of his cross" (v. 20), where believers are "raised with Christ" as they die to the old life, "and your life is hidden with Christ in God" (3:1–3). We are to live our lives in Christ (2:6) since Christ is our life (3:4). In fluid imagery that melds the life of the believer to the death and resurrection of Jesus, Colossians combines stirring reflection on Christ's preexistence with concrete recommendations for living in light of the new life Christ has given. Central to this is the injunction to "clothe yourselves with love, which binds everything together in perfect harmony" (3:14), love that is made possible because of Christ's love for us, a theme that gains even greater prominence in 1 John: "We love because he first loved us" (1 John 4:19). Indeed, for 1 John, the impetus for the Son is love: "God's love was revealed among us in this way: God sent his only Son into the world so that we might live through him" (4:9). Those who follow him are likewise commanded to love one another, just as God has loved us. Christ is made known, in short, through love, a marker that has affected nearly every Christology ever since.

Revelation

No depiction of Jesus in the New Testament would be complete without some reflection on its last book, Revelation. Densely and richly symbolic, and notoriously difficult to interpret, the Bible's concluding apocalyptic vision is driven by a dual portrayal of Christ. On the one hand Jesus is the victim of the world's violence, the one who suffers and dies because of it. He is the lamb who is slain (5:12), whose blood cleanses and makes pure (7:14). Jesus does not counter the world's violence (much of Revelation is code-speak polemic against the violence of the Roman Empire) by greater violence, but overcomes it by succumbing to it and rendering it empty. Jesus's nonviolence is the antidote to the world's bloodthirstiness.[10] At the same time, Revelation includes imagery of the risen Christ complete with triumphal power. The book opens with a vision of the Son of Man who has a sharp, two-edged sword coming from his mouth (1:16); those who do not repent will experience war from "the sword of my mouth" (2:16). Jesus, symbolized as the Word of God, summons armies of heaven who "strike down the nations, and he will rule them with a rod of iron; he will tread the wine press of the fury of the wrath of God the Almighty" (19:14–15). Much of the momentum of Revelation stems from a triumph or vindication of the righteous: Though the righteous are not exhorted to take up arms on their own, they are promised that the power of God and the Word will vanquish sin, death, and the devil and judge the dead (see 20:4–15). In depicting this triumph, Revelation does resort to military imagery. J. Denny Weaver, an Anabaptist theologian, interprets these passages in light of a final rejection of violence:

> The supposed battle scenes are not really battles at all. In chapter 12, the language of battle between the forces of God and the forces of Satan is really a depiction of the cosmic significance of the resurrection of Jesus. . . . They are "killed by the sword of the rider on the horse, the sword that came from his mouth" (19:21). . . . The beast and the kings and their armies are defeated not by violence and military might. They are undone—defeated—by the Word of God.[11]

The pacifist reading of the Jesus of Revelation, however, has tended to be muted in the tradition. The passages of Revelation have also fueled a vision of Christ as a crusading triumphalist. Indeed, the combination of imagery in the Bible's final chapters feeds into both streams: both the slain Lamb who defeats violence through nonviolence and the triumphant Judge and Warrior who brings about the final defeat of the powers of evil. Depending on the context, depending on the times, people have read the book of Revelation and drawn a different portrait of Jesus from those pages. Both visions of Jesus have had a tremendous impact on subsequent theology.

Noncanonical Visions of Jesus

Most of the earliest and most influential portrayals of Jesus that we still can access are contained in the New Testament. The power of their enduring legacy is vast, since nearly all interpretations of Jesus that the church has ventured since then have had to grapple with these canonical portrayals. Yet the canonical Scriptures do not exhaust the earliest portraits of Jesus. Other sources offered interpretations of Jesus, nearly all of which sought to speak to communities gathered in Jesus's name. It is important to note that these noncanonical or "heterodox" interpretations of Jesus were written for and by communities of faith, groups of people who sought to follow Jesus. Even if subsequently many of these depictions were deemed defective, they were not intended to spawn heresies. The earliest centuries of the Christian church reflect a lengthy process of sifting and clarifying what portraits of Jesus were acceptable or not. Only over time were some interpretations of Jesus rejected. I will not attempt an exhaustive survey of multiple noncanonical sources. This select examination, however, is intriguing. What is most noteworthy about some of the noncanonical sources are the details they supply about Jesus that were eventually rejected.

We have seen from our survey of the Gospels that the New Testament offers scant detail about the period between Jesus's birth and the beginning of his public ministry. The vast majority of Jesus's life, in other words, is unrecorded in the Scriptures. Some noncanonical sources address this gap. The second-century Infancy Gospel of Thomas, for example, offers some distinctive vignettes on Jesus's childhood. In one of these, a young Jesus crafts twelve sparrows from clay, claps his hands, and gives them life. Later in this story, occurs this puzzling incident: "After this again he went through the village, and a lad ran and knocked against his shoulder. Jesus was exasperated and said to him: 'You shall not go further on your way,' and the child immediately fell down and died."[12] The purpose of such stories, it seems, was to demonstrate Jesus's power even as a child. But such portraits ultimately seemed out of bounds to a more orthodox position in which Jesus doesn't wield power for power's sake. The power of Jesus is meant to empower others and give life, not to take it away.

Several other noncanonical sources take pains to demonstrate that Jesus was untainted by the hurly-burly affairs of the world. The so-called gnostic gospels offer a vision of a docetic Jesus, a Savior of humanity who is fully divine, but only appears to be human. His human form is simply a guise that allows us access to him. The portrait of Jesus that emerges from many of these depictions is a placid Jesus who hovers above the affairs of humanity. In the Gospel of Thomas, we encounter these words: "Jesus said, 'I stood in the midst of the world, and I appeared to them in flesh. I found them all drunk. I found none among them thirsting.'"[13] The Gospel of Peter contains a vignette of the actual event of Jesus's resurrection (a detail, like Jesus's childhood, that the canonical Gospels are silent on). In it, the stone to Jesus's tomb rolls away on its own and a voice utters from heaven, "Thou hast preached to them that sleep?"[14] The portrayal of an otherworldly Jesus, as much as it sought to preserve Jesus's divinity, eventually was deemed inadequate in addressing his humanity. As we will see in the next chapter, it was essential (for soteriological reasons) to stress Jesus's full humanity. In this regard, many noncanonical interpretations of Jesus stand out by mentioning aspects of Jesus's life that ultimately seemed inconsistent with his ministry.

Conclusion

The earliest images of Jesus are widely varied, and the New Testament itself reflects this variation: Four Gospels with four distinct emphases; Pauline Letters that connect Christ to salvation; Revelation with its dual portrait of Christ as slain Lamb and the sword-like power of the Word. In this earliest period no single depiction of Jesus emerges dominant. Some interpretations of Jesus do get excluded, however, such as a child who kills others out of sheer annoyance. What is perhaps most striking about the visions of Jesus that emerge in the New Testament is that they invite further interpretation. Though the writings connect Christ and salvation, they do not offer much reflection on *how* salvation in Christ takes place. The portraits, in other words, supply the grist for subsequent theological reflection. There is no way to avoid the canonical depictions of Jesus; the question is how to engage them, how to make the portraits of Jesus contained therein speak anew to each successive age. On some questions—such as the relationship of

Jesus to other religions—the New Testament devotes almost no attention. On others—such as the relationship between faith in Jesus and the pattern of discipleship—the New Testament offers abundant reflection. As time goes by, however, different questions come to the fore. Whatever the question, however, there is no way to avoid the earliest portrayals of Jesus because they lay the foundation for those that follow.

Notes

1. J. Kameron Carter argues perceptively in *Race: A Theological Account* (Oxford: Oxford University Press, 2008) that the church's understanding of Israel affects its understanding of "difference" writ broadly, most distinctly in its interpretation of race. To risk oversimplifying Carter's nuanced argument, he claims that because the church got its understanding of Israel wrong (in supersessionist theology), it got its understanding of race wrong, privileging one race over others, seeing one race as normative. Carter's analysis points to the ways in which Christology is never an isolated discipline. How we understand Jesus affects our understanding of others.
2. E. P. Sanders, *Paul: A Very Short Introduction* (New York: Oxford University Press, 1991), 91.
3. Sallie McFague, *Speaking in Parables: A Study in Metaphor and Theology* (London: SCM, 2002), 6.
4. Martin Kähler, *The So-Called Historical Jesus and the Historic, Biblical Christ*, trans. Carl E. Braaten (Philadelphia: Fortress Press, 1964), 80.
5. Though in quoting these words from Psalm 22, Jesus also invokes memory of the entirety of the psalm, which moves from lament and abandonment to praise for God's mighty deeds of deliverance.
6. Luke Timothy Johnson, *The Writings of the New Testament: An Interpretation* (Philadelphia: Fortress Press, 1986), 168.
7. The Gospel that emphasizes Jesus's Jewishness as much as any other thus seems to lay blame for the crucifixion squarely on Jewish shoulders.

8. Lewis R. Donelson, *From Hebrews to Revelation: A Theological Introduction* (Louisville: Westminster John Knox, 2001), 15.
9. Here the author makes a stunning claim. Though the author assumes the framework of Israel's practice of sacrifice, he or she concludes, in the end, that such a system never really worked: "It is impossible for the blood of bulls and goats to take away sins" (10:4). Doubtless, this argument—like some of the strands that color John's Gospel—has fueled countless Christian readings of Judaism as being incomplete or defective.
10. For a fuller theological account of this "nonviolent atonement" see J. Denny Weaver, *The Nonviolent Atonement* (Grand Rapids: Eerdmans, 2001), especially 20–33.
11. Weaver, *Nonviolent Atonement*, 32–33.
12. "The Infancy Story of Thomas," in *New Testament Apocrypha*, vol. 1, *Gospels and Related Writings*, ed. Wilhelm Schneemelcher (Philadelphia: Westminster, 1963), 393.
13. "The Gospel of Thomas," in Schneemelcher, *Gospels and Related Writings*, 514.
14. "The Gospel of Peter," in Schneemelcher, *Gospels and Related Writings*, 186.

2

Patristic Portrayals of Jesus

The first several centuries of the Christian church, roughly constituting the period between the end of the first century and the dawn of the sixth, were astonishingly productive in theology. This is the period during which major questions about the nature of Christ and his relationship to God were asked, and during which rough consensus over those questions was hammered out in church councils. Some of the most formative (and ecumenical) statements of faith in the church stem from this period, such as the Nicene Creed and the Chalcedonian "definition" of Christ's nature. This is also the period in which influential views of the nature of Christ's "work" of salvation are ventured. Theologians in this period draw from the rich and varied imagery of Jesus in Scripture, expanding on this imagery to offer accounts that address core questions of faith: Who is Jesus Christ? How is he related to God? What is the nature of his lordship? What does it mean to say that Jesus saves? What does he save humanity from? Though Christology proper begins with the New Testament, the patristic period gives birth to Christology as a discipline: extended theological reflection on the life, death, and resurrection of Jesus Christ becomes a part of the church's ongoing work at this point in history.

The results of this work are remarkably varied. Some accounts of Jesus are rather one-sided and emphasize divinity at the expense of humanity. To explore this period is to explore an era when much is up for grabs. The movement that gathered in the wake of Jesus's death and resurrection was hardly homogenous in theology or culture. Different interpretations of Jesus vied for attention. Whatever emerged as "orthodoxy" took several centuries to establish, and even then alternative depictions of Jesus continued to gain traction. Highly speculative versions of Christology (such as Origen's) took root alongside terser and more concrete visions (such as Ignatius of Antioch's). The period is probably best seen as the age in which the broad parameters for reflection on Christ's person and work are made explicit. Though some of the figures in this period gain outsize influence (such as Augustine), no single portrait of Jesus emerges as *the* orthodox portrait. Though some portraits are eventually judged deficient (and even heretical), a plurality of images emerges, each highlighting different emphases that are necessary to affirm about Jesus the Savior.

Ignatius of Antioch (ca. 35–ca. 107)

Early Christian bishop Ignatius is perhaps most well-known for his martyrdom. His extant letters impress the reader that martyrdom is not to be feared, but welcomed as a means to true discipleship and openness to God. In his *Letter to the Romans*, Ignatius seems to equate martyrdom with true Christianity: "It is not that I want merely to be called a Christian, but actually to be one. . . . The greatness of Christianity lies in its being hated by the world, not in its being convincing to it."[1] Martyrdom is also analogous to baptism, and cleanses sin in a way akin to being born: "I would rather die and get to Jesus Christ, than reign over the ends of the earth. That is whom I am looking for—the One who died for us. . . . I am going through the pangs of being born."[2] Reunification of the believer with Christ is thus possible through death, which gives rise to new birth.

Christologically, Ignatius focuses significant attention on defending the bodily nature of Christ's incarnation and resurrection. The stress is that Christ possesses a human body, and that this body undergoes real suffering in the crucifixion. This counters a gnostic claim that Christ only *appeared* to have a human body and did not really suffer on the cross. In his *Letter to the Smyrnaeans*, Ignatius writes: "He suffered all these things for us; and He suffered them really, and not in appearance only, even as also He truly rose again." For Ignatius, the resurrection does not represent an escape from embodiment (as gnostics would have it), but an eschatological extension of his human body: "I know that He was possessed of a body not only in His being born and crucified, but I also know that He was so after His resurrection, and believe that He is so now."[3] Beyond these somewhat terse affirmations, however, we do not have a devel oped Christology coming from the pen of Ignatius. What he wrote about Christ was designed chiefly to combat gnostic distortions. The net effect of his brief christological reflections is a reaffirmation of Jesus as fully human, whose sufferings are real, and whose bodily nature extends to resurrection life.

Justin (ca. 100–ca. 165)

The early Christian martyr who left the most extensive record is Justin. His extant corpus is far greater than Ignatius's and focuses on two concerns: (1) the relationship of Christian faith to the faith of Israel; (2) the relationship of Christian faith to the classical, pagan world. Justin's *Dialogue with Trypho* contains an extended, imagined dialogue between Justin and a Jewish leader. One of the main thrusts is that Jesus is the fulfillment of Old Testament prophecy. Countering various objections, Justin points to numerous images and types in the Hebrew Scriptures as heralding Christ's birth, death, and resurrection. The passages he cites have become part of the common parlance of Christians throughout the ages. Prominent among these texts is Psalm 22, a psalm that Mark and Matthew include in Jesus's last words. For Justin, "the whole Psalm refers thus to Christ."[4] Justin adds to this account words from Isaiah, Malachi, Moses, and Joshua, bolstering his argument. His point is not so much that these old prophecies are abrogated in the new covenant of Jesus (though he does argue that Jews need to convert to Christian faith). Rather, his point is that the faith of Israel is fulfilled in the coming of Jesus Christ. "Nor do we think that there is one God for us, another for you, but that He alone is God who led your fathers out from Egypt with a strong hand and a high arm." Christ, for Justin, is "an eternal and final law . . . after which there shall be no law, no commandment, no ordinance."[5] The argument here is a double-edged sword. Jesus is the one promised in the Scriptures of those who adhere to the law, but after his coming, the law is no longer necessary. Justin thus makes extensive use of Hebrew Scriptures in arguing for Christian supersessionism: arguments that have become common coin in many quarters of the Christian church. In the end, Jesus the Jew is the one who demonstrates that there is no more continued need for Judaism. The consequences of this interpretation for Jewish-Christian dialogue and understanding have been legion and often destructive. The Christology outlined here leaves no doubt: the faith of Israel plays a preparatory role for the coming of Jesus. Israel's faith is valid, but only for a time.

In his *Apologies*, Justin engages other dialogue partners: the wisdom of pagan tradition. His arguments here display a similar trajectory to those outlined in the *Dialogue with Trypho*: Christ is the summation of pagan wisdom as well as Jewish wisdom. Justin nods to some of the classics of paganism, such as the Stoics, Socrates, and Plato, offering an account of broader pagan culture as anticipating Christian faith. The overarching depiction of Christ in the *Apologies* is Christ the eternal Word (Logos). Echoing the Johannine Prologue, Justin claims that Jesus Christ is the incarnation of God's eternal Word, the One through whom all things came to be. All wisdom in the world, wherever it comes from, has its ultimate origin in God's wisdom, the eternal Word. "For each man spoke well in proportion to the share he had of the spermatic word [*logos spermatikos*], seeing what was related to it." What pagans have in part, Christians have in full, thanks to the coming of the eternal Word in Christ. Pagans have partial truth, anticipatory truth. Justin thus does not argue against pagan wisdom, but for the inclusion of pagan wisdom within a broader span. "Whatever things were rightly said among all men, are the property of us Christians. For next to God, we worship and love the Word who is from the unbegotten and ineffable God, since also He became man for our sakes, that, becoming a partaker of our sufferings, He might also bring us healing."[6] Justin's Christ might be dubbed an "inclusive" Christ, insofar as his vision of Christ absorbs and includes whatever is right and true, whatever its source. By claiming Christ, the Logos, as the primeval source of wisdom, Justin's Christology encompasses a thoroughly theological examination of culture. Jesus, in this vision, does not stand against culture, but speaks within it and points to its fulfillment in him.

Justin thus bequeaths the church two legacies, both in the name of his "fulfillment" Christology. Because his Jesus is the fulfillment of Jewish and pagan wisdom, Christian faith is both capable of absorbing and including other perspectives within it, but is also the apex of truth. Whatever is dimly perceived elsewhere is clearly perceived with Christian vision. If Justin's Christology is inclusive, it is a bounded inclusivity. Other religious traditions and paths ultimately are destined to disappear. It is hard to overestimate the impact of this perspective on subsequent Christologies. Until the past hundred years, it was hardly questioned.

Irenaeus of Lyons (?–ca. 202)

Irenaeus offers one of the most intriguing depictions of Christ in the early church. Less immediately influential than some others of this period, Irenaeus has been rediscovered in contemporary theology, in no small part because of his compelling, holistic christological vision. Jesus Christ, the Word, is active in creation. Irenaeus's preferred image here is that God works through the "hands of the Father,"[7] which are Son and Spirit. This image conveys a unity of divine purpose (what is accomplished in the Father is also accomplished in the work of Son and Spirit) and the embodiment of God's work in the world. God the creator does not hover above the created order, but enters into relationship with it, works within it through the incarnate Son. The Son carries out God's work of gracing, shaping, sustaining, and redeeming creation. This is a direct refutation of a gnostic vision in which creation is the "problem" that needs to be overcome. God's work in Jesus Christ does not result in an escape from creation, but the redemption of the entire created order.

If there is one word that captures Irenaeus's Christology, it is *recapitulation*. This theme is integral to how he conceives of Christ's person and work, creation and salvation. Jesus Christ is the one who recapitulates, or sums up and gathers together the entire history of humanity and all creation. In relation to human beings recapitulation means this: We are created in the likeness and image of God, humanity (in Adam) falls from grace through disobedience—this long history of disobedience is acted out in history in each human being ever since. Christ emerges on the scene as the incarnate Word, who takes this entire history of disobedience as his own and enacts a great reversal. Through his perfect obedience to God, Christ reverses the curse of disobedience. This is the additional meaning of recapitulation, in that Christ does not simply sum up the history of the cosmos but establishes a new headship in his incarnation. In Jesus Christ a new humanity and a new creation begin. Christ is "the recapitulation" that takes place "in his own person of the effusion of blood from the beginning." Christ "summed up these things in Himself . . . saving in his own person at the end that which had in the beginning perished in Adam."[8] We are redeemed through Christ's summing up of the tragedy of human history, his taking it as his own, and reversing it for us. For Irenaeus, moreover, all of creation (and not just humanity) is included in this story of redemption. The coming of Jesus Christ is good news for the whole world. Salvation in Christ is not merely a fix-it job, or a restoration of Eden. Rather, it is the fulfillment of God's ongoing creative work, encompassing all that is. Irenaeus's vision of Christ's saving work is remarkably resonant with contemporary ecological concerns for the healing of creation. At the far horizon of Christian hope is a vision where "creation, having been renovated and set free, shall fructify with an abundance of all kinds of food, from the dew of heaven, and from the fertility of the earth."[9] Animals, sun, moon, and stars are all renewed in this vision: "The whole creation shall, according to God's will, obtain a vast increase, that it may bring forth and sustain fruits."[10] Redemption in Christ does not simply restore what was lost because of sin, but brings creation beyond Eden into more intimate communion with the Creator. "The Word of God, our Lord Jesus Christ, who did, through His transcendent love, become what we are, that He might bring us to be even what He is Himself."[11] Here are clear signs of divinization in the understanding of salvation: Christ enters into the human condition in order to bring us into greater likeness to him.

For Irenaeus, the entire trajectory of Jesus's life, death, and resurrection accomplishes this. He does not isolate salvation in Christ to a single moment on the cross, but spreads it to cover the entire Christ event, which is akin to a second creation. This is a thoroughly *incarnational* Christology (rather than a sacrificial one) that is often a minority voice in the tradition until the nineteenth century, and it is thoroughly consistent with Irenaeus's stress on embodiment. In strong resistance to the strains of Gnosticism in his midst, he stresses Christ as the Word made flesh. It would not be possible for us to be saved unless the incarnate Word took our flesh. Irenaeus stresses the full humanity of Christ, and takes pains to elaborate what this means, by meditating on his blood, organs, physicality, and emotions. Christ has a body; we have bodies; and this body is redeemed by the living God. Christ became "an actual man, consisting of flesh, and nerves, and bones,—that [flesh] which is nourished by the cup which is his blood, and receives increase from the bread which is His body."[12]

One oddity of Irenaeus's Christology is that he is almost alone among the early church fathers whose writings we still possess in claiming that Jesus lives into later adulthood. The cross still figures in Irenaeus's theology, but the Jesus who dies on it is not a young man. Likewise, he maintains a ministry of Jesus that lasts at least a decade (rather than the three years or one year suggested in the Gospels). Odd as these aspects might seem, they are consistent with his view of the saving trajectory of Christ's *life*. What is important about Jesus is not one isolated instance (such as birth, death, or resurrection), but the entire trajectory of Jesus's saving sojourn throughout creation. This understanding of Jesus's life also serves as a reminder that at this point in Christian history there is no fixed biblical canon. Irenaeus may have had access to other traditions about Jesus that included his death as an old man, traditions that have now mostly evaporated from collective memory. Just as Christology was coming into sharper focus, the books of the Christian Bible were only beginning to be collected into a recognizable form.

Irenaeus presents one of the most distinctive early Christian interpretations of Jesus. His work plows the field for future harvests, even when they yield different fruits. His emphasis on the entire trajectory of Jesus's life, ministry, crucifixion, and resurrection resists reductionism. The saving work of Christ cannot be isolated to a single moment. This makes Irenaeus's understanding of Christ *comprehensive*, both in its emphasis on the full span of the incarnation and in its effects on the life of the cosmos. In this vision, there is no aspect of the cosmos untouched by the One who recapitulates all things. The One who comes in the flesh really is good news for all creation.

Tertullian (ca. 155–ca. 220)

Native to Carthage, Tertullian was enormously influential for subsequent theology. Many historians herald Tertullian as a "first" in several arenas: the first to starkly contrast Christian faith with predominant philosophies of the time, the first to employ language of "three persons" in the discussion of the Trinity, the first to reflect explicitly on the "two natures" of Christ's person. Though it is difficult to determine whether Tertullian was, in fact, the first to utter these maxims, his Christology does presage much of what becomes orthodoxy later. Most of Tertullian's work was occupied with combating various heresies he discerns in the wider Mediterranean world. In this regard, he helps clarify what being Christian *is* by ruling out what it *is not*.

Some of the chief culprits, in Tertullian's eyes, were Marcion and those influenced by him. Marcion made a rigid distinction between the God of the Old Testament (who created the material world) and the God of the New Testament (who transcended materiality). This distinction led him to characterize the former God as angry as opposed to the loving God of the latter (a tendency that is evident in popular Christian piety even today). And it further led Marcion to be suspicious of anything regarding the "flesh" or the "material" as getting in the way of salvation offered in Christ. In contrast to this, Tertullian offers a robust defense of materiality, especially in relation to Christ's incarnation. In language that ridicules Marcion and gnosticism, Tertullian writes: "You are horrified also at the infant, which is shed into life with the embarrassments which accompany it from the womb; you likewise, of course, loathe it even after it is washed . . . and yet, in what way were you born? You detest a human being at his birth; then after what fashion do you love anybody?" Christ, by contrast, "has loved even that man who was condensed in his mother's womb amidst all its uncleanness. . . . For his sake He came down (from heaven), for his sake He preached, for his sake 'He humbled Himself even unto death—the death of the cross.' . . . He loved his nativity also, and his flesh as well. Nothing can be loved apart from that through which whatever exists has its existence."[13] By taking on our flesh, Christ restores and redeems it, reforming our death "by a second birth from heaven," restoring us "from every harassing malady," cleansing, renewing, and reanimating us in the flesh.[14] For Tertullian, the real Word really became real flesh.[15]

As equally important for Tertullian's Christology is his conception of the twofold nature of Christ's person. In his work *Against Praxeas*, this pivotal formulation becomes clear. The incarnation does not mean that Christ's humanity envelops his divinity, nor that his divinity overcomes his humanity. Rather, "the Word is nothing else but God, and the flesh nothing else but Man." In Jesus Christ are "two substances" or a "twofold state, which is not confounded, but conjoined in One Person—Jesus, God and Man. In one *Person* they no doubt are well able to be co-existent. Of them Jesus consists—Man, of the flesh; of the Spirit, God."[16] Tertullian is not concerned with *how* this occurs so much as he is occupied with upholding divinity and humanity as equally important to the person of Christ. We have hope for salvation because Christ is divine (only God can save); we have hope that Christ saves *us* because Christ is human (in the incarnation, Christ takes on our flesh).

Tertullian's theological work is also memorable for how it revels in seeming contradiction. What makes Christian faith compelling, for him, is not its logical consistency, but the necessity of faith. This is, after all, the theologian famous for asking the question, "What does Athens have to do with Jerusalem?" hinting that the gospel becomes adulterated if it relies too much on pagan philosophy. The affirmations about Jesus Christ—his incarnation, his two natures—cannot be demonstrated along the terms of alien modes of thought. They are truths of faith and ought to be recognized as such. Tertullian's insistence on this point can make him sound at times like an absurdist, as in the following: "The Son of God was crucified; I am not ashamed because men must needs be ashamed *of it.* And the Son of God died; it is by all means to be believed, because it is absurd. And He was buried, and rose again; the fact is certain, because it is impossible."[17] Tertullian seems most leery of reducing Christian faith to one or the other prevailing philosophies of the time; he is concerned with maintaining the uniqueness of Christian faith and its signal affirmations. Yet his insistence on making the distinctions so stark makes him quite different from a spirit such as Justin (who claimed that whatever is "true" elsewhere could also be claimed by Christian faith). The legacy of Tertullian's more stark terminology has led, in some cases, to Christian anti-intellectualism, or the carrying out of Christian theology in an intellectual vacuum. It is one thing to insist on this stark polarity when the church is threatened with its own survival; it is something else completely to maintain this attitude in a position of relative cultural privilege. Christian faith is paradoxical, especially in its claim that the divine becomes human, and the human divine, in the person of Jesus Christ. But paradox does not always mean contradiction or raw cultural confrontation. In Tertullian, we see the implications of the paradox of the incarnation being worked out at its most significant extent (at least to this point in history).

Origen (ca. 185–254)

A native of Alexandria, one of the premier centers of learning in the early church, Origen was undoubtedly the most productive church father. The sheer volume of his writing is astonishing: some six thousand volumes, an output that dwarfs the contributions of any other early theologian. Born to a Christian family, Origen became attracted to a rather austere interpretation of the Christian life. His asceticism was reflected in his simple attire, a tendency to study late into the night, to sleep on the bare floor, and to fast frequently. Most famously, his odd reading of Matthew 19:12 and his discomfort with his own sexual desire led him to castrate himself. Origen's theological legacy for the church is manifold: in biblical interpretation (where he proposed a threefold schema—literal, moral, and spiritual); in his embrace of Platonism and willingness to put theology in conversation with philosophy (unlike Tertullian); in his speculative vision, which incorporates imagination as a Christian virtue.

Origen's Christology bears traces of speculative philosophy and a universal, cosmic vision. Without doubt, he goes beyond any of his theological predecessors. Though some of his christological reflections were later deemed heretical, it is important to understand the scope of his speculative vision. His understanding of the Logos (Word of God) is distinctive. According to Origen, God begets the Logos eternally, such that there never was a time when the Logos did not exist. But unlike later formulations of the Father eternally begetting the

Son, Origen indicates that the Word is not God in Godself. This eternally begotten Word, though divine, is not the complete expression of God the Father, and is in some way subordinate to the Father. There is some tension here: on the one hand, the Logos might be described as the first act of creation, but on the other hand, this Logos is coeternal with the Father, an expression of the Father's divinity or divine wisdom. This first act, or eternally begotten Logos, becomes incarnate in the person of Jesus Christ.

The incarnation, however, is the result of a twofold process of creation. Origen posits an original, spiritual unity of all created entities. This first creation is purely spiritual, a world of rational spirits, or souls, who exist in constant obedience to the Father. "All souls and all rational creatures . . . were formed or created, and all these, according to their proper nature, are incorporeal."[18] These souls are genderless, or beyond gender. All of these souls, except one, turn away from the Father in disobedience and experience a "fall" into materiality and the distinction between male and female. The material creation that human beings are born into is the result of this primal fall, which is in effect a second-best cosmos, a cosmos populated with beings of differing physical characteristics and capacities: angels, human beings, and animals. Origen's primal fall is thus a fall from eternity to time, from the immaterial to the material, from communion with God to rupture. The diversity of creatures points to the different degrees to which each soul turns or departs from God. The "second" fall, for Origen, occurs when material human beings (Adam and Eve) turn away from God in another act of disobedience. This twofold sense of creation has consequences for how Origen views salvation: The healing that Christ brings is not simply to restore what was lost in Eden, but to bring souls back to their original perfection, beyond gender, in purely spiritual obedience to the Father.

The one soul who does not turn away in the primal fall becomes united with the Logos, and incarnate in Jesus Christ. The incarnation then is the embodiment—coming to creation—of the one rational spirit (soul) that continues to obey God. Like Origen's account of creation, his understanding of the incarnation is twofold: This obedient soul is first united with the Logos in a spiritual union, and only thereafter is born in the flesh as Jesus of Nazareth. Jesus's embodiment is only necessary because the creatures whom he saves have bodies. But the salvation that Jesus brings is beyond the body. Jesus Christ, the Word made flesh, offers a route back to God by offering a double mediation: The Logos mediates (bridges the gap between) God and the one rational soul that did not fall away (the soul that eventually becomes Jesus of Nazareth); and Jesus's soul mediates the Logos to us, offering us a way to recover our spiritual obedience to the Father. Here Origen's Christology displays its bold speculation. Though he takes cues from various biblical texts (such as the creation narratives in Genesis and the Prologue of John), much of his theology relies on Platonic cosmology and accounts of hierarchy in creation.

In this account, salvation in Christ might best be described as deification. Origen says that the "highest good is to become as like to God as possible."[19] The incarnation, at the far horizon of its reach, makes it possible for us to participate in the divine nature and the immortality of God. Human beings can become more like God, as they are saved by Christ. This work of the incarnation will not rest until salvation extends to all creation, so that God becomes "all in all," where our identity is saturated by the presence and life of God. The end result of salvation is to "arrive at a condition of perfect spirituality," where souls "discern all things by their perfect illumination in all holiness through the word and wisdom of God, and are themselves altogether undistinguishable by any one."[20] In the end, this saving work nullifies the material and gender distinctions that divide the human race and separate us from God. Like the Charles Wesley hymn written more than a millennium after Origen, the salvation that Christ brings evokes eternal bliss and communion, where souls are "lost in wonder, love, and praise." For Origen, salvation in Christ is "participation in the Son of God," through which we are "adopted as a son, and by participating in that wisdom which is in God rendered wise."[21] In this way, Origen recalls earlier conceptions of Christ as the Wisdom of God.

Nothing in creation is exempt from the reach of Christ's salvation. So pervasive is Christ's work that salvation is irresistible. This leads Origen to embrace a version of universal salvation, or *apokatastasis* (restoration). Everything that exists in its present fallen form will be restored to its primal form. Even the devil (who is also a fallen soul) is restored to his former glory in obedience to the Father. "Whether any of these orders who act under the government of the devil . . . will in a future world be converted to righteousness . . . is a result which you yourself, reader, may approve of."[22] This tentative universalism, though a minor theme in some eras of the church, has echoed throughout the ages, and has gained even greater attention in the modern era. He reaches this conclusion not because he has an optimistic view of creation, but because he has a pervasive sense of God's purposes, achieved in the restorative work of Christ, which draws all that is back to the being of God. The end in Origen's conception is like the beginning, an account that has led some to charge Origen with having a cyclical view of salvation history, rather than a linear one.

Origen suggests as much: "The end is always like the beginning: and, therefore, as there is one end to all things, so ought we to understand that there was one beginning."[23]

The sheer volume of Origen's work meant that some of his writings would be viewed with suspicion. Write enough and you will rile someone. Origen's reception, accordingly, has had varied seasons in the church's history: from significant early influence, to subsequent condemnation as heresy, to later rehabilitation. Some of Origen's Christology proved heterodox: Both his understanding of the nature of the Son being begotten and his understanding of embodiment as the result of a primal "fall" were eventually rejected by the broader Western church, in part because it exhibited gnostic and subordinationist tendencies. But the very thing that was subsequently dubbed heretical is integral to his Christology. The fullness of Origen's account of salvation in Christ, where all is drawn back into the life of God, depends on a view that understands materiality as distinct from the nature and being of God. The incarnation is necessary because we have fallen from our original spiritual state, and only the Logos who becomes incarnate in the one remaining spiritual, rational soul can lead us back to where we belong, in communion with and obedience to God. But if Origen in this way disparages the body, his account of salvation encompasses all bodies, for the Christ who comes to save really comes to save *all*, no exceptions. If our bodies are "left behind" in this process, no soul is forgotten, for all are redeemed.

Arius (ca. 250–336)

If Origen occasionally hinted at subordination, Arius wholeheartedly embraced it. An influential preacher in Origen's hometown of Alexandria, Arius generated significant attention for his theology. Because Arius's work was subsequently condemned, we have access to much of it only through the writings of his opponents. Nonetheless, his Christology is important to understand, if only because what subsequently came to be known as orthodoxy was defined primarily *against* it.

Arius consistently emphasizes God's utter transcendence in relation to creation. His theology is strictly monotheistic: God alone is God; nothing else is. Arius warns against confusing the nature of the Father with the Son who becomes incarnate in Jesus Christ. The Son "has nothing proper to God in proper subsistence. For He is not equal, no, nor one in essence with Him."[24] Arius recognized that when Christians emphasized the divinity of Christ, they were saying something novel about the nature of God. His theology warns against claiming *too much* about that divinity. His theology is Triune, but not in the sense that came to be embraced later: "Thus there is a Triad. . . . Not intermingling with each other are their subsistences. . . . Foreign from the Son in essence is the Father, for He is without beginning."[25] If the Father is "without beginning," the Son is not: "Hence the Son, not being (for He existed at the will of the Father), is God Only-begotten, and He is alien from either."[26] This claim is what makes Arius's theology most controversial: There was, indeed, a time when the Son did not exist. Arius upheld the divinity of the Son, but clearly this divinity is of a different order from that of the Father. This led ultimately to the charge that, for Arius, the Son is a creature rather than divine (a claim that Arius himself never makes). Yet, in the name of preserving a strict monotheism, Arius claims that the Trinity is not composed of equally eternal persons. The Jesus that emerges from his Christology is divine, but is clearly subordinate to the Father: talk about an eternally begotten Son, in

Arius's eyes, compromises the nature of God and runs the risk of making Christian faith polytheistic.

Though Arius's theology was rejected at the Council of Nicaea, the impulse of his theology is important to understand. He, perhaps more than most in his time, was aware of the specter of polytheism that haunted the edges of Christian theology. From his perspective, Christian faith ought to proclaim Christ as divine Savior, but in claiming him as such, they need not confuse the Son with the Father. The danger of Christology, in his eyes, is that we claim too much about the Son. The only thing that can save Christology from this is to claim the Son as noneternal. When faced with the choice of compromising God's oneness or placing Christ in a subordinate role, Arius invariably chooses the latter. Anything else risked compromising the otherness of God. But in making this claim, Arius left his Christology open to another charge. If the Son is subordinate to the Father, and if Christ saves, then is it really the case that *God* is saving in and through Jesus Christ? Because Christian theology wanted to emphasize *God's* salvation in Christ, Arius's theology became increasingly viewed with suspicion.

Nicene Christology

Arius's influence in many quarters of the church was strong. His position engendered controversy, and led—at least in part—to a council of bishops that gathered in Nicaea in 325. The council—subsequently dubbed the first ecumenical council—came at the behest of the emperor Constantine, the most formidable political figure in the Christian East. Constantine sought to resolve some of the controversy that had arisen in the church in Arius's wake. But he also had political motivations: a more unified theology could result in a more pliable and governable realm. This council signaled the most emphatic rejection of Arianism to date. In vivid imagery, the creed that emerged from it (which is now the most widely cited and shared creed in Christian churches across the world) is unequivocal in establishing Christ's full divinity. Jesus is "The Son of God, begotten of the Father as only begotten . . . God from God, Light from Light, true God from true God." To make matters even clearer, the Nicene Creed offers a formulation that is not found in the Scriptures: Jesus Christ is "begotten not created, of the same reality [or same essence: *homoousios*] as the Father, through whom all things came into being."[27] This extrascriptural nomenclature, *homoousios*, provided a defense against Arianism and benchmark against which later Christologies are judged. Though the council did not put an end to Arianism, it did effectively marginalize any position that claimed the Son was created by the Father or did not share in the fullness of divinity.

Alexandrian and Antiochene Christologies

If the Nicene Council sought to suppress Arian theology in the name of a more unified Christology, other disputes arose in its wake. The competing "schools" of thought both grappled with the question of how the divine and human natures in Christ were related. Both sought to affirm Nicene orthodoxy: namely, Jesus's full divinity and full humanity. These schools of thought were centered in two of the most prominent cities of the emerging Christian world. In Alexandria (in present-day Egypt), theologians such as Athanasius emphasized the unity of Christ's two natures—a unity that can even rightfully be said to affect, or mutually indwell, the dual natures. Alexandrian theologians held the divine natures in Christ in close proximity, even intimacy. Their position has been dubbed a Word-flesh Christology, whereby the two natures inform each other. By contrast, the Antiochene theologians (such as Theodore of Mopsuestia and Nestorius) insisted on preserving the distinction between the two natures. Alexandrian Christology, in their view, risked blurring categories and compromising divinity. The two natures in Christ do not affect one another. Their position came to be known as a Word-man Christology. Both schools sought to uphold ideas that proved pivotal in later Christology: on the one hand, the Antiochene school was insistent on preserving the distinction between Christ's natures. Jesus Christ was not a tertium quid. But on the other hand, the Alexandrians were conscious of preserving the unity of the person of Jesus Christ. A stance that disallowed the communication of attributes (*communicatio idiomatum*) risked rendering Christ schizophrenic: acting as God in one moment and as a human in another. The influence of each school abided. And unlike the disputes that arose with Arianism, the eventual settling of this dispute in the Council of Chalcedon, as we shall later see, winds up affirming aspects of *both* positions.

Athanasius (ca. 295–373)

Like many others of this period, Athanasius hailed from Alexandria, where he served as bishop. He is best known as the primary formulator and defender of Nicene orthodoxy. Much of his work is consumed with debunking the theology of Arius, whose influence had grown over time. In his stringent critique of Arius, Athanasius attacks the root of the Arian position: Rather than preserving monotheism, Arius's theology actually promotes a version of polytheism, since it posits a divine Son who is a different kind of god than the Father.[28] Throughout his christological writings, Athanasius argues for the fundamental equality of Father and Son. The Son is begotten eternally from the Father, and is not subordinate in time or status: "Being the Son, he is inseparable from the Father, and never was there when He was not, but he was always; and being the Father's Image and Radiance, He has the Father's eternity."[29] Father and Son are coeternal, sharing all things. Whatever the Father possesses is also the Son's; whatever the Son possesses is eternally in the Father. This does not mean, however, that there are no distinctions between Father and Son. Even though there is no priority in time between them, there is a distinction in how each person possesses life and exhibits deity: "While the Father does not possess life from anyone, the Son possesses it from the Father. . . . The Son's deity is the deity of the Father, and in this way the Father carries out his providential care for all things in the Son."[30] For Athanasius, there is a priority of the Father in the order of salvation and providence, though this priority should not be considered in temporal or ontological terms. He employs the analogy of light and radiance, whereby the Father is compared to light and Son to radiance. Light does not precede radiance temporally, but radiance occurs because there is light. As there is no radiance without light, so too is there no light without radiance.

Athanasius also devotes considerable attention to the flesh of Jesus and its implications for the divine life. This human flesh is not partitioned off from the work of God in Christ, but interconnected with all that the Son accomplishes. Athanasius attends particularly to the suffering of Jesus in this regard. The flesh of Jesus is not immune to the suffering of all human bodies, but is part of the work of Christ: "When the flesh was suffering, the Logos was not apart from it. That is why the suffering also is said to belong to him. When he was doing the works of the Father in a divine way, the flesh was not external to him. On the contrary, the Lord did those things in the body itself."[31] When Jesus suffers in the flesh, the divine life suffers *in the Son* (in distinction to the Father). Jesus does not in some cases "act as divine" and in others "as human"; rather, in him, the divine work is accomplished in one who is also fully human. Here Athanasius guards against gnostic tendencies that were likely still afoot. His Christology emphatically rejects any view that would imply that Jesus *appeared* to possess flesh or merely *appeared* to suffer. Instead, in the flesh of Jesus, suffering and humanity itself are incorporated into the divine life. "He was true God in the flesh, and he was true flesh in the Logos. That is why, by his works, he revealed both the fact that he is God's Son and his own Father and, by the passions of his flesh, that he bore a real body and that his body was his very own."[32]

At the same time, Athanasius is careful to avoid confusion between the divine and human person in Christ. Though there is intermingling, interconnection, and a sharing of the human in the divine in Jesus Christ, there are yet distinctions. The divine is rightly called "impassible," while the flesh is not:

> Let no one be scandalized by the human characteristics [of Christ]. Rather, let people see that the Logos himself is impassible by nature and that he nevertheless has these passions predicated of him in virtue of the flesh which he took on, since they are proper to the flesh and the body itself is proper to the Savior. Furthermore, he remains as he is—impassible in nature. He takes no hurt from these passions, but on the contrary destroys them and brings them to nothing.[33]

Athanasius is careful to avoid claiming God suffers in the passion of Christ. To state as much would negate impassibility. Nonetheless, suffering belongs to God in the passion and flesh of the Son, a suffering that is overcome in the victory of Christ over sin, death, and the grave. His interpretation of the passion avoids patripassianism (the suffering of the Father), a position mostly considered heretical during this period (though it has resurrected as the new orthodoxy in the present age), while at the same time upholding the suffering of the Son as real and consequential for divine life, and for human salvation.

Athanasius's understanding of Christ's flesh is critical for his view of salvation. He depicts salvation history in terms of humanity's creation in the image of God, a rebellion that leads to the loss of that image, and Christ's incarnation, which leads to the restoration of that image. Christ accomplishes this for us in his flesh: "What was to be done save the renewing of that which was in God's image, so that by it men might once more be able to know him? But how could this have come to pass except by the presence of the very image of God, our Lord Jesus Christ?"[34] This threefold schema of an unmarred *imago Dei*, loss of the image because of sin, and recovery of the image through Christ has been enormously influential in subsequent theology, so much so that it has become the standard pattern of conceiving this history. Earlier configurations (such as Irenaeus's, which stress an original incompleteness of humanity) are, by comparison, relatively minor chords in the development of orthodoxy. There is the sense that salvation, for Athanasius, restores humanity to Eden.

But that is not all. For Athanasius, salvation in Christ does not merely recover what was lost because of human sin; salvation brings humanity closer to God: "Who will not marvel at this? Who will not agree that it is truly something divine? If the works of the Logos's Godhead had not been done by means of the body, humanity would not have been divinized. Furthermore, if the properties of the flesh had not been reckoned to the Logos, humanity would not have been completely liberated from them."[35] Salvation in Christ is restoration *and* new creation, a renewal of flesh that divinizes our broken lives. Salvation does more than repair the damage wrought by sin; it draws Eden into more intimate communion with the divine.

Perhaps best remembered as the chief combatant against the Arian position, Athanasius offered more than a simple "no" to Arius. He considered the coeternity of Father and Son to be essential components of Christian monotheism; he imaginatively conceived of salvation history; and he deftly considered the implications of the flesh of Jesus as good news for a humanity wracked by sin, who were guaranteed new life in the flesh of their bodies. Salvation thus conceived is not an escape from the flesh, but its renewal. This insistence on embodiment as the way to divinization is critical for subsequent theology. Even when it was minimized, Christian theology offered hope for the body, not an escape from embodiment.

Gregory of Nazianzus (ca. 330–ca. 390)

One of the foremost theologians of the Christian East, Gregory of Nazianzus (along with the siblings Basil of Caesarea and Gregory of Nyssa, collectively known as the Cappadocian Fathers) helped entrench Nicene orthodoxy. Gregory of Nazianzus was a friend of the other two fathers, and their collective work (though it has differences of theme and emphasis) is best taken together. Hailing from Cappadocia, Gregory's theological studies took him to Palestine, Alexandria, and Athens. He resisted ordination, but eventually agrees to it, and eventually became bishop of Constantinople, helping to combat resurgent Arianism.

Gregory's Christology is emphatic in its embrace of Jesus's humanity. He is probably remembered more for his dictum "that which he has not assumed he has not healed"[36] than anything else he ever wrote. Any suggestion that compromises Jesus's humanity undermines human salvation: "If only half Adam fell, then that which Christ assumes and saves may be half also; but if the whole of his nature fell, it must be united to the whole nature of Him that was begotten, and so be saved as a whole. Let them not, then, begrudge us our complete salvation, or clothe the Savior only with bones and nerves and the portraiture of humanity."[37] Since the fall of Adam is total, so too must the totality of Jesus's humanity be. Christ is no mere half Savior, but the One who redeems the *whole* person. In his humanity, he embodies what needs to be saved; in his divinity, he provides salvation. Without Christ's full humanity, the human race is lost.

In his conception of the Son's relation to the Father, Gregory is remembered not so much for his innovation as for his reinforcement of emergent Trinitarian orthodoxy. In explicit rejection of any suggestion of Arianism, Gregory reiterates the eternity of divine persons: "When did the Father come into being? There never was a time when he was not. And the same thing is true of the Son and the Holy Ghost. . . . When was the Son begotten? When the Father was not begotten."[38] Father and Son share in the same divine nature; moreover, the distinction between Father and Son does not merely signify different modalities of God's activity. The "Son" does not simply name the "mode" of God when God is redeeming. In maintaining the distinctions between the Trinitarian persons, Gregory is mindful of preserving divine unity. The divine persons, in this view, signify *relations* rather than distinct essences or modes. The three persons are what they are in relationship to each other, and not abstracted from each other. "Father is not a name either of an essence or of an action . . . but it is the name of a relation in which Father stands to the Son, and the Son to the Father . . . so in the case before us too they denote an identity of nature between him that is begotten and him that begets."[39] This description is pivotal for subsequent Trinitarian reflection, as it addresses the often-mounted charge against Trinitarian faith that it effectively promotes tritheism. In Gregory's view, the God who is One is the God who is eternally related.

The unity of Son with Father in relation is coupled with Gregory's equally insistent stance that Jesus possesses two natures in his person. Jesus's full humanity includes a rational soul—an aspect that others of this era questioned. Though there is unity in Jesus's person, Gregory takes more pains than most theologians of this period to distinguish between those aspects of Jesus's life that reflect his divinity and those that reflect his humanity. "What is lofty, you are to apply to the Godhead, and to that nature in him which is superior to sufferings and incorporeal; but all that is lowly to the composite condition of him who for your sakes made himself of no reputation and was incarnate."[40] Thus Jesus was "baptized as a man—but he remitted sins as God. . . . He was tempted as man; but he conquered as God. . . . He hungered—but he fed thousands. . . . He is sold, and very cheap, for it is only for thirty pieces of silver; but he redeems the world, and that at a great price, for the price was his own blood. . . . He dies, but he gives life, and by his death destroys death."[41] Gregory's Christology revels in this juxtaposition between what must be redeemed in order for humanity to gain salvation and what divine activity accomplishes it. Jesus Christ embodies in his person lowliness and loftiness.

The resultant view of salvation, like many others in the East, tends toward divinization. Christ becomes lowly so that we might be exalted. Christ "still pleads even now as man for my salvation, until he make me God by the power of his incarnation, although he is no longer known after the flesh."[42] Such language ("make me God") is rather bold, suggesting at the very least a transformation of the human person into the likeness of God, or the incorporation of humanity into the divine life. Many theologians throughout the ages have resisted this kind of language, because it risks blurring the distinction between God and humanity. But for Gregory, it is essential to uphold. Salvation is total, encompassing all of the human person. There is no partial salvation, or even reckoning humanity as saved, in this perspective. And it is important to note that this view has roots in select biblical texts.[43] For Gregory, to claim that humanity is *not* divinized as it is saved is to effect only an incomplete transformation.

Gregory's fourth theological oration concludes with an abundance of christological titles, emphasizing the depth of Christ's saving riches. Jesus is Son, Word, Wisdom, Power, Truth, Image, Light, Life, Righteousness, Sanctification, Redemption, Resurrection, Way, Door, Shepherd, Lamb, and Priest.[44] All of these titles have roots in New Testament narratives. The fact that Gregory enumerates these titles rather than opting for a few favored ones leads toward an expansive rather than restrictive Christology. When it comes to interpreting Jesus, Gregory is convinced that the Savior has many names.

Gregory of Nyssa (ca. 335–394)

A native of present-day northern Turkey, Gregory of Nyssa's theological education is not as thoroughly documented as that of the other Cappadocian Fathers. Nonetheless, his theology has arguably had greater subsequent impact than either of his colleagues. His brother Basil was instrumental in having him named bishop of Nyssa, and he later assumed the bishopric in Sebaste, also in what is now northern Turkey. But it is his work as a theologian that proved most enduring.

The baptism of Jesus has often proved a stumbling block for theological reflection. If Jesus was without sin, then why was he baptized by John the Baptist? The Gospels give the impression of apologizing for this fact of Jesus's life, taking pains to demonstrate Jesus's superiority to John. (In Matthew, for example, John the Baptist says "I baptize you with water for repentance, but one who is more powerful than I is coming after me; I am not worthy to carry his sandals. He will baptize you with the Holy Spirit and fire," 3:11). Yet in each Gospel, Jesus *submits* to baptism by John. For Gregory, Jesus's baptism is essential for human salvation, because in it *we* are baptized. "To-day he is baptized by John that he might cleanse him who was defiled, that he might bring the Spirit from above, and exalt man to heaven, that he who had fallen might be raised up and he who had cast him down might be put to shame."[45] Jesus's baptism is *for our sake*, further testament of the way Jesus relinquishes himself and becomes lowly, so that we might be transformed. He undergoes in baptism the trajectory of the Christian life: dying to sin, being raised into new life.

Like his colleague of Nazianzus, Gregory emphasizes the unity of Christ's activity with that of God. The distinctions among the persons are not to be mistaken as modes of different actions. God's entire activity is unified. "Every operation which extends from God to creation . . . [has] its origin in the Father, proceed[s] through the Son, and reach[es] its completion by the Holy Spirit. . . . [It is] the same life which is produced by the Father, prepared by the Son, and depends on the will of the Holy Spirit."[46] Furthermore, "no activity is distinguished among the Persons, as if it were brought to completion individually by each of them or separately apart from their joint supervision. Rather is all providence, care and direction of everything, whether in the sensible creation or of heavenly nature, one and not three."[47] All that Jesus is, all that he does, stems from the will of the Father. In his person, Jesus is transparent to the divine life. If one wants to know what God looks like in action, one need look no further than the life of Jesus.

If Christ is one with God, Gregory is nonetheless careful to preserve the distinction between the divine and human natures in Christ. J. N. D. Kelly avers that Gregory "tended to hold the two natures apart," with the divine being active and the human passive.[48] Christ's humanity begins to be absorbed into his divinity at the resurrection, like a drop of vinegar being absorbed into the ocean.[49] In this view, Christ's humanity—ever distinct from his divine nature, eventually disappears. True humanity does not abide forever, even for Christ. And this foreshadows our own glorification at the end of days.

Though the patristic period is not particularly known for its elaboration of atonement theories (which appear more robustly in the medieval period), this period employs a variety of images to capture "how" Jesus saves. As previously noted, Jesus's baptism is pivotal for Gregory. Another prominent image that he employs is how Jesus "ransoms" sinful humanity. In imagery appropriate for a culture familiar with fishing, Gregory depicts Jesus as a veiled human who entraps the devil:

"God, in order to make himself easily accessible to him who sought the ransom for us, veiled himself in our nature. In that way, as it is with a greedy fish, he might swallow the Godhead like a fishhook along with the flesh, which was the bait."[50] In this account, the devil demands a ransom over sinful humanity, whom he has gobbled in his maw. Consumed with greed, the devil sees the incarnate Jesus as yet another human person over whom he has "rightful" claim. The real flesh of Jesus disguises his divine nature. Hence, the devil overextends himself, gets trapped on the hook that is Jesus's divine nature, while Jesus frees those who have been claimed by the devil, effectively ransoming humanity. In short, the trickster gets tricked and we are freed. Iterations of this idea of "ransom" reoccur at various points in Christian history. The main point here is that Gregory identifies salvation as connected not merely to an internal struggle against sin within each person, but in some ways a cosmic struggle between real powers of evil (personified in the devil) and the saving activity of God, given for the world in the incarnate Savior.

But if the trickster gets tricked, there is also hope in Gregory's view for even the trickster's redemption. "For the one practiced deceit to ruin our nature; but the other, being at once just and good and wise, made use of a deceitful device to save the one who had been ruined. And by so doing he benefited, not only the one who had perished, but also the very one who had brought us to ruin."[51] The cosmic battle between good and evil is not a battle of equals. In Jesus, we see the triumph of good who brings evil to naught, whose salvation can even transform the great deceiver. The overarching image for the salvation that Jesus offers, then, is healing: "When, then, evil had reached its highest pitch and no form of wickedness had not been daringly attempted by man, he healed the disease.

Not, indeed, at its onset but when it had fully developed, so that the healing might encompass the total ailment."[52] Though it might be tempting to dismiss this cosmic imagery as a relic of a worldview that is no longer shared (the devil rarely factors into modern Christology), it is critical to uphold several aspects of Gregory's Christology: first, the salvation that Jesus offers is total and pervasive, encompassing all of humanity and all creation; second, it is part of the tragic nature of evil itself that it tends to overextend itself and thus help bring about its own demise. If we can no longer find the fishhook imagery convincing in depicting how Jesus saves, it is certainly helpful in helping document how evil tries to encompass all in its grasp and eventually turns its destruction in on itself. This does not mean that every evil will destroy itself if we only wait for it to; but it does mean that evil's destructive grasp does not offer the final word in the cosmos. And for this insight, we have much to thank in Gregory of Nyssa.

Augustine (354–430)

This survey of patristic Christology concludes with arguably the most influential of all, Augustine, who was born in North Africa to a devout Christian mother and a pagan father. He came to Christian faith somewhat slowly, the result of a restless search for truth and his mother Monica's continued influence. Augustine was initially captivated by Manichaeism, a rigidly dualistic cosmology that maintains that evil is due to an evil principle on earth that is set against a principle of good. Though he eventually rejects this philosophy, some have claimed that traces of Manichaeism remain even in his later theology. A scholar of rhetoric, Augustine converts to Christian faith as an adult in Milan, in an episode in a garden where he hears the words "take and read" that he describes in his *Confessions*. This episode leads to further study of Paul's Letter to the Romans, baptism, and eventually his ordination as bishop of Hippo. Augustine's theological output was prodigious, often dealing with pastoral concerns facing his bishopric and threats to the wider church. In these writings he combats Manichaeism, Donatism (a view that held that the efficacy of the sacraments depended on the integrity of the person administering them), and Pelagianism (which asserted that after the fall human beings still had the capacity to choose the good apart from grace). Augustine's greatest theological influence lay not in Christology proper, but in other areas: his formulation of the doctrine of original sin, his account of salvation by grace, and his account of the origin of evil. But his Christology also contains elements that were important pivots for subsequent interpretations of Jesus and his work.

Compared to many of the other figures we have encountered in this chapter, Augustine devotes relatively little space to discussing the person of Christ. The debates over the two natures of Christ, his relation to the Father, and other christological controversies had quieted by the time Augustine becomes bishop. When he does reflect on the person of Christ, his writing is straightforwardly Nicene. His most enduring influence came in his conception of Christ's saving work. Though one can find traces of multiple understandings of the atonement within Augustine (such as a ransom account), it is the focus on Christ's sacrifice and passion that is key. Augustine offers a survey of Old Testament accounts of sacrifice, the offerings that human beings make to atone for sin. Each of these offerings is partial, pointing to the need for a more encompassing sacrifice. These sin offerings foreshadow the offering that is complete—the offering of the sinless one for the sake of all. This is who Jesus is: "'Him who knew no sin,' that is, Christ, God . . . hath made Him a sacrifice for our sins, by which we might be reconciled to God."[53] Sin costs something; it requires the giving up of something valuable to put ourselves in right relation to the God who gives life. Jesus is the One who makes the ultimate sacrifice, giving of himself freely: "By his death he offered for us the one truest possible sacrifice, and thereby purged, abolished, and destroyed whatever there was of guilt."[54] In this understanding of salvation, Augustine is responsible for an important shift that proved enormously influential for the Western church. The essence of Christ's saving work occurs in the passion of Jesus, who becomes both priest and offering (the priest who offers himself). Where other earlier theologians (e.g., Irenaeus) focused on the incarnation as the locus of salvation, Augustine collapses that focus to Jesus's suffering and death. Since Augustine's time, moreover, this focus has held the greatest sway. With very few exceptions, it is only recently that the recovery of a broader, incarnational perspective has occurred.

Augustine's account of Christ's saving work, to be sure, is closely related to his understanding of sin. The root of the fall, for him, is human pride—the willful desire to live apart from God and to choose creatures instead of God. In the fall, humanity arrogates to itself what belongs to God. Jesus, in his willing sacrifice of himself, is the antidote to the fall in his act of utter humility: giving up of himself and rendering all to God.[55] What makes Jesus Savior is not his might, but his relinquishment of power for our sake: the priest who in humility winds up conquering sin, death, and the grave. Evil is thus conquered not in some kind of cosmic battle, but in an offering that shows how evil is, in fact, empty. Since all things have their existence from God, and all exist in fullness in their proximity to God, evil (which is the absence of the good) only is what it is in distance from God, a distance in the end that renders it into nonbeing. Jesus is the humble king of creation who shows in the trajectory of his obedience to God a pattern for the Christian life. Those baptized in his name are called to follow this path of humility for others. This reading of the Christian life becomes enormously influential for medieval monasticism.

Another important aspect of Augustine's Christology is how it bleeds into ecclesiology. Jesus Christ is head of the church, and the church is Christ's body. Speaking directly against the Donatists (who held that the inadequacies of some members of the church rendered their leadership null), Augustine enjoins the church to love and cherish the body, for in doing so we love Christ. "Nor can any love the Father except he love the Son, and he that loves the sons, loves also the son of God. What sons of God? The members of the Son of God. . . . For when the members love one another, the body loves itself."[56] The gathering of the faithful, in its sacraments, in its preaching, is where we meet Christ. This both contemporizes Christology (by being specific about how we encounter Christ today) and institutionalizes it (by making a strong connection between the ongoing presence of Christ and the institutional church). Both of these moves are significant as the Christian church becomes more firmly established in Western culture.

Augustine's impact on subsequent Christology is hard to overestimate. By focusing on Christ's passion as the locus of salvation, he paves the way for the more detailed atonement theories that occur in the Middle Ages. By combining Christology and ecclesiology, Augustine foreshadows a long era of "establishment" Christianity that institutionalizes a faith that began as a rather fringe movement. Though one could critique Augustine for narrowing the christological focus to passion and sacrifice, it is impossible to understand Christology without his interpretations. After all, it is the cross that Paul claimed as a stumbling block to the gentiles. If Christian faith was to gain a foothold in the gentile world, one had to come to grips with Christ's passion. For that focus, the contemporary church continues to stand in Augustine's debt.

John Chrysostom (ca. 347–407)

If Augustine is considered the most influential "father" of the Christian West, one could make a similar argument for John Chrysostom in the East. A rough contemporary of Augustine, Chrysostom (which means "Golden Mouth") was perhaps the most influential preacher of his day. Born in Antioch, raised by a Christian widow, educated by pagans, Chrysostom became attracted to an ascetic life soon after his baptism at age eighteen, a stint that included two years of living in a desert cave. He is later drawn into church leadership, in some cases against his will. Soon after he was appointed bishop of Constantinople in 398, he embarked on a series of homilies against materialism and the corruption of the city's elites. These sermons put him at odds with the ruling classes, leading to the stripping of Chrysostom's ecclesial title by the emperor (and reinstatement the next day, because of public outcry).

In matters of Christology, Chrysostom is a key representative of the Antiochene school, which preserves the distinction between Christ's two natures. God indwells humanity in Christ, but does so without confusing the divine with the human. What is perhaps most distinctive about Chrysostom's Christology, however, is how it conceives salvation in Christ. He differs most from Augustine in terms of how he interprets the sin overcome in Christ. Unlike Augustine, who conceives of original sin as guilt transmitted from one generation to the next, in part through sexual reproduction, Chrysostom understands original sin as the propensity toward corruption unto death. For Chrysostom, sin is less a guilty sentence needing to be overcome by Christ's righteousness as it is a sickness needing to be healed by Christ the great Physician. For Chrysostom, the fall introduces death onto the scene: Sin is the desperate grasping of humanity in the face of death. Adam corrupts humanity, and we sin in the wake. Christ doesn't simply make us innocent in the face of a guilty sentence; he tackles sin at the root by redeeming us from deathly corruption. Jesus saves us from death, allowing us to grow once again into the image of God, in which we were originally created. Physical rather than forensic images rule in this christological understanding. The West, particularly since the Reformation, has been ruled by forensic understandings of Christ's saving work. And in many respects this can lead to distorted understandings of sin and salvation. (What, for example, does it mean to claim an infant as "guilty" of sin, as strict Augustinians insist?) In Chrysostom, we glimpse an alternative path that avoids some of the problems of lumping all humanity as guilty of sin before they gasp their first breaths.

If Chrysostom's alternative conception of Christ's saving work holds much promise for contemporary restatements of soteriology, his understanding of Jesus's distinction from his Jewish heritage is one of the most damaging legacies of the patristic period. Here we encounter Chrysostom at his most haunting. In a series of sermons preached at a time when some Jews in Antioch were engaged in proselytizing (one of the few times in history when this was the case), Chrysostom urges his audience not to partake in Jewish worship and tradition (such as celebrating Passover as a preparation for Easter). Such practices were unwarranted syncretism and obscured the "fact" that Jesus began something new. The "old" was to be suspended. This conception, which is hardly unique to Chrysostom, has been prevalent throughout the history of the Christian church. It understands Jesus as the inaugurator of a new covenant that effectively ends the old. Clinging to the old represents a stubborn refusal to accept and embrace the promises given to the world in Christ. With Chrysostom, however, this typology of "old" and "new" takes a venomous turn: "Where Christ-killers gather, the cross is ridiculed, God blasphemed, the Father unacknowledged, the Son insulted, the grace of the Spirit rejected. If the Jewish rites are holy and venerable, our way of life must be false. But if our way is true, as indeed it is, theirs is fraudulent."[57] The fault for Jesus's death, in this view, is solely that of the Jews. For this crime, Jews are to be punished, and their ways exposed as false. This conception of old and new leaves no room for coexistence of traditions. If one is true, the other must be false. Indeed, for Chrysostom, the otherness of Judaism is essentially a threat to be destroyed. Most fearful of all is his implication that adherents of Jewish tradition are "fit for slaughter."[58] This is Christology at its most dangerous: where the blessing of Jesus's person and work are twisted into threats against others. By fixating on a monolithic vision of truth, which leaves no room for other truths, the way of life in Jesus Christ degenerates into a way of death. Chrysostom's complicated legacy involves both an important counter to Augustinian views of salvation in Christ and the burdensome and destructive presence of Christian anti-Judaism. The contemporary church must, of necessity, continue to grapple with what is life-giving and what is death-dealing in its interpretations of Jesus. In John Chrysostom, both of these strands are clearly in view.

Nestorius (?–ca. 452)

A survey of patristic Christology would not be complete without at least a cursory glance at Nestorius, a figure who has been charged with adoptionism (the idea that God and/or the Spirit "adopts" Jesus at a certain point in his earthly life so that he becomes divine) and Nestorianism (a heresy named after Nestorius that asserts that a human man and a divine Word exist simultaneously in Christ without affecting each other). As is the case with most historical figures dubbed heretical, Nestorius is more complex than his eponymous heresy implies.

Nestorius, schooled in Antiochene theology, insisted on maintaining the distinction between Christ's divine and human natures. He claimed, "I divide the natures, but I unite the worship."[59] Blending of these two natures invariably compromises one at the expense of the other. To claim that Jesus suffers on the cross is one thing, but to claim that the divine Word also suffers in Christ is tantamount to compromising divinity. Kelly considers Nestorius in this way: "Hence the two, divinity and humanity, must have existed side by side, each retaining its peculiar properties and operation unimpaired. Each was a 'nature,' a term which in his vocabulary connoted, not simply a collection of qualities in the abstract, but the concrete character of a thing."[60] What Nestorius resists is the idea that there is a communication of attributes between the divine and human in Christ, sometimes dubbed the *communicatio idiomatum*, or exchange of properties in Christ. For subsequent orthodoxy, it was important to affirm that all that occurs in Christ is attributed to the selfsame person (and not to parcel out between two persons). Christ's suffering might be described in this way as the human experience of the divine Word. But for Nestorius, even this formulation seemed problematic. In his theology, what Jesus experiences as a human being belongs to his human nature, while his divine attributes belong to his nature as Word of God. "To attribute to [Christ's] divinity the properties of the united flesh, I mean birth, suffering, and death, is . . . the act of a mind truly led astray like the pagans. . . . [We] are dragged into error by the word relationship [by making] the Word God partake of the nourishment of milk."[61] Confusion in Mariology, according to Nestorius, led to confusion in Christology.

Indeed, what proved most problematic about Nestorius's Christology, at least among his contemporaries, was his rejection of the idea that Mary was God-bearer, or Theotokos. This formulation that Mary, as the mother of Jesus, gives birth to a divine redeemer had become significant in early Christian liturgy and piety. Nestorius's resistance to this formulation is consistent with his stark distinction between Jesus's human and divine natures. Mary, as a human being, could not be the bearer of divinity, but only the bearer of Christ's human nature. His polemics against Theotokos were blunt: God cannot have a mother.[62] Mary gave birth to a child who, in turn, manifests the nature of God. Mary in Nestorius's view "is called the Mother of Christ, not the Mother of God."[63] For Nestorius's opponents, this formulation proved too much, since it compromised the unity of Christ. It is primarily on this basis that the Council of Ephesus condemns Nestorius in 431.

This condemnation led to further distancing between eventual orthodox positions and Nestorius's own views. Though Nestorius was careful not to claim that a human person and a divine person exist side by side in Jesus Christ (a rigid separation of the two natures that eventually gets dubbed Nestorianism), his Christology eventually becomes identified with this position. Nestorius's primary motivation seems to be a resistance in confusing Christ's two natures. But in resisting such confusion, he swings the pendulum in another direction, risking a depiction of Jesus that is not unified. For subsequent theology, it became important to claim that Christ's human nature was indeed affected by his divinity. Indeed, this claim is bedrock to a proper understanding of salvation. If Christ's human nature is not affected by God's activity and action in him, then what hope do sinful human beings have of being transformed in the light of Christ?

Chalcedonian Christology

The disputes between competing interpretations of the relationship between Christ's divine and human natures are eventually "settled" (if that is the right term) at the Council of Chalcedon, convened in 451. Like its predecessor, Nicaea, Chalcedon was convened by imperial power (in this case Emperor Marcian and Empress Pulcheria). The bishops gathered for lengthy deliberations and wound up emphatically rejecting monophysitism (the idea that Christ embodies one nature, not two), while hanging on to elements of both Alexandrian and Antiochene positions. The Chalcedonian position affirms (unlike Nestorius) Mary as Theotokos and Christ as "Son, Lord, Only-begotten, recognized in two natures, without confusion, without change, without division, without separation."[64] The use of these phrases effected a brilliant compromise. By describing Christ as without confusion and change, the council warns against the extremes of Alexandrian Christology that could compromise the integrity of Jesus's divinity and/or humanity. But by also describing Christ as without division or separation, it warns against the hard-line Antiochene position that could hold the two natures at a distance from one another. Part of the brilliance of Chalcedon is not in how it narrowly defines Jesus, but in its outlining of the boundaries within which orthodox reflection on Jesus can take place. It excludes extremes, but makes room for varying positions. Perhaps this is the enduring lesson of Chalcedon. At its best, it listens to the wisdom of competing theological positions and sees integrity in both. In this regard the Chalcedonian "definition" is hardly a definition at all. Rather, it opens up a space for continued theological dialogue, whereby differing perspectives might inform each other. If, after all, Christology gives shape to the audacious claim that God enters into human flesh and transforms us into greater likeness to God, then it is certainly the case that no one definition or even Christology can do that claim justice. Perhaps Chalcedon is best seen as a tent-widening rather than tent-restricting theological movement.

Conclusion

On this read, Chalcedon leaves a promising legacy. The patristic period is bewildering in its theological diversity. This is the period when so much seems up for grabs. The skeleton that is New Testament Christology began to take on flesh. But in the process, some formulations get excluded, at least in terms of subsequent orthodoxy. Arius's interpretation of Jesus, which holds that the Son is created, seemed to undermine the grounds of salvation: that God saves in Jesus. But amid the interpretations of Jesus that get excluded is true christological abundance: from Irenaeus's deeply enfleshed theory of recapitulation to Augustine's more juridical interpretation of how Jesus saves; from Origen's imaginative portrayal of the incarnation to Justin's stark and pithy claims. The patristic period, in other words, settles some matters and leaves others open.

It constricts Christology at the same time that it makes room for christological diversity. If the ugliest side of its Christology shows a tendency to distance Jesus from Judaism (hence, the horrors of Chrysostom), its most promising side underscores the need for others in the "doing" of Christology. No one does the work of interpreting Jesus alone.

Notes

1. Ignatius of Antioch, *Letter to the Romans*, in *Callings: Twenty Centuries of Christian Wisdom on Vocation*, ed. William C. Placher (Grand Rapids: Eerdmans, 2005), 34.
2. Ignatius, *Letter to the Romans*, 35.
3. Ignatius of Antioch, *Epistle to the Smyrnaeans*, in *Ante-Nicene Fathers* [hereafter *ANF*], ed. Alexander Roberts and James Donaldson (1885–1887; repr., Peabody, MA: Hendrickson, 1994), 1:87.
4. Justin Martyr, *Dialogue with Trypho*, in *ANF* 1:248.
5. Justin, *Dialogue with Trypho* 1:199–200.
6. Justin Martyr, *Second Apology*, in *ANF* 1:193.
7. Irenaeus, *Against Heresies*, in *ANF* 1:531.
8. Irenaeus, *Against Heresies*, 1:541.
9. Irenaeus, *Against Heresies*, 1:562.
10. Irenaeus, *Against Heresies*, 1:564. "In the resurrection of the just [the words shall also apply] to those animals mentioned. For God is rich in all things." Irenaeus, *Against Heresies*, 1:563.
11. Irenaeus, *Against Heresies*, 1:526.
12. Irenaeus, *Against Heresies*, 1:528.
13. Tertullian, *On the Flesh of Christ*, in *ANF* 3:524.
14. Tertullian, *On the Flesh of Christ*, 3:524.
15. This memorable phrase is from the title of my colleague Cynthia Rigby's doctoral dissertation at Princeton Theological Seminary: "The Real World Really Became Real Flesh: Karl Barth's Contribution to a

Feminist Incarnational Christology" (PhD diss., Princeton Theological Seminary, 1998).

16. Tertullian, *Against Praxeas*, in *ANF* 3:624.
17. Tertullian, *On the Flesh of Christ*, 3:525.
18. Origen, *De principiis*, in *ANF* 4:262.
19. Origen, *De principiis*, 4:344.
20. Origen, *De principiis*, 4:266.
21. Origen, *De principiis*, 4:379.
22. Origen, *De principiis*, 4:261.
23. Origen, *De principiis*, 4:260. "When the end has been restored to the beginning, and the termination of things compared with their commencement, that condition of things will be re-established in which rational nature was placed, when it had no need to eat of the tree of the knowledge of good and evil." Origen, *De principiis*, 4:345.
24. Arius, quoted in Athanasius, *De Synodis*, in *Nicene and Post-Nicene Fathers*, Second Series [hereafter *NPNF* 2], ed. Philip Schaff (1886–1889; repr., Peabody, MA: Hendrickson, 1994), 4:457.
25. Arius, quoted in Athanasius, *De Synodis*, 4:457.
26. Arius, quoted in Athanasius, *De Synodis*, 4:457.
27. The Nicene Creed, in *Readings in Christian Theology*, ed. Peter C. Hodgson and Robert H. King (Minneapolis: Fortress Press, 1985), 205.
28. See Justo L. González, "Athanasius," in *The Westminster Dictionary of Theologians*, ed. Justo L. González, trans. Suzanne E. Hoeferkamp Segovia (Louisville: Westminster John Knox, 2006), 27.
29. Athanasius, *Four Discourses against the Arians*, in *NPNF* 2 4:409.
30. Athanasius, *Orations against the Arians*, in *The Christological Controversy*, ed. Richard A. Norris Jr., Sources of Early Christian Thought (Philadelphia: Fortress Press, 1980), 96.
31. Athanasius, *Orations against the Arians*, 90.
32. Athanasius, *Orations against the Arians*, 101.
33. Athanasius, *Orations against the Arians*, 93
34. Athanasius, *On the Incarnation of the Word*, in *Christology of the Later Fathers*, ed. Edward R. Hardy, Library of Christian Classics (Philadelphia: Westminster Press, 1964), 67.
35. Athanasius, *Orations against the Arians*, 91.

36. Gregory of Nazianzus, *To Cledonius against Apollinarius*, in Hardy, *Christology of the Later Fathers*, 218.
37. Gregory of Nazianzus, *To Cledonius against Apollinarius*, 218–19.
38. Gregory of Nazianzus, *The Theological Orations*, in Hardy, *Christology of the Later Fathers*, 161.
39. Gregory of Nazianzus, *Theological Orations*, 171.
40. Gregory of Nazianzus, *Theological Orations*, 173.
41. Gregory of Nazianzus, *Theological Orations*, 174–75.
42. Gregory of Nazianzus, *Theological Orations*, 187.
43. "But to all who received him, who believed in his name, he gave power to become children of God, who were born, not of blood or of the will of the flesh or of the will of man, but of God" (John 1:12–13); "Be perfect, therefore, as your heavenly Father is perfect" (Matt 5:48).
44. Gregory of Nazianzus, *Theological Orations*, 190–93.
45. Gregory of Nyssa, *On the Baptism of Christ*," in *NPNF* 1 5:518.
46. Gregory of Nyssa, *On Not Three Gods*, in Hardy, *Christology of the Later Fathers*, 262.
47. Gregory of Nyssa, *On Not Three Gods*, 263.
48. J. N. D. Kelly, *Early Christian Doctrines*, 5th ed. (New York: Harper & Row, 1978), 299.
49. Kelly, *Early Christian Doctrines*, 300.
50. Gregory of Nyssa, *Address on Religious Instruction*, in Hardy, *Christology of the Later Fathers*, 301.
51. Gregory of Nyssa, *Address on Religious Instruction*, 303.
52. Gregory of Nyssa, *Address on Religious Instruction*, 307.
53. Augustine, *Enchiridion*, in *Nicene and Post-Nicene Fathers*, First Series [hereafter *NPNF* 1], ed. Philip Schaff (1886–1889; repr., Peabody, MA: Hendrickson, 1994), 3:251.
54. Augustine, *The Trinity*, trans. Edmund Hill, Works of St. Augustine (Hyde Park, NY: New City Press, 1991), 165.
55. Augustine, *On Faith and the Creed*, in *NPNF* 1 3:324.
56. Augustine, *Homilies on the First Epistle of St. John*, in *NPNF* 1 7:521.
57. John Chrysostom, *Discourses against Judaizing Christians*, trans. Paul W.

Harkins, Fathers of the Church (Washington, DC: The Catholic University of American Press, 1979), 10–11.

58. Chrysostom, *Discourses against Judaizing Christians*, 8.

59. Nestorius, *First Sermon against the Theotokos*," in Norris, *Christological Controversy*, 130.

60. Kelly, *Early Christian Doctrines*, 313.

61. Nestorius, *The Birth of the Messiah*, in *Jesus*, ed. David F. Ford and Mike Higton, Oxford Readers (Oxford: Oxford University Press, 2002), 96.

62. Nestorius, *First Sermon against the Theotokos*, 124–25.

63. Nestorius, *Birth of the Messiah*, 95.

64. The Chalcedonian Definition, in Hodgson and King, *Readings in Christian Theology*, 210.

3

Medieval Christologies

The dawn of the medieval period marks an era of "establishment Christianity" that is difficult to overestimate. This period, covering approximately eight hundred years (from the seventh to the end of the fifteenth centuries), witnesses an ascendant church that has moved beyond Constantine's official decree of toleration in the Edict of Milan (promulgated in 313) to an institution that permeates nearly every aspect of society. In much of Europe and the broader Mediterranean world, the church—and Christian faith in general—gives shape to the broader culture. As time marches on, the church seizes the reins of greater power. Though this era includes the Great Schism of 1054, which marks the definitive split between the Western (Roman Catholic) and Eastern (Orthodox) churches, it is an era that, for the most part, assumes some degree of unity in the Christian communion. This is not to say that there were not disagreements. Indeed, disagreements in theological matters continued unabated: Monastic movements emerged, which served to critique some other forms of the institutional church. Mystics offered other perspectives on "orthodoxy." But nearly all of these movements occurred under a rather "big tent" view of the Christian faith.

The portrait of Jesus that emerges during this pivotal period is likewise varied. On the one hand, this is the era where christological orthodoxies get more firmly established and even hardened. This is the age when more fully developed atonement theories arise. A movement known as scholasticism also appears in this era, centered in monasteries and in budding universities. The scholastics sought to establish more firmly the precise words of faith, the ways to interpret Jesus, moving beyond some of the imagistic and imaginative language and symbolism of the patristic era. Hence, the scholastics commented on others' interpretations of Jesus, leading to a burgeoning literature of interpretation. In order to come to grips with Jesus, one had to come to grips with others' interpretations of him. Precision of interpretation led to precision in language and care about words. In order to know Jesus, one had to speak the right words about him. On the other hand, this era also gave birth to widespread Christian mysticism. Also often centered in monasteries, the Christian mystics sought to give voice to the Jesus who was beyond words. Instead of seeking precise language, the mystics expressed the transformative experience of the new life in Jesus. To know Jesus, in the mystical framework, is to know how all language for him falls short.

Perhaps the best way of understanding medieval portraits of Jesus is to see them as reflecting twin impulses: the impulse toward verbal precision on the one hand and the poverty of all words on the other. We must speak about the eternal Word using our words, but also know that our words perennially fall short. The other tension in this period is that between the growing institutionalization of an establishment church and the call to life in Jesus that necessarily critiques any establishment. In this period, Jesus emerges both as king and a humble servant. This is, after all, the same period that witnesses a church amassing unfathomed riches while it also gives birth to movements (such the one inaugurated in St. Francis) that stress the importance of poverty. There is a push and pull in this period between the institutional church, growing in power, and groups that issue periodic critiques of that institution. Being mindful of this tension is critical to understanding this period. The medieval Jesus is multifaceted. Much of what is assumed as common knowledge about him takes place during a flourishing period of theological reflection that has often misleadingly been referred to as the Dark Ages.

John of Damascus (ca. 670–749)

The first theologian we will examine in this period is unique on at least two accounts. John of Damascus, a native of present-day Syria, is the only theologian we will encounter who lived and worked in a context shaped by Islam. Indeed, he served as an official in the caliphate, the Muslim regime in that part of the Mediterranean world. His portrait of Jesus thus emerged in a context where others held rather different views of Jesus. Second, whereas many of the interpretations we will consider focus explicitly on words, John paid close attention to the significance of *images* of Jesus. His portrait of Jesus was shaped perhaps most distinctly by the artistic portrayals of Jesus widely used in Christian worship.

Images, or icons, of Jesus played a part in Christian worship for much of its early history. By the eighth century, however, their use proved controversial. Several theologians and even emperors began to criticize the practice and even banned their use in some quarters. Their position, which came to be known as iconoclasm, attracted a significant following and in many parts of the Mediterranean world led to the destruction of any visual depiction of Jesus. Few icons of Jesus, in fact, exist from the eighth century, and hardly any from periods prior to that. The primary motivation for the iconoclasts was not a philistine antiaesthetic; rather, it stemmed from theological grounds. They claimed that the use of icons in Christian worship led invariably to idolatry, the worship of the image rather than what the image signified. The iconoclasts also operated with a fairly restricted view of the incarnation, and indeed God's activity in the world. In order to emphasize the distinctiveness of the incarnation in Jesus, one had to avoid concrete representations of Jesus (which suggested, at worst, other incarnations).

John addresses the iconoclasts on both of these grounds and argues that their incarnational theology is ultimately defective. In his view, God's incarnation in Christ leads not to a restriction of images and interpretations, but to their proliferation. God has made Godself in Christ visible, and we are to underscore that visibility:

> In former times God, who is without form or body, could never be depicted. But now when God is seen in the flesh conversing with men, I make an image of the God whom I see. I do not worship matter; I worship the Creator of matter who became matter for my sake, who willed to take his abode in matter; who worked out my salvation through matter. Never will I cease honouring the matter which wrought my salvation! I honor it, but not as God.[1]

Icons of Jesus enable worship to flourish, and are not to be tolerated, but encouraged. John makes the distinction between worship (which is properly due to God in Christ alone) and reverence (which we show to icons), which enables us to worship God truly. As people composed of matter, living in a material world, it is the material that helps direct our senses to the spiritual, revealed in the God who comes in the flesh. To smash idols is tantamount to despising Christ's incarnation. To forbid their use is to cut short the dynamic of incarnation: "You who refuse to bow before images also refuse to bow before the Son of God who is the living image of the invisible God, and his unchanging likeness."[2] The iconoclasts, in short, operate with a truncated sense of God's pervasive activity throughout creation. Because God reveals Godself uniquely in the flesh of Jesus, we—as creatures in God's image—access Christ through the material. For John, there is no end-run around matter, no escaping the flesh. Reverence of icons displays an aspect of the good news that Jesus comes to save all flesh.

John further codifies and consolidates the results of the preceding centuries' christological controversies. He is as incarnational (in terms of embodiment) as Irenaeus: "Taking to Himself the first-fruits of the human clay, the very Word became person to the body. Thus, there was a body which was at once the body of God the Word and an animate, rational, intellectual body. Therefore, we do not say that man became God, but that God became man."[3] John echoes Chalcedon in his insistence that the divinity and humanity in Jesus compromise neither nature. In Jesus there is unity but not confusion, a fullness without the creation of a third category that is neither fully human nor fully divine: "The whole He, then, is perfect God, but not wholly God, because He is not only God but also man. Likewise, the whole He is perfect man, but not wholly man, because He is not only man but also God."[4] The good news revealed in Jesus is that in him we have the union of God and humanity, a life given for all, so that all might take part in the abundance that is the divine life. This is good news because only God can save (hence the full divinity) and because it is human flesh that needs redemption (hence the full humanity).

In John of Damascus, we encounter a theologian who reveres the material. God comes in Jesus Christ to the material creation, not in order to escape it, but in order to redeem it. God embraces the flesh in Jesus, and relishes the visual, which is a delight for the eyes and good news to a fallen world. His interpretation of Jesus indicates a subtle aesthetic (which is often minimized in other interpretations of Jesus). Christ is the revelation not only of the good and the true, but of the beautiful as well. In Christ we see what is truly beautiful: a life given for all flesh. The images we create of Jesus do not lead away from beauty, truth, and goodness, but orient us toward them when used rightly. Whereas many other theologians are overly suspicious of the material and visual, John reminds us that without these, the incarnation never touches the earth and the bodies that long for redemption. This may be the most enduring significance of his Christology: In a tradition that has even leaned toward despising beauty, John's portrait of Jesus leads us to recognize what true beauty is.

Anselm of Canterbury (1033–1109)

Our portrait of Jesus moves rapidly forward several centuries to consider one of the most influential voices of medieval Christianity, Anselm of Canterbury. A native of Italy, Anselm enters a monastery in Normandy after travels take him away from home. He soon distinguishes himself as a theologian, writing several of his most significant works while in the monastery. While traveling in England, he is appointed archbishop of Canterbury (somewhat against his will), and experiences a difficult term in this post, often in conflict with the king. During one period of self-imposed exile from his bishopric, he writes his most influential christological work, *Cur Deus homo?* (Why God became human). Anselm is significant in the history of Christian thought for several reasons: First, he embodies the scholastic method, which places a premium on a reasonable faith, the use of the human mind in establishing what is true (or not true) about faith. His most memorable phrase, perhaps, is "faith seeking understanding," a brief formulation for what theology itself is. In Anselm's scholasticism, it is not enough to cite Scripture or other theologians in establishing a true claim about the faith; one instead must *demonstrate* its truth through the proper use of reason. The most famous example of this is Anselm's "proof" of God's existence in what has been dubbed the ontological argument: God exists because God is the greatest that can be conceived. But, second, he is also remembered for his thoroughgoing defense of the necessity of the incarnation and Christ's sacrifice for humanity, through an analogous use of reason. In Anselm, we have the most fully developed atonement theory yet to arrive in the church. And in this respect the turn in medieval Christology is more toward the "work" of Jesus than to his "person." To know Christ, in other words, is to know Christ's benefits—the salvation that he brings and *how* he brings that salvation.

Anselm offers an approach to understanding the necessity of Christ's incarnation and sacrifice that is consistent with his scholasticism. *Cur Deus homo?* proceeds along the lines of question and answer—questions posed by an inquirer that are resolved through a consistent use of reason. His Christology also reveals the fault lines of his medieval culture, a time of lords and vassals, kings and subjects, where those "lower" on the societal rungs owed fidelity and allegiance to those higher up. Medieval order was predicated on proper deference of a subject to his or her lord; and when persons of lower standing made an affront against one higher up on the rungs, they had to seek proper remedies. Anselm's Christology thus displays two prominent cultural trends of his time: a penchant for reason and a penchant for preserving honor. The problem that Christ comes to address is the malady wrought by human sin, a sin that is an affront to God's honor.[5] Anselm's first premise is that sin is *infinitely* serious. It is the ultimate affront to honor because it introduces a stain, a marring, on something that is originally perfect: the created order. Furthermore, sin is an affront against the Ruler and Creator of the universe—the One at the pinnacle of the entire created order. Sin is something that humanity has done on its own, and in sinning, human beings pervert what is just into injustice, distort what is perfect into a twisted and flawed shadow of itself. Humans have only themselves to blame for sin, and in sinning they have made the ultimate affront to God. Anselm then considers the proper response to such an affront. On the one hand, God might simply forgive or ignore sin, by restoring perfection and forgetting the stain that humans have wrought. But this potential response, according to Anselm, flouts the kind of God who God is. Why? Because it ignores divine justice: When honor is affronted, honor needs to be restored by the one who has done the affront. God does have the power to restore creation to its perfection, but if God were to do that, God would be acting in ways contrary to God's justice. In Anselm's words, "Either the honor that was taken away must be repaid or punishment must follow. Otherwise, God will be either unjust to himself or powerless to accomplish either; but it is impious even to imagine this."[6] Something, in short, must be done.

The evil that human beings have done, in short, requires *satisfaction*. "Everyone who sins must repay to God the honor that he has taken away, and this is the satisfaction that every sinner ought to make to God."[7] Furthermore, the satisfaction that is required needs to exceed the impact of the original act of sin: "You do not make satisfaction unless you repay something greater than that for the sake of which you were obliged not to commit the sin."[8] But this recognition creates a further dilemma. On our own, we cannot provide the necessary satisfaction. We cannot restore original perfection; we cannot offer something to the One who already has everything. We already owe God everything that we have, and all that we are: "If I owe him myself and all that I can do, even when I do not sin, lest I should sin, I have nothing to repay him for sin."[9] If the affront had been committed to someone lesser than God, the sinner could provide satisfaction through acts of recompense, penance, and the like. But such acts are ineffective when the One we have affronted is God. Only God can provide the necessary satisfaction: The One who does not need to provide satisfaction is the only one who can do it. Hence, the need for a "God-man" who can perform what humanity cannot do on its own. This resolves the dilemma of providing satisfaction. In Anselm's words, "none but true God can make [satisfaction] and none but true man owes it."[10] Jesus provides the necessary satisfaction by laying down his life for sinful humanity. Yet he is the one human being who is sinless; he is, in short, the one human being who does not need to offer satisfaction to God. He is the perfect One who offers the perfect sacrifice. This perfect act, in turn, merits a divine response. It is in accord with divine justice for this one perfect act to be rewarded or compensated. For it to go unacknowledged would be for God to ignore goodness and sacrifice. But this recognition poses another dilemma:

Because Jesus is fully divine, he already has everything and cannot be compensated. There is no way to make more perfect the One who already is perfect. The result is a superabundance of good and grace: an infinite compensation for a perfect sacrifice. Jesus does not and cannot receive this. Yet it abides. And Jesus, who is all perfect and all good, then transfers this superabundance of good to sinful humanity: an infinite goodness that is God's forgiveness of all sin. Jesus's perfect sacrifice thus makes the necessary satisfaction, whose recompense is transferred to all people across all time. Jesus does not simply restore creation to a status quo ante, but brings it into closer and more intimate relation with the God of all.

In this tightly logical (and somewhat elaborate) theory, Anselm offers an *objective* understanding of the atonement. Jesus's entry into the created order changes realities *external* to the human heart. Anselm emphasizes less the change *in us* and more the change in creation itself and the fulfillment of requirements of divine justice. It is also a theory that focuses less on the life and teaching of Jesus and more on his sacrificial death. What matters most, in the end, is Jesus's willingness to lay down his life for others. The theory is more cross-centered than it is focused on the entire span of Jesus's life. In the end, what saves in Jesus's life is his death. It is hard to overestimate how influential Anselm's theory has been in subsequent history. Versions of this account have become common coin in many quarters of the Christian church: from medieval artwork depicting Christ's perfect sacrifice to contemporary tent revival meetings that stress the goodness of Jesus's death. But Anselm's theory betrays more than a focus on a "good death." From start to finish, it betrays the traces of medieval honor codes. His entire argument is premised on the notion of a fixed social (and created) order with rigid hierarchies and roles for persons—and that when an affront is made against one higher on the social rungs, an act of compensation, or restoration, is required. One question to ask, at least in our day, is this: In contemporary societies that often bristle against such social hierarchies, how much of Anselm's theory is appropriate? Does the notion of rigid hierarchies run against the Pauline claim that in Christ there is neither slave nor free and that the dividing lines between humans begin to wash away? What, in short, is salvageable from this theory? It is most effective, perhaps, in making a persuasive case for how Christ saves, but is perhaps defective in its perpetuation of the divisions in society that Christ came to wipe away.

Peter Abelard (1079–1142)

A generation younger than Anselm, Peter Abelard is often paired with his predecessor because of their contrasting Christologies. Nearly all of his life was spent in France, in urban centers of learning such as Paris, as well as more isolated retreats, such as the abbey in Cluny at the end of his life. His biography is doubtless more colorful than those of most theologians. He alienated several of his teachers, then became a popular teacher himself, only to fall in love with one of his students, Heloise. Their relationship was scandalous, resulting in a secret marriage and the birth of a child, Astrolabe. After being castrated by distraught members of Heloise's family, he and Heloise eventually settle near each other in similar religious communities. Abelard's theology proved nearly as controversial as his biography during his life, and included official condemnation of much of his work in 1141, a mere year before his death. Earlier condemnations include decrees to burn some of his writings in 1121.

Despite (or perhaps because of) the controversies surrounding his person, Abelard's Christology has stood the test of time, and has undoubtedly experienced a renaissance in the contemporary era. It differs markedly from Anselm's, and is critical of many christological assumptions of the patristic era. The broad outlines of Abelard's Christology are notably present in his commentary on Romans. In it, he asks the same question that Anselm poses: Why is it necessary, for the sake of our salvation, for Jesus to become incarnate and die? Many earlier answers to this question, as we have seen, hold some role for the devil. Jesus comes to rescue or ransom humanity from the clutches of Satan. According to some of these approaches, the devil has a rightful claim on humanity because humanity has fallen into sin. But for Abelard, any claim of Satan's rightful claim is nonsensical. "The devil acquired no right against man whom he had seduced simply by seducing him, except perhaps (as we have said before) in so far as it was a case of the Lord's permitting it."[11] The prime exchange, for Abelard, is not some cosmic struggle between God and Satan. Jesus comes, as we shall see, to set the human heart free.

Upon first glance, the death of Jesus seems unjust, even cruel. Abelard is not afraid to poke some of the suppositions of his contemporaries' piety. He begins not by lauding Christ's suffering but asking critical questions of it: "How cruel and wicked it seems that any one should demand the blood of an innocent person as the price for anything, or that it should in any way please him that an innocent man should be slain—still less that God should consider the death of his Son so agreeable that by it he should be reconciled to the whole world!"[12] The theological target is at least an indirect critique of Anselm. While his predecessor sees as a necessary death to restore honor and dignity to remove the stain of sin, Abelard asks whether making the death of Christ "necessary" renders the love of God negligible. His solution to the question, *cur Deus homo*, thus zeroes in on divine love radiating out to humans.

For Abelard, there is no divine decree that sends Jesus to the cross, in order to satisfy the demands of justice. Rather, what we witness consistently in the incarnation, which culminates in the cross, is the extent to which divine love is *for us*. In his life, in his teaching, in his death, we glimpse the radical reach of God's love: a love that does not hold back to preserve oneself, even unto death. God will endure anything, in Jesus Christ, for humanity, because God loves us. "Through this unique act of grace manifested to us—in that his Son has taken upon himself our nature and preserved therein in teaching us by word and example even unto death—he has more fully bound us to himself by love."[13] In Jesus Christ, God wills to be with humanity, showing us the way of love, kindling our hearts to love anew. When we witness the transformative love of Jesus on the cross, God empowers us to live and love anew. This is what is changed by the incarnation; this is how we are healed. Unlike Anselm, Abelard has a *subjective* understanding of the atonement: What changes are not the external factors such as a victory over Satan or satisfaction of divine justice, but the internal realm of the human heart. Jesus saves and frees us from sin by making us capable of loving anew. When we witness the full extent of divine love in Christ, we are transformed and made participants in that love for others. "Our redemption through Christ's suffering is that deeper affection in us which not only frees us from slavery to sin, but also wins for us the true liberty of sons of God, so that we do all things out of love rather than fear."[14]

Abelard's approach to the atonement is sometimes dubbed the moral exemplar theory: Having seen the example of God's blazing love for humanity in Christ, we are inspired to follow the example of Christ in all of our lives. When the theory is posed in that way, it can readily be charged with Pelagianism: that it is we who muster ourselves to love when we are inspired by Jesus. But Abelard's articulation of the theory is not, strictly speaking, Pelagian. The entire initiative begins with God's grace: a divine love that kindles and inflames our love. The love that we are capable of is because of divine love, and there is no way to love apart from grace.

It is also easy to psychologize Abelard's theology: The fated, star-crossed lover of Heloise finds its ultimate resolution in a theory of how Jesus "saves" by love. Where Abelard fails to find fulfillment in love on earth with his beloved, he is compensated with the fulfilling love of Christ. Such readings of his theology, though important, are ultimately reductionistic. It is no surprise that some of Abelard's biography might be reflected in his theology. (Good theology, after all, pays attention to context.) But it is quite another matter to reduce theology to biography. Nonetheless, we witness in the theology of Abelard a testament to an increasing focus on love in wider Christian practice and devotion. And we have also a hint of the budding practices of courtly love: the beginnings of romantic paeans to love, the rituals that became celebrated among medieval nobility about the power of romantic love. In an era that was beginning to celebrate the power of romantic love, it is perhaps no surprise that a portrait of Jesus emerges as lover par excellence. Abelard's portrait of Jesus raises several questions, but perhaps chief among them is, what aspect of God do we most emphasize? Any portrait of atonement relies on some divine attribute: for Anselm, it is justice; for Abelard, it is love. No single theory can attend to everything one wants to claim about the God revealed in Jesus Christ. Abelard, in this case, makes a wager: It is better to overemphasize love than something else (such as justice). For a justice without love quickly degenerates into cruelty. If Christians, following John, want to claim that "God is love" (1 John 4:8), then perhaps Abelard's wager is a good one to make. Even if this risks sentimentality, it is better to hold on to the love of God than to lose it altogether. Whatever Christology one winds up embracing, one test of it is whether or not it points us, in the end, to divine love.

Bernard of Clairvaux (1090–1153)

A contemporary, fellow countryman, and frequent opponent of Abelard, Bernard also makes a wager for divine love revealed in Christ, though he makes it on different terms. Drawn to an austere version of the Christian life at an early age, Bernard enters a Cistercian monastery in Cîteaux. A mere year later, he is asked to establish a new house for the monastic order in Clairvaux. From this post, Bernard exercises great leadership, not only among the Cistercians, but also in the wider church, weighing in on multiple theological controversies of his time, and most memorably as the chief theological exponent of the Second Crusade.

Much of Bernard's Christology is reflected in his experience of the Christian life. Jean Leclercq claims:

> The point of departure for Bernard's entire doctrine is an intense, personal experience of the interior struggle. All of his theology is merely a reflection of this primary fact in light of the Gospels and St. Paul. . . . Man had lost the perfect spiritual freedom that permitted continual union with God through an unwavering adherence to the divine will, but he can still regain that freedom. He does not despair for he knows that God became man and saved us in Jesus Christ. Thus, there are always two sides to the question: a deep realism that causes humility, and a sure hope that gives rise to courage and optimism.[15]

Paul's autobiographical remarks, in Bernard's eyes, are enacted in every person: "I do not understand my own actions. For I do not do what I want, but I do the very thing I hate" (Rom 7:15). Christ is the only resolution to this struggle, for he has taken the struggle as his own.

Jesus's struggle for our sake is revealed fully on the cross: "For that death, that Cross, the opprobrium, the scorn, the beatings which Christ endured, what else were they but outstanding examples of obedience for his body, that is, ourselves?" When we witness what Christ endured for our sake, we learn to "imitate his obedience" and "suffer deeply for the sake of obedience."[16] The cross represents the vanquishing of the struggle to do what is not in accordance with God's will, the submission of the self to what is God's will. Jesus's life, in this sense, presents the pattern for the redeemed life. And, in this sense, it is not primarily a cross-centered approach. Bernard echoes Irenaeus—and offers a different perspective from both Anselm and Abelard—by claiming that it is the incarnation that saves. Leclercq puts it this way: "Through the Incarnation, Christ the Mediator brings God's mercy to man in his distress. Filled with God's presence, the soul, while remaining fully human, is no longer in distress. . . . The incarnation is the fundamental Christian mystery from which the other mysteries unfold."[17] Jesus comes to creation not to die, but to enact the pattern of a life spent in submission to God. In Jesus, we know that God has taken our broken lives as God's very own, redeeming them by grace, enabling us to live in obedience to God once again.

One of the radical implications of this vision of Jesus is how it gives expression to the transformative work of Christ in each human life. In this regard, though Bernard stresses incarnation more than crucifixion, he is more akin to Abelard's subjectivism than Anselm's objectivism. What happens in Jesus also happens *in us*. In a Christmas Eve sermon, Bernard notes, "To-morrow, therefore, we shall see the majesty of God, not indeed in himself but in us. . . . A man must make himself a Bethlehem of Judah if he would have Jesus to be born in his heart."[18] Though each person undergoes an intense spiritual struggle, rebelling against divine favor, embodying sin, the struggle is overcome in the One who, as divine, takes it as his own. Because Christ is human, the struggle he undergoes is also ours; because he is divine, the struggle does not supply the final word.

In stressing the incarnation, Bernard runs up against a development in popular piety. It had long been established as orthodox that Jesus himself was born of a virgin. One of the sidelines of this doctrine was the development of traditions which claimed that Mary, too, was conceived without original sin (the immaculate conception). Bernard was one of the most vociferous opponents of this development (which, incidentally, was not defined as Catholic dogma until 1854), because he thought it detracted from the uniqueness of Jesus. Furthermore, Bernard resists the idea that the flesh of Jesus was somehow created *de novo* in Mary's womb and did not stem from her flesh. Bernard resists this tendency since it undercuts the conviction that Jesus, like all human beings, was born of the mother's flesh: "Flesh was assumed from the origin from which the Virgin came forth and was not created new in the Virgin; for it was derived from the same root."[19] Mary's uniqueness lay in the fact that she gave birth to Jesus, not because her own conception and birth were unlike all others. And the Son she gives birth to is flesh of her flesh. Bernard's incarnationalism, in short, does not avoid the flesh.

The most memorable of Bernard's reflections on the life and passion of Jesus are, no doubt, his reflections on Jesus's passionate love for God and humanity. This aspect of his Christology emerges not in his reflections on the Gospels, but in his sermons on the Song of Songs. In this period of the church, the erotic poetry of the Song was extremely popular, generating perhaps more writing and sermons than any other book in the Bible. Bernard composed and preached eighty-six homilies on the Song of Songs, a series designed to follow the sequence of the Song, and never finished making his way through the book. Many of these sermons are devoted to a few verses. In these sermons, Jesus emerges as the consummate lover, who consummates his love affair with us, which is itself a reflection of the passionate Triune love. Commenting on the Song's opening words, "Let him kiss me with the kisses of his mouth!" (Song 1:2), Bernard writes: "The mouth which kisses signifies the Word who assumes human nature; the flesh which is assumed is the recipient of the kiss; the kiss, which is both of giver and receiver, is the Person which is of both, the Mediator between God and man, the Man Christ Jesus."[20] Bernard employs allegory in this interpretation: The Song's male character stands for Christ, while its female character stands for us. But whereas other forms of allegory can minimize the eroticism of the Song, Bernard's seems to revel in it. The love of Christ for humanity is not only agape, it is eros; it is love in the shape of desire and longing, a love that kindles our own longing for the Redeemer. Jesus is not a disinterested observer of humanity who loves without passion; he is passionately involved in the case of humanity, longing for us as his beloved. The kisses are really kisses, and we are promised in love to be enthralled by Christ's kisses. Salvation in Christ, in the end, is ecstasy. But ecstasy does not come immediately. Instead, it is marked by a long journey. Leclercq states this succinctly: "Jesus comes so that the soul will cling to him; he goes away so that the soul will call him back. He wants us to love him and takes certain steps to win our love: He gives himself so that we will enjoy his presence; he then leaves us so that we will long for it even more."[21] Just as the lovers of the Song are more characterized by physical absence from each other and longing than intimate presence, salvation in Christ is marked by kisses and longing for kisses. In these sermons more than any other place, Bernard makes plain the case for Christ as Lover.

Bernard of Clairvaux offers a multifaceted portrait of Jesus. He is an icon for the Christian life insofar as he depicts the struggle against sin that is each person's, One who offers resolution to that struggle in submission to God. And as flesh of Mary, he saves not primarily through the cross, but through the long course of his life, a life given even now to those who would follow him. But most vividly, and perhaps most influentially, Jesus is the lover of humanity, the One who is the mirror of God's passion for creation. The One who is the incarnation of divine Love longs for all to partake in that Love. If many portraits of Jesus have emphasized agape at the expense of eros, Bernard's portrayal reminds us that eros is a component of God's love for the world in Christ.

Hildegard of Bingen (1098–1179)

A German abbess and polymath, Hildegard entered a Benedictine convent as a child and grew to study and write on a wide number of subjects. Her writings are saturated with reverence for creation, which has led some in the contemporary church to regard her work as a precursor to ecological theology. If the medieval church was assuredly patriarchal, one of the avenues for women's voices was in mystical strains. Hildegard, like most of the other women noted in this chapter, is best described as a mystical theologian. Her chief christological points are contained in a series of visions, the most famous of which is *Scivias*, a report of these visions in Trinitarian outline.

One of the visions contained in this book (which also contains Hildegard's illustrations of these visions) focuses on an edifice with pillars. One pillar represents the Trinity and another stands for the Son who "holds up the whole edifice of the Church." Hildegard exposits the traditional categories of Christ's divinity and humanity, but her description of his humanity is most intriguing. Here she bleeds Christology into ecclesiology: Christ's humanity "is manifested in the ardent faith of its stones, which are the faithful people who work hard by the goodness of the Supernatural Father when the Trinity has been revealed to them." She further explains that "the incarnate Son of God, who is true God with the Father and the Holy Spirit, is now inherent in his members, that is, the faithful people who will be born up till the end of the world and made members of their head through living works."[22] This is more than saying that Christ's humanity is revealed in members of the church, the body of Christ; rather, it is claiming that his humanity is *present* in the church, in the faithful. If one wants to know what the humanity of Christ looks like, one need look no further than the faithful. This is not to claim that the faithful are without sin; the entire course of *Scivias* is a call to confession; but it does say that Christ's humanity draws so near to the church that it becomes the humanity of its members. Again, the tones of intimacy are strong. Christ does not keep his body to himself, but gives it to the world.

Like any true mystic, Hildegard claims that Christ, in the end, is not strictly knowable. He cannot be grasped by human knowledge because he is divine. But if Christ cannot be known, one can have relationship with him through faith: "For the great and incomprehensible holiness of the true Incarnation is so obscure to human minds that it cannot be contemplated, except insofar as it can be done by faith. It can be understood in faith and works by those who labour in the divine cult."[23] Knowledge of Christ does not reside in the recesses of the human mind; but he becomes visible to us through the faith of the church, and in "works." This emphasis on works is also significant, as it foreshadows later debates in the church. For Hildegard the mystic, it is clear that knowledge of Christ is not limited to faith as a passive reception; we can also come to know Christ when we are caught up in work for the sake of the kingdom he proclaimed. This is consistent with her emphasis on Christ's humanity: For Hildegard, Christ is the One who draws near—present in the members of his body, unable to be grasped by human knowledge, revealing himself to us in faith and works. The ecstatic visions of this mystic reveal a vision of Christ who is solidly grounded in this earth, in these people.

Clare of Assisi (1193–1253)

Born into a relatively prosperous family in Assisi, Italy, Clare came into contact with the teachings of Francis, the founder of a monastic movement that stressed poverty, simplicity, and care for creation. When family members arranged her marriage, Clare spurned these arrangements and instead sought the counsel of Francis. Soon thereafter, Clare decides to follow Francis and become a part of the movement he inaugurated, eventually becoming the prioress of "Poor Ladies" that emphasized poverty, chastity, and contemplation. Though not a prolific writer, much of Clare's correspondence has been preserved, most significantly in her letters to Agnes, the daughter of the king of Bohemia who had also refused an arranged marriage. In these letters her Christology comes into fullest view.

One of the most prominent images for Jesus in this correspondence is that of the bridegroom. In refusing to marry a man (as their families had urged), these sisters of poverty consented to marry Christ. This marriage is a paragon of virtue: "When you have loved [Him], You shall be chaste; when You have touched [Him], You shall become pure; when you have accepted [Him], You shall be a virgin. . . . You are *the spouse and the mother and the sister* of my Lord Jesus Christ."[24] This latter portion is a remarkable statement: While bridal imagery is common in depicting the believer's relationship to Christ (most allegories of the Song of Songs, for example, consider the female lover to be the church or the believer and the male lover to be Christ), Clare also suggests that the chaste believer is analogous to the mother of Christ. This is both an analogue to Mary, Jesus's own mother's, chastity, but it is also something more. In later correspondence, Clare claims that the chaste believer will "always carry Him spiritually in your chaste and virginal body."[25] The believer makes room for Christ in her body akin to the womb. Our relationship to Christ spins out in multiple relations: akin to the intimacy of the nuptial bed, the familial bond of a sibling, and the gestating warmth of pregnancy. And in this transformation of the "normal" ways of viewing such relations, it is in chastity that one is nuptially bound to Christ and in virginity that one carries Christ within.[26]

The One to whom we are bound in marriage is also poor. In hallmark Franciscan fashion, Clare also interprets Jesus through abjection. Jesus, the high priest and king, becomes poor on our behalf so that we might be exalted through him: Jesus "chose to appear despised, needy, and *poor* in this world, so that people who were in utter poverty and want and in absolute need of heavenly nourishment might become *rich* in Him by possessing the kingdom of heaven. . . . The kingdom of heaven is promised and given by the Lord only to the poor."[27] This great reversal, which echoes across Franciscan practice, has sometimes been heralded as presaging the "preferential option for the poor" that is found in twentieth-century liberation theology (which we will explore later in this book). What is significant here is that Jesus becomes poor not in order to praise poverty, but so that poverty might be glorified (i.e., transformed into spiritual richness). The Jesus who glorifies us is the Poor One who is rejected by the wealth and power of this world, but who reveals the nature of true riches. In their rejection of material wealth, the Franciscans sought to indicate where true wealth lay.

Coming into contact with the prestige and power of this world, however, Christ also suffers. His suffering, Clare writes, is a result of the world's contempt: "Look upon Him Who became contemptible for you, and follow Him, making yourself contemptible in the world for Him. Your Spouse, though *more beautiful than the children of men*, became, for your salvation, the lowest of men, despised, struck, scourged untold times throughout His whole body, and then died amid the sufferings of the Cross."[28] As in her interpretation of Christ as bridegroom, this imagery is filled with contrasts: Jesus's glory is in his humiliation; our exaltation is possible because of the world's rejection of him. But his sufferings also mean that we are never alone in ours. The believer enters into relationship with Christ also through imitation, which is achieved both by undergoing physical sufferings, but even more so through contemplation: "*Transform* your whole being *into the image* of the Godhead Itself through contemplation! So that you too may feel what His friends feel as they taste *the hidden sweetness* which God Himself has reserved from the beginning for those who love Him."[29] Clare's interpretation of Christ is not masochistic, the delight in suffering; rather, it is contemplation and suffering so that we might partake in greater glory. Indeed, the imagery here is sensuous: tasting (the most intimate of the senses) the sweetness God has reserved. Though Clare and the Franciscans stressed simplicity, the end of life in Christ was intensely pleasurable.

This recognition is important to salvage Franciscan traditions from the charge of undue austerity. Though Clare, like others, was resolute in stressing Christ's poverty (and the poverty of those called to follow him), it was not for the sake of suppressing bodily senses. Instead, relationship with Christ awakens the senses, intensifying them. Jesus is the one who redirects our passions, not by smothering them, but by making them flourish in relation to him. Jesus is the one "whose beauty all the heavenly hosts admire unceasingly, whose love inflames our love, whose contemplation is our refreshment."[30] Jesus is the fulfillment of desire, the one in whom our desire finds rest, so that we might love even more. The crucified and despised One is also the vision of true beauty.

Clare's interpretation of Jesus revels in contrasts: chastity and marriage, wealth and poverty, humiliation and glorification, desire and restraint. Jesus is the one who bridges what is seen as separate, who shows us the shape of the fulfilled life, who orients us not to the evanescent promises of earthly desires, but their fulfillment in his life for the world. Those who follow him are shown the path of fulfillment, even if that path is a difficult one.

Bonaventure (1221–1274)

Bonaventure is often considered the second founder of the Franciscans. Like the founder of the order, Bonaventure was Italian. His chief theological studies were at the influential University of Paris. A gifted scholar and teacher, Bonaventure was also conscripted for various ecclesial leadership posts, including general minister of the Franciscan order, and eventually a cardinal in the church. In these leadership capacities, Bonaventure often played a mediating role, resolving disputes between the more extreme Franciscans, who advocated adherence to the letter of Francis's *Rule*, and more liberal accommodationists, who sought to assimilate into the life of the universities. He also was important in lessening the impact of followers of Joachim of Fiore, an apocalyptic mystic who prophesied that a new age would be inaugurated in 1260, an "age of the Spirit," which would signal the beginning of the end times. Bonaventure was an unapologetic institutionalist who saw the rise of Joachim's thought as a threat to the burgeoning infrastructure of Christendom, not to mention its heady speculation about the end of time. His most influential christological reflections come from two sources: *The Soul's Journey Into God*, a contemplative manual, and *The Tree of Life*, a meditation on the Gospels.

Bonaventure is sometimes described as an "emanationist," who understands all things flowing from God and ultimately returning to God. Though this characterization can be misleading, it can also help understand the significance of

Bonaventure's basic theological orientation. Zachary Hayes describes that orientation in this way:

> Bonaventure can speak of a center in God. And it is through that center that God reaches out to form the created world. That world with its history, then, moves outward in a circular movement from its origin in God to find its final end in its return to God. This circular movement is mediated by the central person of the Trinity, who became incarnate in the form of Jesus of Nazareth, thereby bringing the center of God into union with the center of the world.[31]

The orientation of the world is akin to our own, as we find our beginning and ending in the living Trinity. *Soul's Journey* depicts this dynamic movement in greater detail, as a detailing of the mystical life and the life of Christ for the world.

Bonaventure's understanding of the spiritual life is governed by the metaphor of ascent. The soul, when properly oriented, rises from the mundane, the terrestrial, and sensible to the celestial, and ultimately is incorporated into the life of God. Jesus Christ is the "ladder" in Bonaventure's vision, the one who provides the way of ascent to the Trinity. In Bonaventure's words, "There is no other path but through the burning love of the Crucified."[32] The journey is possible only by grace. Technically speaking, we do not climb the ladder, but are lifted up it by the love of Christ.[33] The journey, though arduous, promises ecstasy as our appointed end. The new life in Christ offers nothing less than transformation, where the life of Christ becomes our own: "Transcending yourself and all things, by the immeasurable and absolute ecstasy of a pure mind, leaving behind all things, and freed from all things, you will ascend to the superessential ray of the divine darkness."[34]

Compared with other theologians of his milieu, Bonaventure spends little time reflecting on dogmatic issues such as the unity of Christ's divine and human natures, or the preexistence of Christ (though his Christology assumes both of these) and more on the life of Christ as gleaned from the Gospels. This might be called Bonaventure's "exemplarism," in which Jesus Christ is the prime example for us in the universe—the link between deity and creation—and the indication of how God extends generosity and grace to the whole world. Jesus's birth, life, passion, and resurrection provide the key that unlocks the mystery of the universe. He is both a personal example, who shows us that we need to carry about his life in our own, and a cosmic example of God's activity in the world. This exemplarism is most evident in *Tree of Life*, a short meditation on the New Testament accounts of Jesus. For Bonaventure, Jesus is a tree, whose lower branches represent his origin and life, whose middle branches represent his passion, and whose topmost branches extol his glorification.

The lower branches of the tree indicate Jesus's lowly birth: "Although he was great and rich, he became small and poor for us."[35] Bonaventure's Franciscan emphases are distinct here: Nearly everything about his understanding of Christ's life is colored with humility, poverty, patience, and obedience. These are the virtues that echo throughout the life of Jesus, and they are ones that we are to incorporate into our own lives. Jesus's earthly life is one of submission, not only to poverty and simplicity, but to the law in order to redeem and free us.[36] One of the more striking aspects of this interpretation of Jesus's life is how Bonaventure interprets Jesus's table fellowship, especially surrounding the Last Supper. Jesus does not simply share food; he becomes food for us, bread that is delightful and pleasant to taste.[37]

If Jesus submits to the law and to others throughout his life, this pattern continues as his earthly life ends. Faced with an unjust sentence and the brutality of the Roman system and some of the religious authorities, Jesus endures his passion with patience, refusing to strike back: "The Lord of all creation was struck on the ears like a contemptible slave, while he with placid respect and submissive speech gently reprimanded one of the servants of the high priest who had given him a blow."[38] Again, this is a pattern for our lives and the life of the world: true power in the cosmos is not tit-for-tat exchange of violence, but the refusal to engage in violence so that it might be overturned. Throughout Bonaventure's depiction, Jesus is placid in his passion. This placidity reverses the order that had been in place since the fall of Adam. When Jesus is given bitter gall as he is breathing his last gasps, he reverses the taste that had been in place since expulsion from Eden. Adam, in tasting the sweet and delightful fruit, brings sin and curse into the world; Christ in tasting the bitter gall, provides the remedy of forgiveness and salvation.[39] He endures bitterness, agony, and suffering so that we might partake in the fullness and sweetness of life again. And, in his death, Christ's body provides yet more: When the soldier pierces Jesus's side, out pours water and blood, symbols of the church's sacraments.[40] In surrendering his life, Christ's body springs forth in abundant life for all.

Bonaventure concludes this depiction of Christ by reflecting on the resurrection. Here the chords begin to sound different. If Franciscan traditions are sometimes depicted as austere and ascetic, this Franciscan's vision of fulfillment in Christ drips with sensuousness. The final notes of Christ's person underscore his beauty. "This most beautiful *flower of the root of Jesse* . . . thus blossomed again in the resurrection so as to become the beauty of all. For that most glorious body—subtle, agile and immortal—was clothed in glory so as to be truly more radiant than the sun, showing an example of the beauty destined for the risen human bodies."[41] The risen Christ thus unveils our destiny, to be incorporated into his beautiful life for the world, to shine as the sun. It is a destiny that rings with marital tones as well, as the believer is united to Christ akin to a bride and bridegroom. Our fulfillment is found as we are "led into the palace of the heavenly court and introduced into that sacred and secret bridal chamber and will be united to that heavenly Lamb [Christ] in so intense a covenant that bride and groom will become *one spirit*."[42] Jesus, the end and goal of all things, is known to us in the end as a lover who makes us participants in God's eternal love.

Bonaventure's vision of Christ is at once mystical and practical: Focused squarely on Gospel accounts of Jesus's life, his reflections also invite the reader into a speculative vision of eternal life in Christ. The poor, simple, scorned Jesus who walked this earth is also a sensuous Savior who makes us partakers of God's eternity. The legacy of this Franciscan thinker is to invite us to retell and draw us into the story of Jesus, to become participants in the life of Christ and not mere observers of it. As we walk where he walked, we take part in the suffering and the beauty of the One who is both scourged and beautiful, simple and attractive. His Christology depicts a Christ who brings the world into the heart of God. One question to ask of Bonaventure is whether his Christology turns our renewed attention to the needs of the world (as his focus on Jesus's life and servanthood does), or whether it encourages us to focus on the things above the world (as his concluding mysticism does). Perhaps this tension is necessary: Too much focus on the here and now can eclipse the dawn of the new day that God is bringing; too much focus on the heavenly or what lies ahead can close our eyes to the needs of the present, to the crying injustice of this earth. Both of these foci are necessary for a full depiction of Christ, the one who is both incarnate and risen. If Bonaventure emphasizes one at the expense of the other, it is probably reflected in the way his Christology ends with an ascent above the terrestrial and mundane. Intriguingly, his focus on the Jesus of the Gospels yields a mystical Christ who rises above all flesh.

Thomas Aquinas (1225–1274)

Italian by birth, encouraged by his family to join the Benedictine order, Thomas Aquinas eventually found a home with the much more recently founded Dominicans. He is undoubtedly the most significant and influential theologian of the medieval period. His *Summa theologica*, a comprehensive, systematic account of Christian faith, has probably not been surpassed as an intellectual and theological achievement since it was written. Though, as is often recollected, Thomas at the end of his life considered it—and everything else that he had written—to be mere straw. While his work did not receive immediate acclaim, it eventually became integral to theological education in the Roman Catholic Church, and he "is the only theologian who is mentioned in the *Codex of Canon Law* of 1918," which notes that all priests are to receive instruction according to Thomistic method.[43] Thomas is notable in the history of theology for his recovery of Aristotelianism, which emphasizes the role of the senses in coming to correct knowledge. And perhaps even more important is his conviction that reason can demonstrate many of the truths of Christian faith (though reason is ultimately fulfilled in revelation). Thomas is perhaps the best exemplar of scholasticism, which relies on the collected wisdom of inherited traditions, synthesizes their contributions, asks questions of nearly every aspect of faith, and employs reason to its fullest in new articulations of faith for the present. In Christology, Thomas is likewise a synthesizer. Anselm and Augustine, in particular, factor heavily in his expression of Christ's identity and work. But he is no mere repeater of this inherited tradition. Instead, he expands the scope of these earlier theological perspectives, crafting what might be described as a narrative interpretation of Jesus.

Perhaps the best way of understanding Thomas's Christology is as a story. Joseph Wawrykow notes, "Aquinas in the ST was the first to make the retelling of the story of Christ, from the beginnings to its culmination, integral to a scholastic treatise on Christ."[44] His interpretation of Jesus is notable in that it does not isolate any one moment as the cause of our salvation. Like many of the earliest Christologies, Thomas takes an incarnational approach to Christology, emphasizing the course of Christ's life, death, and resurrection. Within this retelling of the story of Jesus, Thomas undoubtedly spends more time than many of his contemporaries in emphasizing Jesus's humanity. Jesus, as a human like all other human beings, had to rely on his senses to come to fuller knowledge of the world. His temptation, as a human being, is also fitting: "Christ wished to be tempted; first that He might strengthen us against temptations."[45] This narrative of Jesus yields an abundance of titles for Jesus, as Thomas refers to him by multiple names, including ones that have not been as developed in the tradition, such as defender, teacher, brother, and food.

Like most any theologian who seeks to uphold orthodoxy, Thomas emphasizes the union of human and divine in Jesus Christ. Jesus is properly known as Mediator who unites us to God "by communicating to men both precepts and gifts, and by offering satisfaction and prayers to God for men."[46] The union of humanity and divinity is not created by the Father, such that the eternal Word becomes a creature. But the human nature taken up "by the Word in the act of the incarnation is creaturely" and, hence, it can be said that "Christ is a creature according to the Word's human nature."[47] The union of divine and human in Christ does not mean that one nature overcomes the other. To know him as incarnate is to know him as the One who represents God to humanity and humanity to God. In this sense, Christ is a double Mediator.

Thomas spends much time (in the *Summa* and elsewhere) reflecting on the necessity of the incarnation. On the one hand, human nature cries out for restoration, for healing, for satisfaction, and for mending the damage caused by sin. In this sense, the incarnation is necessary. "It was appropriate that God became a human being, so that the one who was able to repair human nature and the one who was able to make satisfaction for sin would be one and the same."[48] But the crying need of the world does not mean that God is *required* to act in any specific way. The necessity of salvation does not constrain or compel the activity of God (as if God could not have acted in any other way). Furthermore, construing necessity as compulsion would mean that Christ did *not* suffer voluntarily, which Thomas holds as essential for the sake of our salvation. Jesus of Nazareth willingly conducted all aspects of his life (a will that accorded with the will of God). Yet Christ's passion "was necessary from necessity of the end proposed,"[49] namely, our salvation. We can only be saved through the action of God, by one who shares in our humanity. But the action of this One is also willing, not constrained by external necessities. Indeed, for Thomas there is no one, isolated moment within the story of Jesus that is *the* pivot for salvation. Resurrection is as integral to this story as Christ's suffering and death. "As Christ destroyed our death by his death, so he restored our life by his resurrection."[50]

Nonetheless, like many of his contemporaries (and those influenced by Thomas), Christ's passion occupies a prominent place in the story. "Christ by His passion merited salvation, not only for Himself, but likewise for all His members."[51] Thomas recalls Anselm, whose understanding of the atonement centers on a willing, meritorious act undertaken by the one who does not need to make atonement for himself. The compensation for this act of merit—submitting to the cross—is transferred to sinful humanity, the members of Christ's body. But Thomas's interpretation of the cross expands the Anselmian view, for in the crucifixion, Thomas also sees ethical consequences for our own lives. The cross, in this view, is an example of virtue that can take root in our lives. And it reverses the transgression of Adam: "This kind of death was especially suitable in order to atone for the sin of our first parent, which was the plucking of the apple from the forbidden tree against God's command. And so, to atone for that sin, it was fitting that Christ should suffer by being fastened to a tree, as if restoring what Adam had purloined."[52] By one tree comes curse and death; by dying on another tree, Christ brings forth forgiveness and life. Christ's passion, however, only "affects" his human nature. Like many who preceded him in the tradition, for Thomas it is improper to ascribe suffering to Jesus's divine nature: "What is impassible cannot suffer. Consequently, Christ's passion did not concern his Godhead."[53] The vulnerability of the cross, in other words, does not compromise divine power.

Another part of the broader narrative that Thomas stresses is Christ's descent into hell. This creedal affirmation, which has often been perplexing, was for the sake of liberation: "He descended into hell to free from punishment others, who were kept there because of the sin of our first parent, for which Christ had already made full satisfaction by suffering death . . . in order to show himself the liberator of the living and the dead."[54] In this descent, Christ reveals salvation that is intended for all: for those who preceded the incarnation as well as those who stand in its wake. In rising from the dead, Christ signals God's triumph over sin, death, and the grave. In his glorified body, we get a foretaste of the glorified bodies that are promised us at the end of days.[55] In this regard, salvation in Christ, for Thomas, is physical as well as spiritual.

Several aspects of Thomas's Christology are significant for future developments. First, it is an attempt to offer a comprehensive portrait of Christ, in which the entire narrative (rather than one moment within it) points to the redemption possible in Christ. Second, by attending to Christ's humanity, Jesus's coming to knowledge through the senses, Thomas offers a portrait of Christ that touches the earth and does not hover above it (or human nature). Finally, he offers a compelling account of the logic of salvation in Christ by carefully accounting for the necessity of incarnation and passion. Even if many of Thomas's questions are no longer prominent today, the way that he wrestles with *every* question leaves an important legacy for contemporary theology: The fullest interpretations of Christ leave room for entertaining alternative perspectives on him. In this regard, it is important to entertain other answers before we answer the question, Who is Jesus Christ for us today?

Meister Eckhart (ca. 1260–ca. 1327)

Dominican mystic Johannes Eckhart, also known as the Meister, received a classical education, studied with several influential teachers, and served as professor in Paris. Also known for his influence on the formation of the modern German language, Eckhart is most memorable in theology for his bold interpretations of Christ and the transformation of the believer by grace. Though often accused of being a pantheist, Eckhart's writings, on closer examination, reveal a profound sense that the work of Christ is nothing less than Christification—the sacramental change of the person like unto Christ. In explaining this transformation, Eckhart pushes the boundaries of orthodoxy. Much of his writing proved controversial in his own time and in the years hence. Most notably, this controversy led to a charge of heresy in 1326, shortly before his death the following year. In 1329, Pope John XXII condemned some of Eckhart's theology, but cleared him of heresy charges. Argument over his varied writings—contained in sermons, commentaries, and treatises—has continued ever since.

Though Jesus's passion and teaching occupy some of Eckhart's attention in these writings, his Christology is most noteworthy for its interpretation of Christ's birth (and rebirth) in each person. This *incarnational* Christology stresses the coming of the Son to heal humanity from its sin and render us adopted children of God. His coming is good news for all. Where Eckhart's interpretation becomes daring is in how he personalizes this coming. He is wholly orthodox in speaking of the Father's eternal begetting of the Son (à la Nicaea and Chalcedon), but pushes the boundaries in the following claim: "He [the Father] has given birth to him [the Son] in my soul. . . . He gives me birth, me, his Son and the same Son. I say more: He gives birth not only to me, his Son, but he gives birth to me as himself and himself as me and to me as his being and nature."[56] Eckhart makes this bold assertion to describe the transformation of the individual, by grace, through Jesus Christ. Christ's work in our lives is nothing less than our rebirth and the rebirth of the Son in us. In this sense, the incarnation is an ongoing event, renewed in each person. Key to this understanding of Jesus's work is the Eucharist. As believers partake of Christ's body and blood in the sacrament, they become sacramental vessels themselves: "What is changed into something else becomes one with it. I am so changed into him that he produces his being in me as one, not just similar. By the living God, this is true! There is no distinction."[57] Here the boundaries of orthodoxy begin to sway. Whether or not one reads Eckhart here eschatologically (that the far horizon of Christian hope is the transformation of the person like unto Christ), the distinctions that have sustained most preceding Christology here begin to fall away. By asserting that there is "no distinction" between the believer and Christ, Eckhart risks the charge of pantheism, or at least pan-anthropo-theism (blurring the boundaries between divine and human).

Eckhart pushes the boundaries even further in his likening of the transformed believer to the Father: "Out of the purity he everlastingly bore me, his only-born Son, into that same image of his eternal Fatherhood, that I may be Father and give birth to him of whom I am born. . . . He gives birth to his Only-Begotten Son in the highest part of the soul. And as he gives birth to his Only-Begotten Son into me, so I give him birth again into the Father."[58] Here the distinctions between divine and human, and between genders, really become blurred: Father gives birth to Son, who transforms us, so that we, in likeness to the Father, give birth to the Son, and render him back to the Eternally Begetting. Even if we read comments like this as rhetorical or poetic flourish, it becomes difficult to sustain this Christology as orthodox. Yet, in Eckhart's defense, he is speaking to the radical change that takes root in life because of Christ. His interpretation stresses deification, a strain that has been present in the Christian tradition since its inception (John 1:12–13) and echoed thereafter in varied voices, especially in the Christian East. Bernard McGinn understands Eckhart along these lines, situating his bold christological assertions among wider, more common themes: "The Word is Son by nature, we are sons by adoption; he is the true image of the Father, we are made to the image; and, finally, we are the members of Christ."[59] Christ comes, in short, so that we may become by grace what he is by nature. The movement, in this case, is always from the Father, through the Son, to us; and though we return this movement by giving "birth" to the Son, God's initiative in Jesus Christ is always primary, always the initiator. In this sense, there is never a complete blurring of categories between Creator and created, even if on the far horizon of Eckhart's Christology, Christ so permeates all things as to render the boundaries permeable. Indeed, from his perspective, our hope is founded on nothing less: Christ is the One who invites all to take part in his fullness, who makes us members of his body, who suffuses our entire being, so that we are no longer bound to sin.

This insight might make Eckhart's the most hopeful Christology we have yet encountered. In Christ, our divinization is complete, and it is enacted whenever we partake of the sacrament. His interpretation of Jesus lingers little on the teaching, witness, or even crucifixion of Jesus, and instead focuses on the eternally begotten Son who is also born in us. This focus on a cosmic Christ can make Eckhart's Christology slippery: He neither offers an account for how this birth of the Son takes place in us, nor does he take pains to preserve distinctions between humanity and divinity that are common to most Christian interpretations of Jesus. At times this also renders Eckhart's Christology unmoored from history, in that the details of Jesus's life as outlined in the Gospels give way to his sacramental presence spread throughout the universe. But this may also be its hidden strength: Jesus Christ is good news for all creation, who enables creation's rebirth wherever his grace is present. Few theologians have spoken as eloquently and persuasively about the new life given by Christ. The change wrought in the soul and in creation is real. And in this regard, for Eckhart, there is no looking back on the old creature.

John Duns Scotus (ca. 1265–1308)

A native of Scotland, John Duns Scotus joined the Franciscan cause in 1280. He studied later in some of the great universities of Europe: Oxford, Cambridge, and Paris. Shortly before his death, he assumed a teaching post in Cologne. Suspicious of some of Thomas Aquinas's theological methods, Scotus argued against what he sensed was an overdependence on Aristotelianism. This argument against Aquinas's method, in part, led to the further distancing of theology from philosophy in the Middle Ages.[60] In matters of Christology, Scotus is important for the way he understands the *predestination* of Christ, anchoring the incarnation not primarily as God's response to or remedy for human sin, but as an expression of God's eternal glory and desire for union with creation.

For Scotus, Christ's coming is not primarily to redeem. This may strike some as puzzling, given the centrality of redemption in most narrations of the Christian story. But by decentering redemption, Scotus wants to avoid rendering the incarnation as a mere bandage or fix-it job for the "problem" of sin. Christ's coming is more than that. God eternally elects the Son as a manifestation of divine glory. Christ is the union of divinity and humanity in his person, the One who is chosen before all time: "It does not seem to be solely because of the redemption that God predestined this soul to such glory, since the redemption or the glory of the souls to be redeemed is not comparable to the glory of the soul of Christ."[61] Election is prior to sin, both temporally and theologically. Election is first extended to Christ, who is in turn the cause of our election. This makes Christ's predestination, and the incarnation itself, something inherently "positive," and not simply a supremely wise divine response to the mess humanity has created. "The incarnation of Christ was not foreseen as occasioned by sin, but was immediately foreseen from all eternity by God as a good more proximate to the end."[62]

Even in a hypothetical scenario of no human sin, Scotus claims that Christ's incarnation would still have occurred and still be good news for the world. The reason for this is that the incarnation does not simply restore what had been lost because of sin, but brings creation to greater fulfillment, because it is the full manifestation of divine glory and love. This glory and love revealed in Jesus Christ makes possible the greater union of God and creation. In Scotus's words, God elects and sends the Son because "he wills to have other colovers, and this is nothing else than willing that others have his love in themselves."[63] And though Scotus generally pays less attention to hypotheticals than other theologians of his time, it is clear that the fundamental reason for Christ's coming is love—the extension of love to all, and the transformation that love brings to each person touched by it. Scotus thus resuscitates one of the oldest themes of Christian tradition, found in the Gospel of John, renewed in Abelard and others, and echoing with special resonance in contemporary theology. Indeed, many medieval theologians fixate on this particular aspect of the incarnation. The era that probably bequeathed more commentary on the Song of Songs is likewise responsible for emphasizing the centrality of love in our depiction of Jesus. This is ultimately where Scotus's interpretation of Jesus shines: By emphasizing the eternal election of Christ in love, we are invited to partake of that love as the pinnacle of what it means to be created in God's image.

William of Ockham (ca. 1280–ca. 1349)

Often identified with the medieval school of nominalism, which questioned the existence of "universals" as opposed to the particular, individual realities that we encounter in the world, Ockham (like Scotus) was a Franciscan from the British Isles. He proved controversial in his time, primarily because of a dispute with Pope John XXII over the nature of ecclesial poverty, a dispute that led to his excommunication. Strictly speaking, Ockham did not deny the existence of universals, but claimed that they were organizing concepts for our encounter with reality, and as such, existed only in the mind. His theological legacy lies primarily in completing what Scotus began: namely, questioning the use of reason as establishing the truth of Christian doctrines. Though Ockham, like any theologian, employs reason, he claims that it alone cannot explicate the faith. His theological stance veers toward voluntarism, which maintains that the will of God has precedence over all else. In this understanding, God does not will the good, but *what* God wills is good. The divine initiative establishes what is good or not. Ockham's reason for asserting thus is that he does not want to constrain the activity of God by any human conception of "the good" established by reason.

In Christology, Ockham is primarily consumed with questions of the union, or the relation of the human and divine in Christ. In this, his voluntaristic tendencies are evident. The incarnation, Ockham claims, "is founded in human and not divine nature, because only human nature is imperfect and hence capable of the union, which is not true of the divine nature."[64] There is no "need" for this union, glimpsed from the perspective of the divine; nonetheless, God wills the union. Indeed, "union" only makes sense from the human perspective, which stands in need of it. This leads to the question of what happens to human nature in the hypostatic union. Ockham rejects the idea that the human becomes divine with a humorous twist:

> One way would be that human nature would *become* the person of Christ. However this understanding is incorrect because it is more repugnant to human nature for it to become the person of Christ than for it to become a jackass. The second way would be that human nature is *sustained* by a divine person, and this understanding is correct because [Christ's human] nature does not subsist as an independent being but is sustained by the Word of God.[65]

Ockham's interpretation keeps the two natures in Christ distinct, emphasizing the primacy of the divine in making the union possible, highlighting the human as the ground of the need for union. But nothing about this union, according to Ockham, can "be proved philosophically; its truth is known only by Faith."[66] Here is represented the terminus of one end of the medieval sensibility: In a period that assiduously employed and embraced reason as a means for greater understanding of not only the person and work of Christ, but all of Christian doctrine, a decidedly scholastic theologian arrives at the conclusion that rather little can be demonstrated as truthful about any doctrine on the basis of reason. Here Ockham sows seeds that begin to flower later in other periods (such as the

Reformation and its subsequent pietism). To understand Christ truly, one must embrace him in faith.

Birgitta of Sweden (ca. 1303–1373)

Perhaps because Ockham and others signaled the limits of reason in interpreting Jesus, the portraits in the latter portion of the Middle Ages often veer toward the devotional: images meant to stir the heart more than the head. Birgitta of Sweden is one of these exponents. After her husband's death, she founded an order that came to be named after her and eventually moved to Rome. Her interpretation of Jesus comes mainly from a series of visions that she experienced. Many of these focus specifically on Christ's passion as a subject of reverence.

Birgitta's vision lingers on the crucifixion of Christ: "His fine and lovely eyes appeared half dead; his mouth was open and bloody; his face was pale and sunken, all livid and stained with blood; and his whole body was as if black and blue and pale and very weak from the constant downward flow of blood." His death was "prolonged and delayed amidst grave torment and great bitterness." No part of his body was immune from this torture: "He then had pale lips, a bloody tongue, and a sunken abdomen that adhered to his back as if he had no viscera within."[67] Birgitta's image of Jesus's brutal death is multilayered. It evokes horror in its graphic depiction of Christ's agony, underscoring the savage nature of Jesus's death. In an age that was no stranger to violence, this is an image that may also have emphasized Christ's connection and solidarity with all victims of violence. The image also evokes sympathy: here laid bare for all is the suffering of the divine Son, the One who bears the brutal consequence of the world's sin on his body. As we witness his torture, we are moved to pity and even reverence that this Son underwent such for our sakes.

This graphic image can overwhelm so that we must turn away; in this sense, the suffering of Christ is too much to bear. Look any length of time and one has to avert one's gaze. But at the same time, Birgitta's image also invites lingering attention: to pay close attention to the wounds, the pain, the suffering of Christ, for they are the cause of our salvation. The image both draws our attention to violence and implores us to find another way beyond violence. But there is no way beyond violence that does not grapple with the horrific consequences of sin's violence. In this sense, Birgitta's image—like a train wreck—both revolts and attracts. We can't bear to look at the same time that we are summoned to look. It is no coincidence that Birgitta's verbal imagery here bears consonance with much medieval iconography that focuses on the wounds of Christ. His wounds show solidarity with all who bear wounds: the downtrodden, the despised, the rejected. In this sense, the imagery might even be subversive: In an era often dismissed for its rigid social hierarchies, this portrait of Christ may show us that God's initiative is consistently with those who are wounded by society's violence. But in the end, Birgitta's portrait is less a theological exposition than it is a devotional image. She draws with her words a suffering Savior who invites all to contemplate and take part in his suffering anew.

Julian of Norwich (1342–ca. 1416)

Not much is known about Julian of Norwich's life, other than a few captivating facts. Her *Revelations of Divine Love* is the first English-language book to have been written by a woman, which contains her reflections on a series of sixteen visions that she received in the midst of a grave illness in 1373. These "revelations," or "showings," according to Julian, came sometime after she had prayed "to receive three wounds, namely, the wound of true contrition, the wound of genuine compassion, and the wound of sincere longing for God."[68] The other striking fact of Julian's life is her position as an anchoress, a life committed to prayer and withdrawal from the world, symbolized by living in a cell. Anchoresses underwent a ritual whereby they were sealed in a cell (symbolizing their death to the world, akin to a tomb) and reborn to a new life of contemplation. Whether Julian received these visions prior to her embarking on an anchorite life is unclear; what is clear is that she writes the revelations while an anchorite in Norwich cathedral.

Like Birgitta, Julian focuses explicitly on Christ's suffering: Nearly all of her expositions of the revelations deal with the passion. And like her Swedish counterpart, she lingers on the physical torment of Jesus, focusing on his discolored and desiccated body and agonizing thirst. Christ was "hanging in the air, like some cloth hung out to dry." These sufferings are meant to kindle our own compassion. In Julian's vision, "All the while he was suffering I personally felt no pain but for him."[69] But they also express Christ's solidary with us in suffering: "For when he suffered, we suffered. All creatures capable of suffering pain suffered with him."[70] In focusing on Christ's solidarity with all suffering creatures, Julian is hardly unique. But her exposition takes a distinctive hue when she suggests that Christ's suffering continues in the resurrection. Typically, the resurrection is interpreted as vindication of the suffering servant, or a triumph over suffering. But for Julian, it represents the continuation of the passion: "Now that he is risen and is impassible, he still suffers with us."[71] This correlation of impassibility and suffering is a bit puzzling, since divine impassibility typically means that one is incapable of experiencing pain. But for Julian (though she does not expand on this), Christ's impassibility involves some incorporation of suffering and pain in the ongoing resurrection life. It recalls, perhaps, the risen Christ's appearance to Thomas in the Gospel of John, where Christ's body still bears the wounds of crucifixion (John 20:27). Resurrection is not to bodily perfection, beyond pain, but to a body scarred by the cross that incorporates pain into God's eternal life. Christ's solidarity with suffering continues beyond the grave.

In some respects, Julian's interpretation of the passion encourages our embrace of suffering as a gift: "The sharper our suffering with him on his cross, the greater our glory with him in his kingdom."[72] The question here is whether Julian's Christology amounts to an undue valorization of suffering. On the one hand, Julian's voice is comforting, in that it promises that whatever agony we experience, Christ is already there with us, taking our suffering as his own. There is no place, in short, where he is not. Knowing that Julian wrote her *Revelations* at the peak of the Black Death in Europe, these words are no empty promise. Her visions occur in a context that knew all too well the finality and horror of a swift, untimely death. Julian's witness in this context was nothing less than radical hope in the face of death: that nothing in life or death can separate the believer from God's love in Christ. But there are also tendencies in Julian's revelations that seem to encourage readers to seek suffering, which anticipates the glory one will ultimately receive. As in much else, it all depends on how the *Revelations* are read. If we keep in mind her context (radical hope in the face of bubonic plague), we avoid masochistic readings of the text. Julian does not advocate a search for suffering at all costs, or suffering as its own good; rather, her christological vision refuses to give up hope even in the face of death. This tension, however, is often the case in Christian interpretations of suffering: Emphasizing the meaning of suffering too much risks rendering it a good to be sought after; avoiding its meaning risks turning a blind eye to the manifold suffering of every age. Julian's Jesus is, at his root, a Servant who suffers in solidarity for the sake of humanity, for the sake of love, for the sake of life.

The most innovative and captivating aspect of Julian's Christology is its turn to the maternal. Jesus is the Mother who nourishes, cares, and tends to her children. Julian first grounds this interpretation of Jesus in the Trinity: "In our Father, God almighty, we have our being. In our merciful Mother we have reformation and renewal. . . . In yielding to the gracious impulse of the Holy Spirit we are made perfect."[73] This captivating twist on gender considers the Son to be Mother as well. And though Julian does not explicate in great detail the consequences of this grammatical shift, her use of maternal imagery opens up other dimensions of Christ's saving work. Indeed, her use of images and metaphor is fluid throughout her vision: the Son is presented as both male and female; the Christ who is our Brother is also our Mother. Julian invokes childbirth as an image for describing Christ's care for the world: Jesus "is in labor until the time has come for him to suffer the sharpest pangs and most appalling pain possible."[74] The eternal Word gestates creation into being; Christ labors on behalf of humanity, culminating in the agony of childbirth, even relinquishing his life so that others might live. Jesus is also the Mother who nourishes us: "The human mother will suckle her child with her own milk, but our beloved Mother, Jesus, feeds us with himself, and, with the most tender courtesy, does it by means of the Blessed Sacrament, the precious food of all true life."[75] Here the Eucharist is compared to breast milk, the basic food that sustains us in infancy. This is the closest analogue to what Christ does in his gestures at the Last Supper: to feed his disciples with himself. For, in feeding the infant with breast milk, the mother does feed her baby with herself. Later in this same exposition, Julian continues the gender-bending. Note the juxtaposition: "The human mother may put her child tenderly to her breast, but our tender Mother Jesus simply leads us into his blessed breast through his open side, and there gives us a glimpse of the Godhead and heavenly joy—the inner certainty of eternal bliss."[76] In feeding us with the blessed sacrament, Jesus invites us to her breast; in feeding us, our Mother also incorporates us into her body. In gestures even more intimate than a mother feeding her child, Jesus our Mother shows us a wound that is also her breast.

The heart of Julian's Christology, however, is a vision of Jesus sustained in love. For her, love is the beginning and end, the why and the how, of the Christian life. Love is the reason why we are here and why Christ has come: "The whole of life is grounded and rooted in love . . . without love we cannot live."[77] Christ comes in order to show the fullness of divine love, a love that will never let us go. This end and aim allows us to make further sense of her interpretation of Christ's suffering and imagery of Christ as Mother. Everything Christ undergoes is for the sake of love. In the conclusion of her revelations, Julian writes, "Who showed it you? Love. What did he show you? Love. Why did he show it? For love. . . . So it was that I learned that love was our Lord's meaning. . . . Before ever he made us, God loved us; and that his love has never slackened, nor ever shall."[78]

Julian's Christology is imagistic; her interpretation of Jesus exposes underemphasized trajectories in the history of theology and is important for subsequent theological reflections for at least two reasons: (1) the way her interpretation (much like Birgitta's) allows the reader to linger at the foot of the cross in order to contemplate Christ's suffering for the sake of love. Her Christology is less concerned with showing *how* Christ's suffering is salvific and more interested in outlining the extent of Christ's suffering for us. In this way, her Christology—like a painting or sculpture—invites readers to become a part of the interpretation of the image. (2) Her novel usage of motherhood in interpreting Christ's coeternity with the Father and his work on behalf of humanity, nourishing us with the food of his breast. In an age like ours (and like hers) attuned to the power of language, Julian offers a holistic perspective of Christ's love, incorporating the range of gendered experience: The One who is Son is also our Mother. In his breast, we are incorporated into her body.

Catherine of Siena (1347–1380)

One of the youngest children from a very large family, Catherine experienced a call to become married to Christ, though she did not enter a religious order. Her writings cover a gamut of topics: politics, popular piety, and mystical theology. She spent much time writing about and mediating ecclesial and political conflicts. (This included her attempts to persuade the pope in exile in Avignon to return to Rome.) A prolific letter writer, Catherine developed a distinctive Christology in her correspondence.

In one of her letters, Catherine employs the metaphor of ascent to describe Christ. "Christ actually made for us a staircase of his body. If you look at his feet, you see that they are nailed fast to the cross to form the first stair. This is because we have first to rid ourselves of all selfish will; for just as the feet carry the body, desire carries the soul."[79] In this imagery, the wounds of Christ are sensual; Catherine—like Birgitta—lingers on the scars of crucifixion, but for Catherine the wounds are less signs of agonizing torture than they are lures for our redemption: "At this second stair, his open side, you find a shop filled with fragrant spices. . . . There your soul is so sated and drunk that you lose all self-consciousness, just like a drunkard intoxicated with wine; you see nothing but his blood, shed with such blazing love."[80] The ascent up Christ's body reaches the mouth, a place of peace, quiet, and obedience. Here the believer experiences the rest of divine love. Sensual imagery permeates this vision: Christ is tasted and touched as well as seen and heard. Jesus is the resolution of desire, for "he has made himself our table, our food, and our servant."[81] We are warmed in his presence by bathing "in the blood of Christ crucified."[82] The body of Christ in this vision is central, for it is the vehicle of our redemption. In Christ's body, agony is transformed into ecstasy, violence into peace. For Catherine, moreover, this is all in the name of union with God. Christ becomes human so that we might enter Christ's pierced side, becoming united to the One who is our meal and Savior. In one of Catherine's visions, Christ places a ring on her finger, symbolizing her betrothal to him. This vision captures much of her Christology: Jesus is the one who woos us, embraces us, and invites us to spiritual marriage. In him, we find our destiny and our ecstasy, our food and our bath.

Thomas à Kempis (ca. 1380–1471)

A native of Prussia, Thomas experienced most of his theological education in Holland, where he became an Augustinian monk. He was a disciple of Geert de Groote, who stressed simplicity, pious devotion, and mysticism. Thomas eventually becomes superior of a monastery, but spends much of his time in solitude, copying manuscripts and composing some of his own. Some have claimed that his most famous work, *The Imitation of Christ*, was authored by de Groote. Most contemporary scholars consider it to be the product of Thomas's hand, but highly influenced by de Groote's teaching. No other Christian book (other than the Bible) has been translated more frequently and widely. Though it is not a Christology per se, but instead a guide to the spiritual life, traces of the author's Christology emerge loud and true. Jesus Christ, in this vision, shows us the shape of a truly human life, the way of salvation. Those who follow him are called to a way of imitation.

One of the most prominent images for Jesus in Thomas is *friend*. Indeed, Jesus is the most faithful friend, the model of friendship. He is the friend who summons all of our love and devotion: "It behooves the lover of Jesus to forsake all other love besides Him, for He will be loved alone, above all others. The love of creatures is deceptive and disappointing, but the love of Jesus is faithful and always abiding. . . . Love him, therefore, and hold Him for your friend, for, when all others forsake you, He will not forsake you, or suffer you finally to perish."[83] In some ways, this is an *exclusive* vision of friendship, in that the friend Jesus focuses all of our attention. But for those who incline toward him, the rewards are immense: "When our Lord Jesus is present, all things are pleasing, and nothing seems hard to do for His love. . . . To be without Jesus is the pain of hell. And to be with Him is a pleasant paradise. If Jesus is with you no enemy can grieve you."[84] Jesus is the beloved lover, who is faithful "beyond all other friends."[85]

The friend we have in Jesus communicates to us, directly and intimately. But to hear him, one must quiet the soul. "Blessed is that man who hears Jesus speaking in his soul, and who takes from His mouth some word of comfort."[86] Christ speaks within, silently and internally to each person, but in order to hear him, we must bridle sensuality and restrain desire. Here Thomas departs from the vision of Catherine and other mystics who stress eros: "O my soul, take heed to what has been said before and shut the doors of your sensuality, which are your five senses, so that you may hear inwardly what our Lord Jesus speaks within your soul."[87] Jesus is the one who tames desire rather than unleashing it; he is discerned in the quiet of the soul's inwardness and focus. We travel this path when we are obedient, taking on ourselves Christ's yoke of humility. Thomas imagines Jesus speaking thusly, "I made Myself the humblest and lowest of all men, so that you would learn to overcome your pride through My humility. Learn, therefore, you who are but ashes, to be docile; learn, you who are dust and earth, to be humble for my sake; learn to break your own will and to be subject to all from the heart."[88] Jesus is the Servant who shows us that a life of fullness comes from emptying the self. The Friend who will not forsake us is the source of unflagging love. This love can be found, however, only when we tame ourselves. If fulfillment is the goal, it must first pass through the fires of restraint. The influence of this portrait of Jesus has been wide, both prior and subsequent to *Imitation*. Jesus shows us the way by never letting go of us, summoning all of our devotion, and calling us to embark on a path of denial and servanthood. Fullness is found in Christ only by letting go of the fetters that constrain us in this world. Riches are found in the poverty of the Servant. Jesus here is the great inverter, who turns servanthood into exaltation, who promises constant friendship and companionship for those who follow his example.

Nicolas of Cusa (1401–1464)

Polymath Nicolas, native to Germany, embodied the Renaissance wing of the church as the Middle Ages were waning. He was a scientist and mathematician as well as philosopher and theologian, whose musings on the universe antedated Copernicus's revolutionary conception of a heliocentric solar system. A mystic who was also involved in church politics, he offered arguments on the scope and limits of papal authority. Yet he is most known for his understanding of the limits of reason, and that authentic knowledge comes when we acknowledge our own ignorance. This insight is developed most fully in his aptly titled work *On Learned Ignorance*.

The christological portrait that emerges in this work is one in which Jesus gathers us as participants in *his* humanity. The problem that Christ comes to address, in this view, is our bondage to sin. The solution is our elevation to God in the humanity of Christ. In becoming united to the divine nature, "the human nature in Christ was exalted to the Supreme Power and was delivered from the weight of temporal and burdensome desires."[89] But what happens to Jesus's humanity, according to Nicolas, is not restricted to him alone. Christ's humanity is "maximal," in that it "encompasses the complete possibility of the species, so that it is . . . united to each man much more closely than is a brother or a very special friend."[90] Christ's humanity, in a very real sense, also becomes *ours*. "In

Christ the faithful are circumcised; in Him they are baptized; in Him they die; in Him they are made alive again through resurrection; in Him they are united to God and are glorified."[91] For Nicolas, our humanity is incomplete without incorporation into Christ's humanity. Jesus comes to redeem and to elevate, offering us fulfillment in the very life of God. This is participatory Christology par excellence: Jesus, who unites finite and infinite, makes us participants in his exalted and resurrected body.

Conclusion

The riches of medieval Christology are impossible to distill into a pithy phrase. Like the patristic period, this era is multifaceted and multivocal. A wide variety of approaches characterize the age, epitomized on the one hand in scholasticism, which seeks doctrinal precision, and on the other hand in mysticism, which stresses the poverty of *all* words in describing Christ. But what all of these varied themes might have in common is what Nicolas of Cusa stresses: *participation.* Jesus Christ comes so that we might become participants in his life. Even the most "objective" accounts of Christ's work (such as Anselm's) stress some kind of participation, whereby the believer is transformed and made unto greater likeness of Christ. Some have argued that participation is the hallmark of the medieval worldview; it is the sign of the "enchanted" universe, permeated by God's grandeur, in which we live, move, and have our being.[92] Like the medieval cathedral that directs our attention upward and outward, summoning our lives into the life of God, medieval Christologies of participation stress our transformation and incorporation into the life of Christ. But as the medieval period began to wane, many of the authorities that undergirded this participatory universe began to be questioned. The various reform movements, as they sought to redress abuses of some ecclesial authorities also led to revolt. As the church convulsed, the participatory universe began to show cracks. As we turn to this period of Reformation, many Christologies began to stress the individual who was sometimes overlooked or subsumed in the enchanted medieval world.

Notes

1. John of Damascus, *On the Divine Images*, trans. David Anderson, Popular Patristics (Crestwood, NY: St. Vladimir's Seminary Press, 1980), 23.
2. John of Damascus, *On the Divine Images*, 28.
3. John of Damascus, *The Orthodox Faith*, in *Saint John of Damascus: Writings*, trans. Frederic H. Chase Jr., Fathers of the Church (New York: Fathers of the Church, 1958), 270.
4. John of Damascus, *The Orthodox Faith*, 283.
5. This interpretation of Anselm's *Cur Deus Homo?* is strongly influenced by the professor of the first graduate-level theology course that I ever took. I still reference my lecture notes from Prof. George Lindbeck's 1992 course on medieval and Reformation theology at Yale Divinity School, which provided me my first glimpse at the wonders of the theology of these pivotal periods.
6. Anselm, *Why God Became Man*, in *A Scholastic Miscellany: Anselm to Ockham*, ed. Eugene R. Fairweather, Library of Christian Classics (Philadelphia: Westminster, 1956), 122.
7. Anselm, *Why God Became Man*, 119.
8. Anselm, *Why God Became Man*, 139.
9. Anselm, *Why God Became Man*, 137.
10. Anselm, *Why God Became Man*, 152.
11. Peter Abelard, *Exposition of the Epistle to the Romans*, in Fairweather, *Scholastic Miscellany*, 281. Anselm's Christology also rejects the idea of the incarnation being necessary because the devil holds a rightful

claim over humanity. Jesus saves, for Anselm, not because he releases humanity from the devil, but because he provides the satisfaction necessary for restoring dignity, honor, and righteousness to creation that had been lost because of sin.

12. Peter Abelard, *Exposition of the Epistle to the Romans*, 283.
13. Peter Abelard, *Exposition of the Epistle to the Romans*, 283.
14. Peter Abelard, *Exposition of the Epistle to the Romans*, 284.
15. Jean Leclercq, introduction to *Bernard of Clairvaux: Selected Works*, trans. G. R. Evans, Classics of Western Spirituality (Mahwah, NJ: Paulist, 1987), 35–36.
16. Bernard, *On the Steps of Humility and Pride*, in Evans, *Bernard*, 107.
17. Leclercq, introduction, 46.
18. Bernard, *Sixth Sermon for Christmas Eve*, in *St. Bernard's Sermons on the Nativity* (Chulmleigh, UK: Augustine, 1985), 117–18.
19. Bernard, *On Consideration*, in Evans, *Bernard*, 165.
20. Bernard, *Sermons on the Song of Songs*, in Evans, *Bernard*, 216.
21. Leclercq, introduction, 52.
22. Hildegard of Bingen, *Scivias*, trans. Mother Columba Hart and Jane Bishop, Classics of Western Spirituality (Mahwah, NJ: Paulist, 1990), 433–34.
23. Hildegard of Bingen, *Scivias*, 434.
24. Clare of Assisi, *The First Letter to the Blessed Agnes of Prague*, in *Francis and Clare: The Complete Works*, trans. Regis J. Armstrong and Ignatius C. Brady, Classics of Western Spirituality (New York: Paulist, 1982), 191.
25. Clare, *The Third Letter to Blessed Agnes of Prague*, in Armstrong and Brady, *Francis and Clare*, 201.
26. In some respects these categories reify patriarchal notions of marriage and motherhood by emphasizing passivity of the bride and mother. But in another respect, they subvert these notions, since the "marriage" does not involve a typical "consummation" and the "motherhood" does not involve a typical pregnancy.
27. Clare, *First Letter*, 192–93.
28. Clare, *The Second Letter to the Blessed Agnes of Prague*, in Armstrong and Brady, *Francis and Clare*, 197.
29. Clare, *Third Letter*, 200.

30. Clare, *The Fourth Letter to Blessed Agnes of Prague*, in Armstrong and Brady, *Francis and Clare*, 204.

31. Zachary Hayes, *Bonaventure: Mystical Writings* (New York: Crossroad, 1999), 15.

32. Bonaventure, *The Soul's Journey into God*, in *Bonaventure: The Soul's Journey into God, The Tree of Life, The Life of St. Francis*, trans. Ewert Cousins, Classics of Western Spirituality (New York: Paulist, 1978), 54.

33. "So our soul could not rise completely from these things of sense to see itself and the Eternal Truth in itself unless Truth, assuming human nature in Christ, had become a ladder, restoring the first ladder that had been broken in Adam." Bonaventure, *Soul's Journey*, 88.

34. Bonaventure, *Soul's Journey*, 115.

35. Bonaventure, *Tree of Life*, in Cousins, *Bonaventure*, 128.

36. Bonaventure, *Tree of Life*, 131.

37. Bonaventure, *Tree of Life*, 139.

38. Bonaventure, *Tree of Life*, 145.

39. Bonaventure, *Tree of Life*, 151.

40. Bonaventure, *Tree of Life*, 155.

41. Bonaventure, *Tree of Life*, 160.

42. Bonaventure, *Tree of Life*, 168.

43. Luis G. Pedraja, "Thomas Aquinas," in *The Westminster Dictionary of Theologians*, ed. Justo L. González, trans. Suzanne E. Hoeferkamp Segovia (Louisville: Westminster John Knox, 2006), 331.

44. Joseph P. Wawrykow, "Jesus Christ," in *The Westminster Handbook to Thomas Aquinas* (Louisville: Westminster John Knox, 2005), 78.

45. Thomas Aquinas, *Summa theologica* III, q. 41, art. 1, trans. Fathers of the English Dominican Province (Notre Dame: Ave Maria Press, 1981), 4:2234.

46. Thomas Aquinas, *Summa theologica* III, q. 26, art. 2, 4:2154.

47. Wawrykow, "Jesus Christ," 79.

48. Thomas Aquinas, *Compendium of Theology*, trans. Richard J. Regan (New York: Oxford University Press, 2009), 150–51.

49. Thomas Aquinas, *Summa theologica* III, q. 46, art. 1, 4:2259.

50. Thomas Aquinas, *Compendium theologiae* 239, cited in Brian Davies, *The Thought of Thomas Aquinas* (Oxford: Clarendon, 1992), 341.

51. Thomas Aquinas, *Summa theologica* III, q. 48, art. 1, 4:2277.
52. Thomas Aquinas, *Summa theologica* III, q. 46, art. 4, 4:2262.
53. Thomas Aquinas, *Summa theologica* III, q. 46, art. 12, 4:2271.
54. Thomas Aquinas, *Compendium of Theology*, 194.
55. One of the more intriguing aspects of Thomas's eschatology is speculation on the glorified body. In the new creation, human beings will rise as specimens of physical beauty: in the vigor of young adulthood, without blemish or scar.
56. Meister Eckhart, *Sermon 6: Justi vivent in aeternum*, in *Meister Eckhart: The Essential Sermons, Commentaries, Treatises, and Defense*, trans. Edmund Colledge and Bernard McGinn, Classics of Western Spirituality (New York: Paulist Press, 1981), 187.
57. Meister Eckhart, *Sermon 6*, 188.
58. Meister Eckhart, *Sermon 22: Ave, gratia plena*, in Colledge and McGinn, *Meister Eckhart*, 194–95.
59. Bernard McGinn, "Theological Summary," in Colledge and McGinn, *Meister Eckhart*, 53.
60. See Orlando O. Espin, "Scotus, John Duns," in González, *Westminster Dictionary of Theologians*, 307.
61. John Duns Scotus, *Concerning the Predestination of Christ*, in *Franciscan Christology*, ed. Damian McElrath (St. Bonaventure, NY: Franciscan Institute of St. Bonaventure, 1980), 149.
62. John Duns Scotus, *Concerning the Predestination of Christ*, 153.
63. John Duns Scotus, *Concerning the Predestination of Christ*, 157.
64. William of Ockham, "The Third Book of the Sentences, Q. 1," in McElrath, *Franciscan Christology*, 197.
65. William of Ockham, "The Third Book of the Sentences, Q. 1," 197.
66. William of Ockham, "The Third Book of the Sentences, Q. 1," 197.
67. Birgitta of Sweden, *Life and Selected Revelations*, ed. Marguerite Tjader Harris, Classics of Western Spirituality (Mahwah, NJ: Paulist, 1990), 189.
68. Julian of Norwich, *Revelations of Divine Love*, trans. Clifton Wolters (New York: Penguin, 1966), 64.
69. Julian of Norwich, *Revelations of Divine Love*, 89–90.
70. Julian of Norwich, *Revelations of Divine Love*, 91.

71. Julian of Norwich, *Revelations of Divine Love*, 94.
72. Julian of Norwich, *Revelations of Divine Love*, 96.
73. Julian of Norwich, *Revelations of Divine Love*, 166.
74. Julian of Norwich, *Revelations of Divine Love*, 169.
75. Julian of Norwich, *Revelations of Divine Love*, 170.
76. Julian of Norwich, *Revelations of Divine Love*, 170.
77. Julian of Norwich, *Revelations of Divine Love*, 137.
78. Julian of Norwich, *Revelations of Divine Love*, 211–12.
79. Catherine of Siena, *Letter 62*, in *The Letters of St. Catherine of Siena*, vol. 1, trans. Suzanne Noffke, OP (Binghamton: State University of New York at Binghamton, 1988), 198
80. Catherine of Siena, *Letter 62*, 198–99.
81. Catherine of Siena, *Letter 62*, 199.
82. Catherine of Siena, *Letter 62*, 199.
83. Thomas à Kempis, *The Imitation of Christ*, ed. Harold C. Gardiner (Garden City, NY: Image, 1955), 84.
84. Thomas à Kempis, *Imitation of Christ*, 85.
85. Thomas à Kempis, *Imitation of Christ*, 86.
86. Thomas à Kempis, *Imitation of Christ,* 103.
87. Thomas à Kempis, *Imitation of Christ*, 103.
88. Thomas à Kempis, *Imitation of Christ*, 124.
89. Nicolas of Cusa, *On Learned Ignorance*, trans. Jasper Hopkins (Minneapolis: Arthur J. Banning Press, 1981), 139.
90. Nicolas of Cusa, *On Learned Ignorance*, 139.
91. Nicolas of Cusa, *On Learned Ignorance*, 139.
92. I have in mind here interpretations of medieval theology (particularly its Thomistic variety) that are common to the movement of Radical Orthodoxy. James K. A. Smith, for example, considers participation to be a hallmark of Radical Orthodoxy's recovery of medieval sensibilities. See James K. A. Smith, *Introducing Radical Orthodoxy* (Grand Rapids: Baker Academic, 2004), 185–229.

4

Reformation Christologies

The age of reform upended the church. Though nearly every age considers itself to be living in transitional times, this judgment is particularly accurate for this pivotal period in Christian history. Perhaps the biggest shift during this critical period was the questioning of established authorities and the lodging of new authorities in their place. Though questioning authority was hardly new to the church, and was presaged by various theologians in earlier ages, in the sixteenth century the questions came with renewed vigor. Many voices in this period discerned corruption in the institutional church, which led in turn to corrupted portrayals of Jesus. But in diagnosing corruption, these varied critics also unleashed a spirit of fragmentation within the church. Though earlier periods also witnessed division (most notably the Great Schism of 1054 between the Eastern and Western churches), the centuries after the age of reform underwent an astonishing proliferation of rival churches, with different polities, authority structures, and confessions.

Perhaps as a result of increasing fragmentation, the age of reform yielded portraits of Jesus that were more acutely political and rhetorical. Exponents of various movements (both within and outside the Roman Catholic Church) selected elements of biblical narratives of Jesus that bolstered their pleas for reform. And thus, in this period, we encounter Jesus the pacifist as well as Jesus the crusader; Jesus the despiser of worldly wisdom and Jesus the embodiment of the world's best wisdom; Jesus the resister of political authority and the Jesus who blesses temporal authority.

Another mark of this era is a move toward interiority: whether exemplified in Reformers such as Luther and Calvin, who stressed the authority of Scripture alone, and hence the authority of conscience in interpreting Scripture; or in voices such as Ignatius of Loyola, who stressed the need for cultivating personal spirituality in following Jesus. And hence, the portrait of Jesus that emerges from this era is not simply a political or rhetorical one, but one that invites disciples on the path of spiritual renewal, as one who, to paraphrase Teresa of Àvila, summons us to the interior castle, a spiritual journey that ends in the glory that is God's very self. This combination of the political and the interior make the varied portraits of Jesus that emerge in these pivotal centuries distinctive. In many respects, we are still living in the wake of their impact.

Martin Luther (1483–1546)

Most narratives of the age of reform begin with the Augustinian monk and professor of Bible Martin Luther, a figure who crystallizes many of the complaints against medieval church authority and structure. Born into a devout German family of moderate means, Luther studied theology in Erfurt and entered the Augustinian order soon after completing his master's degree in law in 1505. He was subsequently selected to study theology in Wittenberg, where he earned a doctorate in 1512. During travels to Rome shortly thereafter, Luther became alarmed at the moral laxity displayed by many of the clerics at the Vatican. This alarm presaged his disputes with other church authorities involved in the selling of indulgences, culminating in his famous posting of the Ninety-Five Theses on the Wittenberg church door in 1517. These theses, intended for public debate, launched an inexorable quest for reform (though Luther did not intend on separating from the Roman church). Excommunicated in 1521, Luther spends the rest of his life writing under pressure, sometimes seeking refuge, articulating a distinctive theology of grace, translating the Bible into vernacular German, repulsing more radical calls for reform, and laying the groundwork for what eventually came to be known as Protestant Christianity. His most distinctive insight is that the righteousness of a Christian is not something that is earned or mustered by individual effort. Rather, righteousness, properly speaking, belongs to Christ, and is given to us by the gift of grace through faith. The human person, hence, is justified (reckoned as righteous by God) because of the righteousness of Christ, which we receive by grace alone, through faith in Christ alonc. Though Luther writes on voluminous topics, nearly everything that he writes grows out of this basic conviction of receiving Christ's righteousness as an unearned gift. It is, for Luther, genuinely liberating, good news, which frees us from the prison of self-reliance, throwing us into the welcoming arms of a truly gracious God, who exchanges our unrighteousness for the righteousness of God's Son.

What is the picture of Jesus that emerges in the hands of the Reformer? Like some of his medieval predecessors, Luther focuses on the crucifixion. But unlike most medieval interpretations of the cross, Luther emphasizes the rhetorical features of Jesus's suffering and death. For him, the cross signals the death knell to a "theology of glory" that emphasizes Christ's majesty along the lines of earthly powers. By contrasting a "theology of the cross" with a theology of glory, Luther claims that Jesus's power is not the elevation of earthly power, but rather the inversion of that power. We know Jesus not as the glorious one, but as one who is humiliated and scorned: "He who does not know Christ does not know God hidden in suffering. Therefore he prefers works to suffering, glory to the cross, strength to weakness, wisdom to folly, and, in general, good to evil. . . . God can be found only in suffering and the cross."[1] The Jesus who comes to us as the incarnate One comes in solidarity with all suffering, and opens our eyes to God's presence within suffering. He turns all earthly powers on their heads: what the world celebrates as glory is in reality nothing; what it despises as weakness is the life-giving power of God revealed in the cross. Jesus comes to critique all earthly powers—including the powers of a corrupt church—and to reveal the saving power of a suffering servant. In this exposition of a theology of the cross, Luther often employs the language of "hiddenness." Earthly power blinds us to the power of God, rendering the presence of God hidden to most. What is hidden to the eyes of power, however, is revealed to the eyes of faith. When Christ comes in the flesh, he reveals the majesty of God in the form of suffering, though for those who do not receive the gift of faith, this majesty remains hidden.

Luther's interpretation of Jesus is revolutionary both in its rhetoric and its locus of concentration. By focusing on the cross, Luther addresses the "severity of Jesus' forsakenness" much more than his contemporaries and his theological predecessors. Bernhard Lohse notes that, by emphasizing Christ's humiliation, Luther "could express in a newer and profounder way than before the significance of the anguished Christ for the Christian."[2] The focus on Christ's agony is thus never a theoretical issue, but always connected to the Christian journey: In Jesus's humiliating death, we see the extent of God's solidarity *with us*. On the cross, Jesus takes our suffering as his own. Luther's *theologia crucis* is also noteworthy in its rearticulation of divine self-emptying, or *kenosis*. Jesus "emptied himself, unwilling to use his rank against us, unwilling to be different from us. Moreover, for our sakes he became as one of us and took the form of a servant, that is, he subjected himself to all evils. And although he was free, as the Apostle says of himself also, he made himself servant of all, living as if all the evils which were ours were actually his own."[3] In Jesus Christ, God holds nothing back for the sake of our salvation. Jesus's self-emptying is for the sake of our fullness as children of God.

The cross, for Luther, does not only reveal majesty as suffering; it also emphasizes the joyful exchange of our sinfulness for the righteousness of Christ. On the cross, Jesus experiences the rejection that we have deserved. Luther's language for this exchange is strong:

> All the prophets saw this, that Christ was to become the greatest thief, murderer, adulterer, robber, desecrator, blasphemer, etc., there has ever been anywhere in the world. . . . He is a sinner, who has and bears the sin of Paul, the former blasphemer, persecutor, and assaulter; of Peter, who denied Christ; of David, who was an adulterer and murderer, and who caused the Gentiles to blaspheme the name of the Lord (Rom. 2:24). In short, He has and bears all the sins of all men in His body.[4]

Christ becomes sin for our sake, and by taking on sin in his innocence, he vanquishes it. The cross presents the ultimate clash between sin and righteousness, law and grace. The one who is rejected overcomes the sin we are burdened with, releasing us to freedom: "For all the curses of the Law were gathered together in Him, and therefore He bore and sustained them in His own body for us. Consequently, He was not only accursed, but He became a curse for us."[5] Some might be tempted to understand this as a rehashing of Anselm's atonement theory. But Luther's emphasis is different. Unlike Anselm, who focuses on the *objective* aspects of Christ's atoning sacrifice (the satisfying of divine justice), Luther focuses on the *subjective* or existential dimensions (what happens to *us*, our transformation). In a word, Luther *personalizes* Christology to a greater extent than his predecessors. In much of Luther's writing, whether in the form of theological treatise, letter, or hymn, the believer comes to the fore. As Lohse notes, "Jesus' redemptive work applies 'to me'; it overcomes 'my' conflict."[6] In Jesus Christ, God comes near to humanity, bringing the agony of our existence into the very life of God.

One of the phrases that best captures Luther's interpretation of Jesus occurs in the Larger Catechism, where he describes Jesus as "a mirror of the Father's heart."[7] We see in Jesus not only God's condescension to consider our plight, we see in "the earthly Jesus . . . how God acts."[8] The humanity of Christ reveals the majesty of God; this abject One shows us the shape of true power in the world: the power of gracious self-giving. This is the heart of God given for the world, and in Jesus we both see and experience it most clearly.

A survey of Luther's Christology, which reveals the heart of God, would not be complete without considering his eucharistic theology. On one level, Luther has a fairly straightforward interpretation of Christ's words recorded in the Gospels: "Take, eat; this is my body" (Matt 26:26). Luther is wary of interpretations of these words (such as Zwingli's) that consider Jesus to be speaking in signs or symbols. Luther's method of biblical interpretation stresses the plain, "literal" sense of words.[9] When Jesus invites his disciples to partake of his body, he means what he says. But Luther, in his avoidance of what he deems a "theology of glory," does not attach a particular philosophical account (such as transubstantiation) to these words. The presence of Christ cannot be fixed according to a precise theological theory. For Luther, Christ is both present *everywhere* (for he is the risen Lord) and *in the sacrament* in particular. "Even if Christ's body is everywhere, you do not therefore immediately eat or drink or touch him. . . . The right hand of God is everywhere, but at the same time nowhere and uncircumscribed, above and apart from all creatures."[10] Luther's account avoids a rigid literalism (whereby Christ's presence would be restricted to the Eucharist) by stressing that Christ is present according to his promise. The presence of Christ is thus tied to the Word: Jesus is present in the sacrament as he has spoken his Word. When we receive the sacrament in the gift of faith, we are recipients of the Word. The presence of Christ, which is everywhere, is made concrete for us in his distinct words of promise: "It is one thing if God is present, and another if he is present for you." Luther imagines Christ saying "I wish to attach myself here with my Word, in order that you may not have to buzz about, trying to seek me in all the places where I am; this would be too much for you, and you would also be too puny to apprehend me in these places without the help of my Word."[11] Luther does not label his account with a particular theory, but many have dubbed it "consubstantiation," whereby Christ's presence is in, with, and under the sacrament, made possible because of the Word of God. Christ surrounds the sacrament and is concretely present within the words, actions, and elements of the Eucharist. We take part in his presence, like all other things, because of the gift of faith.

Perhaps the language of gift captures Luther's Christology best. Jesus is God's gift to the world: a gift that overturns our assumptions about what constitutes glory; a gift that becomes sin for our sake; a gift that we receive because he has experienced the rejection we deserve; a gift of grace made known in faith; a gift that unveils what had remained hidden to eyes clouded by sin; a gift whose righteousness becomes our own by being imputed to us. But in becoming our gift, Christ also highlights the ongoing paradoxical nature of human life. Even in faith, our story is complex. The gift does not completely transform us (at least in this life). In Christ, the believer remains simultaneously a sinner and justified before God. Life in Christ is not a simple triumph over all that stands in the way of God's grace. Rather, in Christ, we are reckoned as righteous even though we are not. Again, this is a freeing notion: We become no longer fixated on our own status before God, or our own spiritual development, but are set free to love God and neighbor, simply because *they are*. The gift of Christ, in this sense, finally enables us to become what we are called to be: persons for one another, persons for God, made in God's image. Even—and perhaps especially—when we fall short, we are thrown back on the arms of the gift. If Luther's Christology at times revels in paradox (and even contradiction), it is because he is trying to make sense of our all-too-human lives in light of God's grace. Jesus embodies this collision between grace and law, sin and forgiveness, showing us the heart of God given for the world.

Huldrych Zwingli (1484–1531)

A Reformer of Luther's generation, heralding from the Swiss cantons, Huldrych Zwingli studied in Basel and Vienna and became ordained as a priest in 1516. Influenced by Erasmus, Zwingli was attuned to some of the abuses in the church, but did not resort to the extremes of Luther's later rhetoric. Nonetheless, his eventual break with the Roman church was as definitive. His most radical and distinctive break with medieval theology centered on his interpretation of the Eucharist, though his exposition of faith and works and various ecclesial practices (such as clerical celibacy and fasting) were equally revolutionary. These theological positions led to his leadership of the reform movement in Zürich, and eventually his death in battle in 1531, in skirmishes against antireform Swiss forces.

In most matters of interpreting Christ's person, Zwingli is somewhat derivative. He assumes standard orthodox positions that he has inherited and does not delve much into the consequences of these positions. He repeats notions of the hypostatic union, for example. In Christ, divine and human natures dwell in harmony: "His divine nature has not in any way been diminished so as not to be truly, properly and naturally God."[12] In Christ, there is no division or separation, because in him "God and Man are one Christ."[13] Nonetheless, we are correct to make distinctions between the natures in attributing origin to Jesus's activity. Jesus suffers as a human being, for example, but not as divine. But the same Jesus who suffers on the cross also utters words of forgiveness: "Father, forgive them for they know not what they do." These words, Zwingli claims, stem from Christ's divine nature, the "voice of the inviolable deity."[14] In some regards, this parceling out of properties and activities is somewhat wooden, running the risk of keeping the qualities of each "nature" in Christ at arm's length. This tendency is amplified in Zwingli's interpretation of the Eucharist. His interpretation of Christ's person is most distinctive in its attribution of that person to us: "All that Christ is is ours and all that he does is ours."[15] The point of the incarnation, in this regard, is personal. Jesus comes in the flesh so that we might partake in his glory: His resurrection is for us, so that we might participate in abundant life.

If Zwingli repeats standard orthodoxy in his interpretation of Christ's person, he departs from that inherited tradition most dramatically in his understanding of Christ's presence (or better said, absence) in the Eucharist. This is where his interpretation of Jesus has proved most influential, in the various church traditions that reject Catholic and Lutheran understandings of the Lord's Supper. Because Zwingli has a rather wooden understanding of Christ's attributes, he is unable to embrace the notion of Christ's body being present "everywhere" in the way Luther does. His basic conviction is that the finite Eucharist cannot contain the infinite power of the risen Lord. Christ's body, furthermore, properly belongs to Christ's humanity, which after Easter is seated at the right hand of God. The body of Christ, properly considered, resides in heaven and not at the Lord's Table. As a glorified, human body, it cannot be in two places at once: "The body of Christ is not in several places at one and the same time any more than our bodies are."[16] Those who ascribe a "real presence" of Christ in the Eucharist, Zwingli claims, drag "Christ down from heaven and from his Father's throne."[17]

We partake of Christ's body in the Supper, then, not physically or literally, but spiritually and sacramentally. What does this mean? Zwingli answers with figurative language: "To eat the body of Christ spiritually is equivalent to trusting with heart and soul upon the mercy and goodness of God through Christ, to have the assurance of an unbroken faith that God will give us the forgiveness of sins and the joy of eternal salvation for the sake of his Son, who gave himself for us and reconciled the divine righteousness to us."[18] The plain language, "Take, eat; this is my body," for Zwingli, stands for something else: accepting in faith the activity of Christ for us. The meal, then, becomes more an act of collective memory than it is a mystical incorporation into Christ's body. The sacrament of the Lord's Supper cannot "create" faith, but it does bear witness to historical memory that sustains faith, namely, the birth and passion of Christ.[19] The Lord's Supper is a means of communal retelling of that story, refreshing our memory. Zwingli's understanding strips away much of the enchantment of the medieval universe. And it presages some of the modern period's understanding of God's activity. Christ's risen body lies ensconced in heaven, not enveloping those gathered in his name. By taking part in the Lord's Supper, we recall what God has already accomplished in Christ, and are wary of attempts to domesticate Christ's body as something to be consumed. If Zwingli's interpretation of Christ is insistent on maintaining the transcendence of the risen Christ, it also runs the risk of making that body inaccessible.

Thomas Müntzer (1490–1525)

A Roman Catholic priest who became attracted to Luther's reforms, Thomas Müntzer spent some time in Wittenberg, learning from the father of Reformation. After a short period, however, he became convinced that Luther's reforms did not go far enough. He departed from Luther's insistence on the prime authority of Scripture, opting instead for the primacy of spiritual and religious experience (which gave rise to Scripture, and through which Scripture must be interpreted). He was also convinced that God was calling a righteous elect, who would usher in a new, egalitarian age by overthrowing the corrupt church and princes who were often hand in hand with ecclesial authorities. Müntzer is most famous for his enthusiastic endorsement of the Peasants' Rebellion, a grassroots movement in which peasants fought against their landlords. This armed struggle proved bloody and was eventually suppressed by the more powerful ruling authorities. At its conclusion, Müntzer himself met a grisly end in brutal imprisonment and beheading. Luther was vociferous in his opposition to both Müntzer's theology and politics, most especially in his denouncing of the Peasants' Rebellion. But for a brief time, Müntzer gained a significant audience, including some secular authorities. His reflections on Christ are mostly in the form of sermons and hastily written tractates.

Müntzer's interpretation of Jesus stresses rejection. One can sense the influence of Luther here, but for Müntzer the scorn heaped on Christ is even more dramatic. Fitting into Müntzer's general view of the struggle between peasants and nobility, Jesus, the crucified Savior, stands against anything elite. He is the One who rejects worldly wisdom: "Christ himself shunned that breed of adders, the biblical scholars."[20] Jesus is the Peasant, the one without formal education who sides with the poor and downtrodden. The world's wisdom clouds our understanding of who he is. Müntzer's Christ can only be encountered from below. "The whole trouble was, then, (as it still is for the world) that Christ was a contemptible person, one of humble parentage. And yet he had the effrontery to instruct and chastise too pointedly the chubby-cheeked people of substance, those who were out for their own pleasures."[21] This Jesus embarks on nothing less than the cause of class struggle, to uplift those whom the powerful and wise have brought low. Perhaps it is no surprise that some subsequent movements in history have seen in Müntzer antecedents, from East German communists who saw in him a Teutonic ancestor, to varied streams of liberation theology that regard him as an earlier, fellow traveler. Regardless of how accurate one deems these comparisons to be, it is clear that for Müntzer, Jesus comes to make the clash between the mighty and lowly clearer, and to show us that God takes the side of those on the bottom of whatever hierarchy is erected.

This sense of a definitive clash makes Müntzer's Christ obsessed with purity. Jesus comes to purge the corruption that has infiltrated society, to make it into the image of the kingdom. "Christ, the son of God, and his apostles and his holy prophets before him, founded a pure and true Christianity, and cast the pure wheat into the field, that is, planted the precious word of God in the hearts of the elect."[22] Müntzer, obviously, sees himself as continuing this struggle, as one elected by God to carry on the work Christ began. There is no doubt narrowness to this vision: Christ calls a select few to follow him, while those who are comfortable cannot walk the walk; the church, likewise, has been corrupted by elites, and only a few will be able to hear the message of purity. But for those who do hear and understand, the appropriate response is to smash. Jesus, in this vision, is not an emissary of peace, but the inaugurator of a righteous war. "The great stone will come crashing down soon . . . as Christ says in Matthew 10: 'I am not come to send peace, but the sword.' But what is one to do with the sword? Exactly this: sweep aside those evil men who obstruct the gospel! Take them out of circulation! Otherwise you will be devils. . . . Have no doubts that God will smash all your adversaries into little pieces—any who dare to persecute you!"[23] Jesus, in this vision, is a militant crusader who gathers the elect to embark on a holy cause. Müntzer fuses Jesus's arguments with the Pharisees with Müntzer's own understanding of the Peasants' Rebellion. In short, he summons Jesus for his own cause, without much self-critique. This is perhaps the greatest danger of this vision: to see Jesus as the espouser of one's own cause, however righteous. Indeed, in Müntzer's vision, any means—even the violent elimination of opponents—is justified in the pursuit of purity. The temptation to see Jesus on one's own side, of course, is a perennial desire and aim. But with Müntzer, that desire turns a blind eye to those on the "other" side.

Ultimately, Müntzer's Jesus comes so that we might partake in the divine life. Here he echoes more orthodox strands in Christian thought, which hearken deification. For those who are caught up in the work of Jesus, the transformation is nothing short of revolutionary. "We must believe that we fleshly, earthly men are to become gods through Christ's becoming man, and thus become God's pupils with him—to be taught by Christ himself, and become divine, yes and far more—to be totally transfigured into him, so that this earthly life swings up into heaven."[24] Jesus does not merely point to the kingdom or to heaven; by his grace he transforms us so that we might partake of heaven in the world. Here Müntzer goes beyond Luther's dictum of simultaneously sinner and justified; for those transformed by Christ, it is possible to become ever more pure, ever more a denizen of heaven while we walk this earth. If the aim is lofty, and the vision of Christ here is compelling, what is ultimately most problematic in Müntzer's portrait of Christ is its departure from the way of the cross, which is also the way of peace.

Martin Bucer (1491–1551)

Dominican priest Martin Bucer became attracted to the cause of Reformation when he heard Luther at the Heidelberg Disputation. Bucer eventually settles in Strasbourg, which had become a city of refuge for many Reformers. There he exercised great influence as a religious and civic leader. More irenic in spirit than many of his contemporaries, Bucer sought to unify Zwinglian and Lutheran branches of church reform and, in later efforts, also tried to mediate disputes between Reformers and the Roman church, even though he had been excommunicated because of his theological views and marriage. At the end of his life, he finds refuge in Britain as a voice for reform in the Church of England. Frank about his openness to changing his theological views, Bucer's theology can be hard to pin down. He wrote mostly on ecclesiology and the need for civic reform. Indeed, many contemporary progressives see in Bucer an early voice for the social gospel. In these writings, however, a discernible Christology emerges, focused on Jesus as teacher, ruler, and reformer.

Bucer's preferred metaphor for Jesus is King. Christ has come to establish a kingdom governed by the gospel, consistent with Jesus's teaching. This kingdom is neither synonymous with the world nor is it seamless with the church (since the church stands in desperate need of reform):

> The Kingdom of our Savior Jesus Christ is that administration and care of the eternal life of God's elect, by which this very Lord and King of Heaven by his doctrine and discipline, administered by suitable ministers chosen for this very purpose, gathers to himself his elect, those dispersed throughout the world who are his but whom he nonetheless wills to be subject to the powers of the world. He incorporates them into himself and his Church and so

> governs them in it that purged more fully day by day from sins, they live well and happily both here and in the time to come.[25]

This Jesus who rules as King calls subjects out of the world to serve *in* the world. The kingdom, in other words, is not purely spiritual, but encompasses all the affairs of life. Even as Christ's subjects are also subject to the governing authorities of this world, they also seek to renew the world. Bucer appeals specifically to ruling authorities to enact social reforms, including better care for the poor, reform of marketing and trade, more wholesome management of inns, and legal reforms. Christ, in this vision, is

> the one dispenser of kingdoms and powers and the preserver of all. . . . Christ the King, gives to this his people also external sovereignty and a free administration of the commonwealth, because they love and worship this their King. . . . He will give them also all political power and all external strength, so that his Kingdom and his pure and genuine religion may grown and flourish among them and prevail everywhere as fully as possible.[26]

Christ's kingdom, eventually, will extend throughout the earth.

Despite the grand reach of Christ's kingdom and the elect's participation within it, Bucer echoes Luther in his claim that we can do nothing apart from the grace of Christ. "Before we are renewed in the Spirit of Christ, we can produce only evil and noxious works."[27] However we seek to follow the One who is King, we cannot confuse our own motivations with those of the King. But Bucer emphasizes the transformative work of Christ—in individuals, in society—more than his Wittenberg contemporary. The work of Christ in the believer is progressive: "Our King regenerates us by his Word and Spirit, so that we are his seed, and he regenerates us unto eternal life."[28] As Bucer explains the nature of Christ's kingdom he notes that

Christ "rules and governs those who have been incorporated into himself and his Church, purging them daily more and more from sins and establishing them in all piety and righteousness and hence eternal life."[29] Apart from Christ, we are nothing more than a bag of bones; but renewed by Christ, we take part daily in the renewal of the world. Nothing in this vision is exempt from the grace of Christ's transformation.

The metaphor of King is not the only one that governs Bucer's Christology. Another, more subtle image combines that of teacher and student. As Bucer emphasizes the need for catechism in the church, he recalls the Lukan story of Jesus as a child in the temple. Here, Bucer claims Jesus as a model student: "Jesus, therefore, then listened. To whom? Undoubtedly to the teachers, who were catechizing him and the other boys. For in all things he always exhibited utmost moderation; he both asked them questions and answered them when they asked him questions, which is really the nature of catechizing."[30] But this Jesus who listens and learns, growing in wisdom and stature, is also the rabbi who teaches. And his method and audience for teaching is indiscriminate. He teaches "heavenly doctrine . . . at home and individually." He teaches friends, disciples, sinners, Samaritans, and Pharisees.[31] He makes his teaching known to anyone who will listen, and as they are touched by Jesus's teaching, the kingdom of Christ grows. This Jesus, who is Ruler of all, does not exert rule primarily by force, but by the power of his teaching invitation. In that regard, he is also a model for earthly rulers, to guide with gentleness, to instruct as molded by the gospel. The gap between this interpretation and Müntzer's is certainly yawning, yielding a humbler and gentler Christ. But it is nonetheless guided by a grand vision of a kingdom that extends throughout the earth.

Ignatius of Loyola (1491–1556)

Born into a wealthy Basque family, trained as a soldier, Ignatius was injured in battle in 1521. His long recovery meant that he had ample time for reading, which led to a discovery of Christian spirituality. When he had recovered enough to travel, Ignatius embarked on a pilgrimage to the Holy Land. A stay-over at the Benedictine monastery of Monserrat was pivotal, leading him to renounce his military life. Soon thereafter, he writes his *Spiritual Exercises*, one of the classics of Christian formation, which becomes the foundation for Jesuit spirituality. When he eventually arrives in the Holy Land, he is not allowed to stay, and returns west. Intensive periods of study then commence at the finest Spanish universities. His writings in this period are imbued with mysticism, and for a brief period of time, he is investigated by church authorities (but is subsequently cleared). In 1537, Ignatius and several others decide to create a new order of Christians, devoted to poverty, chastity, obedience, and allegiance to the pope. The new order, the Society of Jesus, is authorized by Pope Paul III in 1540. Ignatius spends the rest of his life as the leader of this order, which devotes itself to missionary work and education. Its imprint is now felt worldwide. One of the primary voices of the Catholic Reformation, Ignatius wrote primarily about the spiritual life: discerning God's will for one's life and finding God "in all things." His Christology is discernible because the *Exercises* take Christ as the model for contemplation in Christian life.

For Ignatius, spiritual development is possible when we focus on the narrative of Christ as given in the Gospels: incarnation, birth, teaching, miracles, crucifixion, resurrection, and ascension. We are conformed to Christ's love for the world as we reflect on the life and passion of Jesus. The *Exercises* do not have a detailed Christology (in one analogy, an interpreter likens the *Exercises* to a book on "how to play tennis,"[32] since it is a manual that walks its readers through the practices of explicit exercises), but it does have prominent emphases in interpreting the narrative of Jesus. One of these is Jesus's humility, which is a guide to the exercitant's own spiritual posture:

> Consider the address which Christ our Lord makes to all his servants and friends whom he is sending on this expedition. He recommends that they endeavor to aid all persons, by attracting them, first, to the highest degree of spiritual poverty and also, if his Divine Majesty would be served and pleased to choose them for it, to no less a degree of actual poverty; second, by attracting them to a desire of reproaches and contempt, since from these results humility.[33]

Later in the same volume, Ignatius makes this emphasis on humility more explicit and connected to material well-being: "I desire and choose poverty with Christ poor rather than wealth; contempt with Christ laden with it rather than honors. Even further, I desire to be regarded as a useless fool for Christ, who before me was regarded as such, rather than as a wise or prudent person in this world."[34] Jesus, in this vision, stands worldly values on their heads, presenting a contrast to whatever those in lofty positions hold dear. Conversion to Christ mirrors something of Ignatius's own journey: from the acclaim of military chivalry to the simplicity of allegiance to the pope and material poverty. The grace of Christ, in this vision, is not merely spiritual, but encompasses all of human life.

Like many of his medieval predecessors, Ignatius lauds Christ's suffering. Contemplation of the passion offers a window to who Jesus is for us and for the world. In the *Exercises* Ignatius instructs his readers to consider the suffering of Christ so closely that they bring themselves "to grief, sorrow, and tears." By considering the suffering of Christ for ourselves, we are compelled to ask what we can do for Christ. And in contemplating suffering, the exercitant considers "how [Christ's] divinity hides itself; that is, how he could destroy his enemies but does not, and how he allows his most holy humanity to suffer so cruelly."[35] The way of Jesus is a way of relinquishment: of power, of privilege, of earthly prestige. And by receiving the work of Christ, we are not passive, but inspired to go and do likewise, to be willing to suffer for Christ's sake as the way of Jesus becomes more fully known.

One final point is worth noting in Ignatius's interpretation of Jesus: how Jesus is the exemplar of God's sustaining presence *throughout* creation. Jesus Christ is sui generis, the one who is fully human and fully divine. But the divine that sustains Jesus is also radically present throughout the universe. This is one of the hallmarks of Ignatian spirituality, to discern God's presence in all things. "I will consider how God dwells in creatures; in the elements, giving them existence; in the plants, giving them life; in animals, giving them sensation; in human beings, giving them intelligence; and finally, how in this way he dwells also in myself, giving me existence, life, sensation, and intelligence; and even further, making me his temple, since I am created as a likeness and image of his Divine Majesty."[36] Some interpretations of Christ in the Reformation period and hence, in the interest of maintaining the distinction between humanity and divinity, have focused all attention on Christ as the lens through which we glimpse God. But these interpretations, in their extreme cases, run the risk of obscuring God's presence throughout creation. Ignatius's Christology bears the traces of a robust natural theology, which is attentive to the God who is present everywhere, no exceptions. We look to Christ to clarify how God is present for and with the world, knowing that there is no place where God is not, where the traces of the divine do not animate all that is. The great strength of Ignatius's Christology is that it does not simply turn our attention to our need for redemption in Christ, it turns our attention to the world.

Melchior Hoffman (1491–1556)

A furrier by trade, Melchior Hoffman did not receive a formal theological education, but was attracted to religious writings and eventually the cause of church reform. Sometimes dubbed the "Baltic Apostle," Hoffman spent parts of his career in Lithuania, Latvia, Denmark, and Sweden. Influenced and encouraged initially by Luther, Hoffman also journeyed to Wittenberg but eventually lost Luther's support and sought closer ties with the Anabaptist movement. There he found his spiritual home, eventually settling in Strasbourg, where he lived out the remainder of his years. Over the course of his life, he was imprisoned ten years. Despite these travails, he was able to produce an impressive amount of theology, which is often tinged with apocalyptic fervor. Convinced, like some other Reformers, that he lived in the midst of the end times, the call of Christ became even more urgent.

Hoffman's Christology combines classic themes, mystical betrothal imagery, and fiery rhetoric. Jesus is the King who holds all power and strength but is also "the anointed peacemaker for all believers, a reconciler, advocate, and high priest." He is the "King of Kings" who "shuts no one out."[37] Jesus invites the entire world to partake of the kingdom he is inaugurating, offering forgiveness to all who would follow. The call is not limited to the elect. Nonetheless, the contrast between Christ's kingdom and the kingdom of this world is striking. A recurring theme throughout Hoffman's work is how the call of Christ is also a call to purity: "They also who have surrendered themselves to the Lord should lead themselves out of the realm of Satan and from the kingdom of darkness and from this world and . . . they should purify themselves and lead themselves into the spiritual wilderness and also wed and bind themselves to the Lord Jesus Christ."[38] Corruption surrounds those who truly follow Jesus; it permeates the institutional church and society at large. The call of Christ is costly, involving renunciation of religious and temporal authorities in the name of Christ. Because his disciples reject the powers of this world, they should expect suffering and persecution from the world.

The marks of the new citizenship that Christ gives are offered in two ordinances: baptism and the Lord's Supper. In Hoffman's eyes, both are akin to betrothal and marital rites. In baptism, we submit ourselves to Christ, our bridegroom, who claims us as his own, uniting ourselves to him in a passionate embrace. And because the "marriage" requires our consent, the ordinance of baptism is reserved for believers, not infants. In baptism, we give ourselves over to Christ, and for this gift to have any meaning at all, we need to claim it for ourselves; it cannot be claimed by others. The Lord's Supper, furthermore, is like the wedding ring: a concrete sign of the mystical union between Christ and the bride, who is us. "The bride is in truth assured the moment she take the bread that she has accepted the true Christ for her Lord and Head and eternal Bridegroom in order that ever thereafter his will, spirit, mind, and good pleasure may be in her and that she on her part give herself over unto his will with all her heart, spirit, feeling, and will."[39] The union is, moreover, passionate: "She [is] in him and, again, he is in her, and they together are thus one body, one flesh, one spirit, and one passion, as bridegroom and bride."[40] Hoffman's language here is intensely physical, focusing on the body and blood of Christ, which are taken intimately into the believer. But at the same time, Hoffman resists the literal sense of the words of institution. He denies that Christ "corporally exist[s] in the bread" or that the wine becomes Christ's blood.[41] But the union remains nonetheless physical. We are incorporated (taken into) Christ's body in these rites of betrothal, so that his life becomes ours. Dying to the old life, we are born again in the new life of Christ's body. Hoffman's Christology thus avoids the physicalism of contemporary accounts of transubstantiation, but embraces the union offered in the Lord's Supper as more than a spiritual union. Christ takes the believer, body and soul, as his passionate lover, equipping the believer in the struggle for purity, against all that would corrupt the union. The result is a striking series of juxtapositions: Christ as militant crusader against corruption *and* a peacemaker; Christ the Bridegroom who gives himself to the beloved; Christ the King who holds all power and relinquishes it. It is difficult, at times, to discern the patterns amid these juxtapositions. Clearly, Hoffman has moved away from the extremes of Müntzer's militancy, but it was up to another Anabaptist, Menno Simons, to clarify how important Christ the peacemaker was for the proper interpretation of Christ.

Menno Simons (1496–1561)

Dutch priest Menno Simons became attracted to the Anabaptist cause because of its articulation of believers' baptism, but he did not formally align himself with the movement until he relinquished the priesthood in 1536. His influence on subsequent Anabaptist movements is substantial, in part because of his rather long life (while many other Anabaptist leaders were martyred at relatively early ages). He is most remembered for tempering the militancy of many strands of Radical Reformation. Peacemaking for Simons was not incidental to Christian faith, but exists at its very core. To forsake pacifism and take up the sword would be to abandon discipleship and profess allegiance to another lord. His Christology thus stresses Christ as peacemaker, even as it betrays some heterodox leanings in its interpretation of the incarnation.

Simons's conception of the difference between the worldly realm and the kingdom of Christ is rather stark. The world displays a "spirit, doctrine, sacrament, worship, and conduct [that] are quite diverse from Christ's Spirit, Word, sacrament, worship, and example, and are alas nothing but a new Sodom, Egypt and Babylon."[42] The community of faith is called apart from this world, not in a posture of withdrawal, but to bear witness to the one who is the prince of peace. They are called into confrontation with the world, but not on the violent terms that the world chooses. Christ is the one who regenerates us, who implants within us a spirit of peace: "The regenerated do not go to war nor fight. They are children of peace who have beaten their swords into plowshares and their spears into pruning hooks and know of no war." They fight those who profess allegiance to another lord, but do so because Christ has "girded our loins with another sword . . . the Word of God."[43] Jesus thus shows the emptiness of all displays of worldly power and might. Their victory, though by many appearances may seem assured, but is in actuality evanescent. It is important to note that Simons's conception of pacifism is not naive; he knows all too well the scope of the sword's power. In the bloodbath that constituted the age of reform, Simon writes of pacifism while experiencing the martyrdom of his Radical Reformation colleagues. The posture of pacifism is not a strategy for achieving earthly victory; rather, it is a wager that the way of peace is the way of Jesus, that the power of Jesus's relinquishment of earthly power in the face of a violent empire (symbolized in the Roman cross) unveils the enduring power of the universe, the power of God's love, which is always nonviolent. Whatever victories violence can achieve are only temporary. Only the power of self-giving love, the power of peace, endures in the resurrection, in the new creation that God has brought into being with his Prince of Peace. This insight, which led to the Anabaptists' rejection of earlier violent means (symbolized in Müntzer and others), has abided in the centuries hence, constituting the core of Anabaptist Christology.

One dimension of Simons's Christology that did not endure across subsequent centuries, however, is his heterodox understanding of the incarnation. His interpretation of Jesus's humanity, indeed, is somewhat suspect. Though he does not deny Christ's full humanity, he resists the idea that Jesus receives his human flesh from Mary. For Simons, Christ's flesh descends from heaven.[44] So Jesus possesses real human flesh (and does not, à la Docetism, simply *appear* to be human), but this flesh comes to dwell on earth from God. Mary only nourishes that flesh. Simons here seems to be resisting devotional practices that elevate Mary. But he does so in a rather extreme way, relegating her to a passive vessel rather than one who shares her humanity with, and gifts her humanity, to her son. Even Jesus's humanity, in Simons's read, is supernatural, only tangentially connected to our own humanity. Perhaps this is why subsequent Mennonites ultimately rejected this interpretation of the incarnation. For in it, Jesus doesn't seem to share the same humanity with us. His is a "special" humanity that is only received from heaven. If this is the case, then Christ doesn't really assume *our* human flesh that cries out for redemption. Another possible reason for Simons's insistence on a "special" instance of humanity in Christ is ongoing Christian discomfort with birth, sexuality, and women's bodies. How could the Savior enter the world amid the fluid, blood, and pain of the birth canal? Simons's answer is that the flesh of the Savior was to a certain degree removed from these earthy, feminine realities. Though Simons's interpretation of the incarnation is somewhat extreme (and was ultimately rejected), the ongoing discomfort with birth and women's bodies has continued in the centuries since.

Philipp Melanchthon (1497–1560)

Professor of Greek Philipp Melanchthon came into contact with Luther at the University of Wittenberg, where both Reformers taught. Influenced by Luther, Melanchthon soon became one of the leaders of the Protestant movement. Mellower than Luther in temperament, Melanchthon sought out dialogue, not only with other Reformers, but also with the Roman Catholic Church. His thought displays a willingness to shift and adapt over time, as he engaged with these dialogue partners. He was even willing to admit the authority of the papacy, though not on terms that were satisfactory to his Catholic interlocutors. Melanchthon is best known for his authorship of two foundational texts: the Augsburg Confession, which holds special prominence within Lutheranism down to this day, and *Loci communes*, probably the first Protestant systematic treatment of Christian doctrine. Widely influenced by humanism, Melanchthon's theology avoids some of the stark polarities between reason and revelation that are sometimes evident in Luther.

Like Luther, Melanchthon emphasizes Christ's role in justification. This is a consistent refrain throughout the Augsburg Confession and the subsequent Apology for the Confession, which Melanchthon also penned. More than a quarter of the Apology, which covers twenty-eight topics, is devoted exclusively to the one topic of justification. Christ matters because Christ renders the believer justified before God: "We cannot obtain forgiveness of sin and righteousness before God by our own merit, work, or satisfactions, but . . . we receive forgiveness of sin and become righteous before God out of grace for Christ's sake through faith when we believe that Christ suffered for us and . . . for his sake our sin is forgiven."[45] Jesus is the One who stands for us before God, who takes our place, undergoes suffering for our sake. Jesus Christ is God's gift to us; we accept the gift through faith *in* Christ.

Throughout Melanchthon's work, he stresses Christ as mediator and intercessor: justifying us before God, praying for us, representing us to God and God to us. Christ is the One who stands between humanity and the divine, embodying the fullness of both, saving humanity for God's sake and ours. Christ is Intercessor, Sacrifice, and Satisfaction, who makes God known to us. And we know Christ through divine promises to us: promises of righteousness, peace, life, and salvation. Christ is the manifestation of those promises for us, as he is the one who bestows us with these gifts of new life. And Christ reveals the Father: without Christ we do not know the Father.[46] This One who stands between is thus both God's promise and the way in which we live into God's promises.

One of the ways that God's promise to us is made known is through Christ's self-humiliation and weakness. Jesus becomes God's promise by taking on our form and status: "The Lord God Almighty clothed his Son with flesh that he might draw us from contemplating his own majesty to a consideration of the flesh, and especially of our weakness."[47] Echoing Luther's theology of the cross, Melanchthon insists that the glory of divine promise can appear as inglorious in the eyes of worldly power. But it is in his becoming lowly like us that we partake in the new life that Christ offers.

At the heart of Melanchthon's Christology is a somewhat functionalist understanding of Jesus. The most memorable phrase in all of the *Loci communes*, and probably the phrase for which Melanchthon is most remembered, is contained in the following: "To know Christ means to know his benefits. . . . For unless you know why Christ put on flesh and was nailed to the cross, what good will it do you to know merely the history about him?"[48] Christ's "benefits" make knowledge of him possible. Melanchthon is not reducing the person of Christ to his works here, as if the only thing that mattered were what Christ does for humanity. But he does claim that we cannot truly know Christ unless we partake in his gift of new life. This makes a full understanding of Jesus not the subject of history, psychology, or anthropology. While various depictions of Jesus enrich our understanding of him, we cannot know him unless we understand the depth of our need for redemption and experience the reality of redemption in him. In other words, we know the person Jesus *because* of his works. This is what makes Melanchthon's understanding of Jesus "functionalist," in that we glimpse the "person" through his "function." Such an understanding is not reductionistic, but it is at the very least experiential. Or, as Melanchthon writes, "We do better to adore the mysteries of Deity than to investigate them."[49] In this regard, Melanchthon anticipates some themes of pietism that emerge subsequently in Lutheranism: themes that stress spiritual knowledge as true knowledge, devotion as knowledge, and that stress the role of experience in coming to know.

John Calvin (1509–1564)

If we consider Luther to be the "heart" of the Protestant Reformation, John Calvin might be described as its "mind." This distinction is not meant to disparage either theologian, but to note a difference in emphasis and temperament. Luther is the passionate rhetorician, the Reformer who calls out abuses, rallies others to the cause, and outlines the theological grounds for protest, zeroing in on justification as the theological core for evangelical faith. But Luther is no systematizer of the emerging Protestant faith. His writing was more occasional, responding to questions and pressing issues rather than presenting a Protestant dogmatics. That role fell to Calvin, who applied the mind (using the critical skills of humanism) to the beating heart of the Reformation. More reserved than Luther, Calvin saw his role as a teacher-writer, advancing the cause of reform through the pen, defending the faith from its detractors, educating those who were caught up in its passion. His signal contribution is his *Institutes of the Christian Religion*, probably the most influential Protestant dogmatics of all time.

Born in northern France, Calvin received an excellent education, in part because of his family's connection to and receipt of ecclesial benefits from the regional bishop. He studies theology, but gravitates toward law and comes into contact with humanism. Eventually, he becomes attracted to the cause of church reform, a stance that leads him to renounce his ecclesiastical benefits and flee France. Finding refuge in Basel, Calvin begins writing his *Institutes*, a short book intended to be a guide to Protestant faith. Later he finds a home in Geneva (which is interrupted by a dispute that causes him to leave that city for Strasbourg only to return again), where he leaves a lasting impact as writer, teacher, preacher, and civil reformer. Revisions of the *Institutes* continue, along with extensive commentaries on most of the books of the Bible. His impact is wide-ranging, including his understanding of church governance (which combines lay and clerical leadership), an emphasis on predestination as a comfort to the terrified conscience, and a stress on sanctification and growth in holiness as a consequence of justification. In christological matters, Calvin was both an innovator and a critical compiler of orthodoxy.

Perhaps most famously, Calvin summarizes the work of Christ under the threefold banner of Prophet, Priest, and King. This threefold name gathers together the accumulated wisdom of christological orthodoxy. This work cannot be reduced to any one theory. Instead, Calvin combines three significant atonement theories: the name of Prophet relates to Abelardian motifs; Priest hearkens Anselm; and King evokes Christus Victor, the emphasis on Christ's cosmic victory over the forces of sin, death, and evil. By heralding Jesus as Prophet, Calvin signals Jesus as the exemplar of our orientation to God, the prophet who is the window to God's presence and revelation. To know Jesus and his commands is to know the will of God. In explicating this role, Calvin stresses Jesus's teaching and prophetic utterances, the things Jesus said during his earthly ministry. And by focusing on Jesus's words, Calvin stresses that Jesus is the end of all prophets and prophecies. Jesus is the resolution of the Old Testament longing for Messiah, the perfection of all teaching, the fulfillment of all divine promises. After him, there is no other; the life of this Prophet causes prophecy to cease.

But Jesus is more than his words, more than his ministry. He is the Priest who conducts sacrifice by laying his life down for others. In articulating Christ's priestly role, Calvin reclaims Anselm. What matters here is not only Jesus's death but also the manner of that death, which occurs as the result of a trial we should have endured ourselves. "To take away our condemnation, it was not enough for him to suffer any kind of death: to make satisfaction for our redemption a form of death had to be chosen in which he might free us both by transferring our condemnation to himself and by taking our guilt upon himself. . . . The guilt that held us liable for punishment has been transferred to the head of the Son of God." Jesus takes the role of a guilty person for our sake, even undergoing a trial before Pilate, a "wicked and profane man."[50] Though we are the ones who are guilty, Jesus assumes our guilt and takes on the consequences of it. Calvin considers this manner of death both substitution and satisfaction. For him, it is critical for Jesus to die as one accursed, as one condemned by "justice." If Jesus had died in old age, was murdered by thieves, or killed by a mob, satisfaction and substitution would not have occurred.[51]

Jesus's saving work, however, is more than his prophetic life and sacrificial death. Jesus as King establishes the eternity of God's dominion. In his life, death, and resurrection, Jesus achieves victory over all earthly powers. Jesus conquers and transforms the powers that bind us to sin and death, giving new life in resurrection power. This "work" of Christ as Victor includes the political, even though his reign is spiritual. "The Father has given all power to the Son that he may by the Son's hand govern, nourish, and sustain us, keep us in his care, and help us."[52] In light of Christ's power, all earthly powers are proved empty, even as Christ is at work transforming earthly powers. One of the differences between Calvin's Reformed ethos and that of most Anabaptists is that whereas Anabaptists tend to opt out of political structures, since they are inherently corrupt, Calvin encourages political involvement, so that civil government might more nearly reflect God's intent for humanity.[53]

In his kingly role, Jesus also reveals himself to be Lord of the church, a lordship that is eternal. For Calvin and others in the Reformed tradition, the church is not an ephemeral waystation on the way to a full relationship with God. Rather, it is the community that mediates our relationship to God, where the Word of God is heard, where we encounter that Word in sacraments, and where the Word governs us through appropriate discipline. The church, for Calvin, abides, which is due not to the faithfulness of the saints, but to God's faithfulness in Jesus Christ as head of the church. As head of the church, Jesus establishes a spiritual kingdom, but not an otherworldly kingdom. The church offers no escape from the world. Jesus does not save by taking us out of the world (à la Gnosticism), but saves us in midst of the world. This allows us to remain firmly enmeshed in the world, while holding all things in the world lightly: "Christ's kingdom lies in the Spirit, not in earthly pleasures or pomp. Hence we must forsake the world if we are to share in the Kingdom."[54]

This emphasis on Christ's kingship bleeds into Calvin's notion of sanctification, the growth and increase in Christian life that is possible when we are justified by faith. Here is yet another contrast with Luther. Luther tends to contrast "law" and "gospel." The law is what condemns us, by showing us that we cannot fulfill it on our own. So the law drives us into the arms of grace. A second use is the restraining function of law: the rules of society that bear a divine imprint and keep us from unleashing further havoc in the world. To both of these "negative" functions of the law, Calvin adds something: a third use, in which law is also a guide for saintly living. For Calvin, the law doesn't only convict us; it enlivens us as we grow into our sanctification, our increase in faith, hope, and love. In this sense, Jesus is not only the bearer of grace and justification; he is also a lawgiver, who shows us how we ought to live. Jesus doesn't simply enumerate rules that are impossible for us to follow; he shows us, in law, the way of holiness, which we can follow by grace. This is further reason why the Reformed tradition has been so insistent on never giving up on the civil sphere, never relinquishing the impetus to reform society from within, even when it has resulted in rebellion against the established order. Perhaps this is why it has witnessed such a bewildering array of attempts to re-form society more nearly in the image of God: from horrendously misguided attempts, such as apartheid in South Africa and Manifest Destiny in North America, to the attempts to atone for those sins, as in the South African Truth and Reconciliation Commission and attempts at the social gospel. As it confesses Christ as King, the Reformed tradition holds both the promise of reforming society in more humane ways as it also runs the danger of imposing on society its own worst aspirations. The transformative impulse, rooted in a vision of Christ as King, is no doubt a double-edged sword.

One final aspect of Calvin's Christology is worth noting, which is often seen as a peculiarity of Reformed Christianity. This is the *extra calvinisticum*, which is an interpretation of the relationship of God the Son to the incarnate Jesus. For Calvin and those in his wake, the incarnation does not exhaust the presence of the divine Son. During Jesus's earthly ministry, the Son is present beyond Jesus's flesh as well as within it. Calvin maintains a rather firm distinction between the divine and the human in matters of Christology. And though his theology highlights accommodation, how God condescends to express God's very self in human words (in the Bible) and in human flesh (in the incarnate Jesus), the presence of God is never fully contained in these human expressions. This, too, has consequences for Calvin's view of the Eucharist, where he is also wary of rendering the Son fully, physically present in the elements at table. For Calvin, the mystery of the Eucharist is not that Christ is physically present; rather, the miracle is that in breaking, sharing, and consuming the meal, those who partake are lifted into a heavenly banquet. Christ is really, spiritually present as he gathers participants at the Lord's Supper into this foretaste of the messianic banquet. The Son, seated at the right hand of the Father, is not contained in the elements of communion, but invites his followers into his heavenly presence.

Calvin's Christology is thematically rich. It is both a synthetic Christology, as it gathers together inherited orthodoxy under the offices of Prophet, Priest, and King; and it is innovative in how it understands the relationship between the eternal Word and the incarnate Jesus. Though strands of this Christology run interpretive risks (Jesus's kingship, in some instances, can simply replicate patterns of earthly kingship—the Reformed tradition is no stranger to triumphalism), the multifaceted nature of Calvin's Christology means that no one portrait of Jesus is sufficient for the life of faith. In this sense, Calvin's Christology invites ongoing reinterpretation and reclamation.

Teresa of Ávila (1515–1582)

Born into a Jewish-Spanish family that had converted to Christianity, Teresa entered the Carmelite order when she was twenty years old. Drawn to austerity and a strict adherence to the rules of the order, she eventually becomes involved in efforts to reform it. These efforts intensify after what she described as a conversion experience nearly twenty years after she joined the Carmelites. This experience also turns her practice in a more mystical direction, resulting in writings that reflect on the soul's journey into deeper relationship with God. Teresa becomes a leader among the Carmelites, resulting in the establishment of more than thirty convents of discalced, or "barefoot," Carmelites. Much of her work aroused the suspicion of the Spanish Inquisition, though she eventually escaped censure (or worse). Her work has since become widely heralded, and in 1970 she was named the first female doctor of the church. Her Christology emerges distinctly in her most renowned work, *The Interior Castle*, which likens the spiritual journey to an entry into a many-chambered house, with God at the center. Christ is the inviter, guide, and companion in this journey, beckoning us into deeper intimacy.

Teresa employs abundant metaphors to describe Jesus, including Brother, Friend, Teacher, Lord, and King. But most central to her depiction of Jesus as the guide of this journey is the Savior who elicits our desire. Jesus awakens our soul to love: "He makes [the soul] desire Him vehemently by certain delicate means the soul itself does not understand."[55] The nature of this desire is intense; once the soul is awakened, it is no exaggeration to say that Jesus ravages us with love. For us, awakening to love is painful as well as the source of pleasure. Teresa likens the pain to an arrow that pierces the skin:

"I do know that it seems this pain reaches to the soul's very depths and that when He who wounds it draws out the arrow, it indeed seems in accord with the deep love the soul feels that God is drawing these very depths after Him."[56] As we journey deeper into the interior castle, guided by Christ, the pain does not immediately subside. Instead, it abides as testament to the intensity of Christ's love.

This symbolism of desire gets more concentrated the further one journeys, as eroticism becomes more visible. Jesus, the awakener of desire in us, is like a pleasing fragrance that "moves the soul to a delightful desire of enjoying Him, and thereby the soul is prepared to make intense acts of love and praise of our Lord."[57] As Jesus enkindles the heart to love, he also enlivens all of our senses. The journey is consummated as Jesus presents himself as our Spouse, who takes into his private chamber: "He brings [the soul], before the spiritual marriage is consummated, into His dwelling place. . . . For just as in heaven so in the soul His Majesty must have a room where He dwells alone."[58] Here the deepest intimacies are shared as we become united to Christ in marriage. Jesus is the Bridegroom, to whom we are knit in union, from whom we live our lives. As we become Christ's bride, we recognize that our life is Christ. Though Teresa's eroticism is less explicit than some of her predecessors', the point of it is similar: Jesus kindles our desire, which generates both pleasure and pain, finding resolution only when we are united in marriage to the One who is our longing, life, and beloved. In the end, Teresa offers an intensely experiential Christology that invites the believer to commence the journey. Its obvious strength is that it invites our experience as we seek to follow Jesus; its potential weakness is that it might not provide sufficient checks on whether the experience we have is actually related to Jesus. Desire, after all, can have many sources and objects, some of which are rather remote from the life of Christ.

John of the Cross (1542–1591)

Strongly influenced by Teresa, and a fellow reformer along with her, John grew up in a very poor family and became a priest in 1567. His involvement in efforts to reform the Carmelites led to a nine-month imprisonment in a monastery resistant to reform. Renowned for his spiritual devotion, John also suffered health problems, but is most remembered for his beautiful, poetic renditions of the spiritual life. Like Teresa, his depictions of Christ focus on desire and longing. In one of his most famous, *The Spiritual Canticle*, John likens Christ to a stag.

The spiritual contemplative pursues Christ like a hunter. But unlike the typical hunt, here the pursued is the one who leaves the wound. In *The Spiritual Canticle*, there is a dialogue between a bride, who represents the spiritual pilgrim, and the bridegroom, who is Christ. Here is how John depicts the bride's speech: "Where have you hidden, Beloved, and left me moaning? You fled like the stag after wounding me; I went out calling you, and you were gone."[59] John's vision of Christ is akin to Teresa's, in that Jesus awakens our desire. But John emphasizes the *absence* of Christ in this longing more than his *presence*. Jesus eludes the hunt; he is always going ahead, calling us to follow, but in ways that leave us longing for more: "Why, since you wounded this heart, don't you heal it? And why, since you stole it from me, do you leave it so, and fail to carry off what you have stolen?"[60] There is less resolution here than there is for Teresa. John attends more distinctly to incompleteness, even the negativity of the journey into God. This is evident in another of his masterworks, the *Dark Night of the Soul*. Jesus awakens our desire, but there is no resolution to this desire in this life for us. Instead, we are always on our way. Jesus, in this regard, tantalizes us with the promise of quenched desire, but short of paradise we are left with increased longing. The soul thus issues a plea to Christ: "Extinguish these miseries, since no one else can stamp them out; and may the vision of your beauty be my death; for the sickness of love is not cured except by your very presence and image."[61] Christ is the one who enkindles desire, wounds us with desire, and exposes the sickness of our soul. As we journey toward union with Christ—which John promises as much as Teresa—we can expect intensified pain rather than pleasure. If Jesus promises eternal rest, he also inflicts wounds as he eludes our grasp. Jesus, in this regard, is one who cannot be contained, who always leaves us aching for resolution. At its best, this Christology avoids a Pollyanna depiction of Christ as the healer of all ills, thus enabling us to recognize the frustration and dark night that invariably accompany any spiritual journey. At worst, it may foster masochism in a way akin to John of the Cross's longing for his own death.

The Council of Trent (1545–1563)

Convened by Pope Paul III, but not concluded until the reign of Pius IV nearly twenty years later, the Council of Trent was interrupted several times by political and military disputes. Its purpose was both to reform abuses within the Roman church and to define Catholic orthodoxy against perceived extremes of the Protestant Reformation. Protestants were invited to take part, but they did not participate for long, and only then as observer delegates. The council emerged with several definitive stances: the importance of traditions (as well as Scripture) in delineating orthodoxy, establishing the Vulgate as the authoritative biblical text, further exposition of the seven sacraments, and establishment of more rigorous and consistent education of clergy. In matters of Christology, the council (which was probably the most important influence on Catholicism until the Second Vatican Council in the twentieth century) is most memorable in how it interpreted justification and the presence of Christ in the Eucharist.

Trent describes justification as "a translation from that state in which man is born as a child of the first Adam, to the state of grace and of the adoption of the sons of God through the second Adam, Jesus Christ, our Savior."[62] Upon this much, there is no disagreement with the Protestant Reformers. But Trent has a stronger view of human agency than is typical for the Reformers. "While God touches the heart of man through the illumination of the Holy Ghost, man himself neither does absolutely nothing while receiving that inspiration, since he can also reject it, nor yet is he able by his own free will and without the grace of God to move himself to justice in His sight."[63] In some respects, the difference is of degree: While for the Reformers, even the human acknowledgment of the need for grace in Christ is itself a gift of grace, for Trent, there is one small thing that humans can do: acknowledge a need for grace, to say yes to the inspiration or to say no by rejecting it. A further difference is evident in how Trent links justification and sanctification. While the Reformers emphasize that God declares us to be righteous (even though we are not) because of Christ's righteousness, Trent stipulates that justification opens up a path by which we are made righteous. The Lutheran dictum "simultaneously sinner and justified," according to Trent, is not completely accurate, because justification means something more than being reckoned *as* righteous; it opens up a way of transformation. The faith and righteousness of Jesus are not just imputed to the believer; they are imparted in a slow process of reorientation. Anything less, according to Trent, cuts short the radically transformative work of Jesus.

Trent also firmly establishes Catholic orthodoxy surrounding the Lord's Supper. First, it claims the Mass as sacrifice, not a memorial, not a testimony. As sacrifice, it exists in continuity with the sacrifices attested to in the Hebrew Scriptures, while bringing them to completion: The Mass is "that sacrifice which was prefigured by various types of sacrifices during the period of nature and of the law, which, namely, comprises all the good things signified by them, as being the consummation and perfection of them all."[64] In a very real sense, Christ's self-sacrifice is reenacted whenever the Mass is celebrated. In eating and drinking of this meal, we too participate in the sacrifice, accepting it for our lives. Christ is really present in the elements and actions at table: Trent affirms transubstantiation as the proper way of interpreting the meal.

Furthermore, the efficacy of the sacrament as a means of grace is not dependent on the faith of the partaker (as it tends to be in Protestant theology). Rather, the grace is in the elements and ritual actions themselves, regardless of the posture of the partaker, because Christ is really present in them. To eat and drink at this table is to be transformed by Christ's life and sacrificial death. Trent even claims that this transformative grace is not limited to those presently gathered at the table: the Mass "is rightly offered not only for the sins, punishments, satisfactions, and other necessities of the faithful who are living, but also for those departed in Christ but not yet fully purified."[65] Masses for the dead, which had come under fire from many Reformers, thus continue to have a valid place in

Catholic understandings of the grace and power of the living Christ present in the Supper: a power and grace that extends beyond the human grave.

Though many Protestant readings of Trent have tended to see in its statements primarily a reactionary motif, focused mainly on defending traditional Catholic christological doctrine in the face of perceived threats, I would suggest that the primary motivation (at least in Christology) is to promote a more expansive view of the grace of Christ. In this sense, Trent resists the limits of transformative grace that it perceives in some Protestant interpretations. Its understanding of justification in Christ, for example, suggests that Christ's righteousness is something more than a forensic category, by which we are merely counted as righteous. To claim as much, at least from Trent's perspective, is to limit the ongoing grace of Christ that will not let us go even as we become more righteous. Likewise, Trent's emphatic pronouncement that Christ is really present in the elements of the Mass means that the grace of Christ is not dependent on our disposition: It is a grace that pursues us whether or not we have prepared ourselves for it, and it reaches beyond the veil of death.

Richard Hooker (1553–1600)

Widely regarded as the most formative and influential of early Anglican theologians, Richard Hooker was educated and taught at Oxford (though eventually dismissed and later rehired). He served churches in London and elsewhere, but is mainly remembered for his defense of the emerging theology of the Church of England, primarily as it contrasted with Puritanism. His *Laws of Ecclesiastical Polity* is a foundational work of Anglicanism, epitomizing a moderate spirit, carving a "third way" between various extremes of Protestantism and its Catholic detractors. He is widely credited with establishing the "three-legged stool" of Scripture, tradition, and reason, as essential for discerning theological truth. His Christology is not extensive, and emerges primarily in relation to his understanding of the Eucharist. Here, like in so many other instances, he carves a middle way.

On the one hand, Hooker emphasizes the transformative power of the Eucharist, because of Christ's grace: The effect of the Eucharist, for us, is "*a real transmutation of our souls and bodies from sin to righteousness*, from death and corruption to immortality and life."[66] In this respect, Hooker's interpretation is akin to Trent's. But the miracle of the Eucharist is not the "real" presence of Christ in the elements; rather, it is in the presence of Christ *in the believer.* "The real presence of Christ's most blessed body and blood is not therefore to be sought for in the sacrament, but in the worthy receiver of the sacrament."[67] Here Hooker sounds more like Protestant interpretations. And in this respect, he renders the presence of Christ even more intimate: Christ is the one who is present that enables the believer to take part in the sacrament. As we eat and drink, Christ is already there, animating our gestures at table.

Hooker likens the Supper to our mystical participation in Christ. When Jesus says, "Take, eat; this is my body," he makes himself wholly ours. Christ is thus present in those who gather at table without being contained or exhausted by it. The real mystery is not that bread and wine take part in this communion, but that *we do*, as we are transformed by the life of Christ that extends beyond the table.

Jacob Arminius (1560–1609) and Arminianism

A pastor and theologian from the Netherlands, Jacob Arminius identified with the Calvinist wing of the Reformation throughout his life, even when he criticized some strands of it. He studied in some of the great centers of Reformed thought, including Leiden and Geneva, and eventually assumed a professorship in Leiden in 1603 (after serving a church in Amsterdam). There he entered into several theological controversies, among them disputes over predestination, the nature of free will, Christ's atonement, and the perseverance of the saints. Though he never sought to leave the Calvinist fold, the theological movement that arose in his wake is often seen as a Protestant alternative to Calvinism. Therefore, the christological statements that we will consider come from a series of "Articles" composed one year after Arminius's death.

Arminius insisted (contra some Reformed stances) that Jesus Christ died for all persons, regardless of their eternal status. This led him to reject the idea of limited atonement—that Christ only died for the elect—that had begun to gain credence in some Reformed circles. To claim that Christ died *only* for some, in Arminius's view, made Jesus something less than the Savior of the world. But to claim Jesus as Savior of the world does not mean that all are saved in him. Here is how the Arminian Articles put it: "Jesus Christ, the Savior of the world, died for all men and for every man, so that he has obtained for them all, by his death on the cross, redemption and the forgiveness of sins; yet . . . no one actually enjoys this forgiveness of sins except the believer, according to the word of the Gospel of John 3:16."[68] Christ came for all, but only faith enables us to receive the gift of salvation. This recognition leads the Arminians to an account of grace and how it operates on the human person. In many contemporary Reformed accounts, grace cannot be resisted: God bestows the grace of Christ, in faith, on those whom God wills. Once showered by grace, there is no way to turn away from it. The Arminians found this idea problematic since it limited the scope of Christ's saving work, limiting it only to the elect. For the Arminians, by contrast, it is likewise "all grace, all the time," but we always have the opportunity to say no to it:

> This grace of God is the beginning, continuance, and accomplishment of all good, even to this extent, that the regenerate man himself, without prevenient or assisting, awakening, following and co-operative grace, can neither think, will, nor do good, nor withstand any temptations to evil; so that all good deeds or movements, that can be conceived, must be ascribed to the grace of God in Christ. But as respects the mode of the operation of this grace, it is not irresistible, inasmuch as it is written concerning many, that they have resisted the Holy Ghost.[69]

The grace of God in Jesus Christ, in other words, enables us to respond—in freedom—to God's offer of salvation in Christ. But it does not compel us to respond to that offer affirmatively. Jesus emerges in this portrayal as the One who continually stands at the door, offering entrance to all. Our response to that invitation is likewise animated by grace. In the eyes of the Arminians, this invitation had become obscured by hardline Calvinism. Jesus seemed only to have eyes for those whom God had already foreordained for salvation. The work of the Arminians thus tries to make Jesus's embrace of all remain at the center of any depiction of him. And for this much, their efforts are significant. If later Arminians began to open the door to more and more human activities that were possible apart from grace, we should remember that for Arminius, even our acceptance of grace is itself a further offer of grace.

George Fox (1624–1691)

Widely considered the founder of the Quakers, Englishman George Fox embarked as a young man on an itinerant preaching tour, which took him throughout Europe and North America. He was a critic of the institutional church who was convinced that God imparts an inner light to all people. Our call is to discern that light and follow it. His theology stresses experience, the work of the Holy Spirit, and the importance of pacifism. Jesus figures prominently in that theology, primarily as the inaugurator of all authentic experience. Much of Fox's christological reflections, appropriately, occur in the form of journal entries.

Fox's Jesus is itinerant and anti-institutional. Jesus cannot be identified strictly with any established church. Fox reflects on the time when he discerned this: "The Lord showed me clearly, that he did not dwell in those temples which men had commanded and set up, but in people's hearts."[70] The ongoing presence of Christ, therefore, is not primarily encountered in the sacrament (contra Catholicism) or in the church (contra Catholicism and most strands of Protestantism), but in the inner testimony of each believer. Jesus takes us as his own, and speaks to us intimately, if we would only listen. He speaks to us, and is present to us, through an inner light, which is the light of Christ himself. This light leads us into all truth,[71] and it is our ongoing task to discern it. Far more than nearly anyone of this period (save Müntzer), Fox personalizes the presence of Jesus. Indeed, the inner light of Jesus is what holds chief authority in this emergent Quaker theology: more important than ecclesial traditions, more important even than the reading of Scripture. To be sure, the Bible still holds a prominent place, but it is the Bible read in response to the light of Christ given in human experience. This leads the emergent Quaker movement to dispense with traditional sacraments and liturgy. The center of Quaker worship forms around believers' testimony and speaking out of the light. When moved by the Spirit or the inner light to speak, believers will offer testimony; when they are not moved, they will remain silent and allow God to speak through the silence.

This Jesus who is itinerant, inhabiting each believer's heart, is also One who calls those who follow him to reject many of the ways of the world. Foremost among these ways is Jesus's rejection of violence. When faced with the sword of the Roman Empire, Jesus chooses another way, showing us that violence does not have the final word. The Spirit of Christ, "which leads us into all Truth, will never move us to fight and war against any man with outward weapons, neither for the kingdom of Christ, nor for the kingdoms of this world."[72] There is no better example of a worldly lust than its endless resorting to bloodshed. For Fox and the Quakers, pacifism is not simply one option among others; it is the primary way we show that we belong to Christ. Jesus is a nonviolent Savior who illuminates all with his light. Our task is to discern that light and follow him, wherever it leads. The portrait of Jesus, is both anti-institutional and intensely personal. But for those who follow, we partake in nothing less than the mind of Christ.

Westminster Confession (1643–1646)

An act of Parliament convened the Westminster Assembly, with the intent of providing theological clarity for the Church of England amid the turbulence of reform. The delegates were chiefly English, though a few Scots were also in attendance. The confession that emerged, as well as two catechisms and a directory of worship, are masterpieces of Reformed scholasticism. They represent one of the last Reformation-era confessions, a high-water mark in establishing the parameters of orthodoxy. Though intended for the Church of England, the documents were never officially adopted by that church. They did, however, prove foundational for the Church of Scotland (replacing the Scots Confession) and especially for the Reformed-Presbyterian movement in North America, where the Westminster Standards held central place for centuries. In matters of Christology, the documents specify rather clearly matters of dispute, such as the mediatorship of Christ, the nature of atonement, the role of predestination, and the presence of Christ in the Eucharist. They also exemplify a manner of doing theology in which the life of Christ tends to be underemphasized in order to specify the importance of his death and resurrection.

One of the overarching themes of Westminster is its articulation of a covenant theology. The good news of Christian faith is that God covenants with humanity, makes promises to us that abide throughout all time. In this sense, the incarnation of Jesus is not an unexpected bolt from the blue, but the manifestation and fulfillment of the promises God has made from the beginning of creation. These promises entail the condescension of God in time, by entering into relationships with the flesh and blood of creation. In the period of law (Old Testament), the covenant was "administered by promises, prophecies, sacrifices, circumcision, the paschal lamb, and other types and ordinances delivered to the people of the Jews . . . which were for that time sufficient and efficacious." In the period of the gospel, "when Christ the substance was exhibited, the ordinances in which this covenant is dispensed, are the preaching of the Word, and the administration of the sacraments of

Baptism and the Lord's Supper. . . . These are not, therefore, two covenants of grace differing in substance, but one and the same under various dispensations."[73] Jesus here exists in continuity with the Jewish context, though he also crowns it and signals the end of the ordinances customary during his own time. He is thus the fulfillment of the old and the establishment of something new. His coming does not signal a new promise of God, but rather the extension of particular promises to Israel that are now present to the whole world. Jesus Christ comes, in this sense, in the fullness of time, for all people.

The chief role of Christ, according to Westminster, is as Mediator. Jesus is the One who stands between God and humanity, bridging the rupture caused by human sin. The Westminster Confession gathers together a body of inherited orthodoxy, focusing mostly on the preexistence of the Word and Jesus's sacrificial death. According to Westminster, Jesus is Prophet, Priest, and King, of one substance with and equal to the Father, conceived by the Holy Spirit, without sin, who endured suffering and crucifixion for our salvation, rose from the dead, ascended into heaven, and makes intercession for us at the right hand of the Father.[74] Westminster, furthermore, rejects the tenets of Arminianism, by defending limited atonement and irresistible grace. It thereby casts the mold for centuries of subsequent Reformed reflection on the person and work of Christ. Indeed, for many centuries—especially in North America and Scotland—one showed how Reformed one really was by demonstrating one's alignment with the Westminster Standards. The Confession and catechisms are remarkable documents, delineating with precision a view of the atonement, offices of Christ, and resurrection that give further specificity to themes drawn out in Calvin and other Reformers. But amid this precision is a conspicuous lack: almost no reflection on the life and teachings of Jesus. For a tradition that emphasizes the centrality of the incarnation, how it is in continuity with God's promises to Israel, and the importance of teaching in the role of ministry, it is stunning that a confession would not offer much interpretation of what the Gospels spend most of their time on: Jesus's parables, preaching, and acts of healing.

Sor Juana Inés de la Cruz (1651–1695)

Born out of wedlock to a mother descended from Spaniards living in Mexico and a Spanish soldier, Juana Inés was a precocious child who sought out education at a time when girls' opportunities were very limited in colonial Mexico. She learned to read at age three, and from then on devoured nearly every book she could find. Adopted by an aunt and uncle at age eight, Sor Juana moved to Mexico City, eventually studying subjects as diverse as theology and botany. She became a polymath, choosing monastic life over marriage, and wrote extensively: dramas, autobiography, letters, and scholarly tracts. Throughout these writings, she is a consistent advocate for the rights of women, especially regarding education. Her Christology is remarkably creative, occurring chiefly in one of her dramatic works, *El Divino Narciso*.

In this play, Sor Juana, retells the story of Jesus by comparing the incarnation to the Greek myth of Narcissus. Juana's eternal Christ beholds his reflection in water, but instead of falling in love with himself, he falls in love with humanity, being captivated by humanity's beauty. Out of this love for the human race, the incarnation of Jesus occurs. Jesus comes in the flesh so that he might complete our beauty, which is imperfect. Jesus desires us to partake in the fullness of divine beauty, and dies because of his great love for us to participate in it. "It was his love that killed him, for nothing else beside the very love of his own could ever overcome him. Through gazing at his likeness, he falls in love and dies, for his image, even copied, wields almighty power."[75] The beginning and end of the incarnation, life, and teaching of Jesus, as well as his death and resurrection, are not primarily for the sake of truth, but for the beauty that is God's love for the world. Jesus falls in love with humanity—no exceptions—and seeks all to participate in that love. This is an especially important theme as the age of colonialism is beginning: When European empires deemed Africans and Native Americans as somehow lesser, the wisdom of Sor Juana is that all are embraced, claimed, and dignified by a God of boundless beauty. By seeing Christ as the source of beauty, Juana's Christology also encourages us to behold the beauty of each human face, just as Jesus does.[76]

Conclusion

Our survey of the Reformation period has ended on an intriguing note. In an era responsible for perhaps the greatest fragmentation in Christian history (witness the birth of a bedazzling array of Christian movements that are no longer in communion with each other), our final christological reflections issue an invitation for all to participate in the beauty of incarnation and to witness beauty in one another. This tumultuous period of Christian history began with a call to reform many abuses in the church that had obscured the beauty of church life and practice. Reformers of various stripes urged their hearers to get back to the basics, underscoring the centrality of Christ in renewing creation, justifying us before God. Subsequent generations of Reformers urged greater specificity in describing how Christ justifies, saves, and heals the sin-sick creation. In the emergent scholasticism of Protestants and Catholics, moreover, the lines of distinction become increasingly sharp. By the end of the Reformation period, the line-drawing seems particularly focused on Jesus's atoning death and its implications for the life of faith. Perhaps along the way, some of the beauty of Christ's life became lost; perhaps Sor Juana's approach—using the unorthodox genre of drama—calls us back to the beauty that is Christ's life for the world.

Notes

1. Martin Luther, *Heidelberg Disputation*, in *Luther's Works*, vol. 31, *Career of the Reformer I*, ed. Harold J. Grimm (Philadelphia: Fortress Press, 1957), 53.
2. Bernhard Lohse, *Martin Luther's Theology: Its Historical and Systematic Development*, trans. Roy A. Harrisville (Minneapolis: Fortress Press, 1999), 222.
3. Luther, *Two Kinds of Righteousness*, in Grimm, *Career of the Reformer I*, 301.
4. Martin Luther, *Luther's Works*, vol. 26, *Lectures on Galatians, 1535, Chapters 1–4*, ed. Jaroslav Pelikan (St. Louis: Concordia Publishing House, 1963), 277.
5. Luther, *Lectures of Galatians*, 289.
6. Lohse, *Luther's Theology*, 224.
7. Martin Luther, *The Large Catechism*, in *The Book of Concord*, ed. Robert Kolb and Timothy J. Wengert (Minneapolis: Fortress Press, 2000), 440.
8. Lohse, *Luther's Theology*, 224.
9. Luther was suspicious of traditions that emphasized fourfold meanings of Scripture, which tended to stress a "spiritual" meaning beyond the plain sense of the text. But in stressing the plain meaning, Luther was not a strict literalist. His method of biblical interpretation avoided prooftexting and sought to interpret particular strands of Scripture in light of the broad trajectory of biblical witness. This approach allowed him to view some books of the Bible with a degree

of suspicion, most notably James, Revelation, and Esther. These books, he sometimes claimed, if not read in light of the broad witness of Scripture could lead readers away from the gospel.

10. Martin Luther, *This Is My Body*, in *Luther's Works*, vol. 37, *Word and Sacrament III*, ed. Robert H. Fischer (Philadelphia: Fortress Press, 1961), 68.
11. Luther, *This Is My Body*, 68–69.
12. Huldrych Zwingli, *An Exposition of the Faith*, in *Zwingli and Bullinger*, ed. Geoffrey W. Bromiley, Library of Christian Classics (Philadelphia: Westminster, 1953), 251.
13. Zwingli, *Exposition of the Faith*, 251.
14. Zwingli, *Exposition of the Faith*, 252.
15. Zwingli, *Exposition of the Faith*, 252.
16. Zwingli, *Exposition of the Faith*, 255. "The humanity of Christ is not eternal, therefore it is not infinite. If it is not infinite, it is necessarily finite. And if it is finite, it is not omnipresent." Zwingli, *Exposition of the Faith*, 256.
17. Zwingli, *Exposition of the Faith*, 255.
18. Zwingli, *Exposition of the Faith*, 258.
19. Zwingli, *Exposition of the Faith*, 260.
20. Thomas Müntzer, *A Manifest Exposé of False Faith*, in *The Collected Works of Thomas Müntzer*, ed. Peter Matheson (Edinburgh: T&T Clark, 1988), 264.
21. Müntzer, *Manifest Exposé*, 318–20.
22. Müntzer, *Interpretation of the Second Chapter of Daniel*, in Matheson, *Complete Works*, 231.
23. Müntzer, *Daniel*, 246.
24. Müntzer, *Manifest Exposé*, 278.
25. Martin Bucer, *De Regno Christi*, in *Melanchthon and Bucer*, ed. Wilhelm Pauck, Library of Christian Classics (Philadelphia: Westminster, 1969), 225.
26. Bucer, *De Regno Christi*, 386.
27. Bucer, *De Regno Christi*, 199.
28. Bucer, *De Regno Christi*, 201.
29. Bucer, *De Regno Christi*, 225.

30. Bucer, *De Regno Christi*, 234–35.
31. Bucer, *De Regno Christi*, 235.
32. George E. Ganss, SJ, introduction to *Ignatius of Loyola: Spiritual Exercises and Selected Works*, ed. George E. Ganss, SJ, Classics of Western Spirituality (Mahwah, NJ: Paulist Press, 1991), 50.
33. Ignatius of Loyola, *Spiritual Exercises*, in Ganss, *Spiritual Exercises and Select Works*, 155–56.
34. Ignatius of Loyola, *Spiritual Exercises*, 160.
35. Ignatius of Loyola, *Spiritual Exercises*, 168.
36. Ignatius of Loyola, *Spiritual Exercises*, 177.
37. Melchior Hoffman, *The Ordinance of God*, in *Spiritual and Anabaptist Writers*, ed. George H. Williams and Angel M. Mergal, Library of Christian Classics (Philadelphia: Westminster, 1957), 184–85.
38. Hoffman, *Ordinance of God*, 186.
39. Hoffman, *Ordinance of God*, 194.
40. Hoffman, *Ordinance of God*, 194.
41. Hoffman, *Ordinance of God*, 195.
42. Menno Simons, *Foundation of Christian Doctrine*, in *The Complete Writings of Menno Simons*, ed. John Christian Wenger (Scottdale, PA: Herald, 1956), 181.
43. Menno Simons, "From *The Writings of Menno Simons*," in *Readings in the History of Christian Theology*, ed. William C. Placher (Philadelphia: Westminster, 1988), 2:33–34.
44. "God's eternal Word (also called God's seed in Scripture) descended from above and entered into Mary by the overshadowing of divine power." Simons, *The Incarnation of Our Lord*, in Wenger, *Complete Writings*, 794.
45. *The Augsburg Confession*, in Kolb and Wengert, *Book of Concord*, 38–40.
46. Philipp Melanchthon, *Loci communes theologici*, in Pauck, *Melanchthon and Bucer*, 103–4.
47. Melanchthon, *Loci communes theologici*, 21.
48. Melanchthon, *Loci communes theologici*, 21–22.
49. Melanchthon, *Loci communes theologici*, 21.
50. John Calvin, *Institutes of the Christian Religion*, ed. John T. McNeill, trans.

Ford Lewis Battles, Library of Christian Classics (Philadelphia: Westminster, 1960), 509–10.

51. Calvin, *Institutes*, 509.
52. Calvin, *Institutes*, 500.
53. The final chapter of Calvin's *Institutes* is thus illustrative. After surveying the breadth of Christian doctrine, Calvin ends his "brief handbook" with a chapter on civil government, illustrating principles that should govern our social and political relationships.
54. Calvin, *Institutes*, 500.
55. Teresa of Ávila, *The Interior Castle*, trans. Kieran Kavanaugh, OCD, and Otilio Rodriguez, OCD, Classics of Western Spirituality (New York: Paulist Press, 1979), 115.
56. Teresa of Ávila, *Interior Castle*, 116.
57. Teresa of Ávila, *Interior Castle*, 118.
58. Teresa of Ávila, *Interior Castle*, 173.
59. John of the Cross, *The Spiritual Canticle*, in *John of the Cross: Selected Writings*, ed. John Farina, trans. Kieran Kavanaugh, OCD, Classics of Western Spirituality (Mahwah, NJ: Paulist Press, 1987), 221.
60. John of the Cross, *Spiritual Canticle*, 222–23.
61. John of the Cross, *Spiritual Canticle*, 223.
62. "Council of Trent," in Placher, *Readings*, 2:45.
63. "Council of Trent," 2:45.
64. "The Sacrifice of the Mass," in *Jesus*, ed. David F. Ford and Mike Higton, Oxford Readers (Oxford: Oxford University Press, 2002), 227.
65. "The Sacrifice of the Mass," 228.
66. "The Sacrifice of the Mass," 225.
67. "The Sacrifice of the Mass," 224.
68. "Articuli Arminiani sive Remonstrantia.The Five Arminian Articles. A.D. 1610," in *The Creeds of Christendom*, vol. 3, *The Creeds of the Evangelical Protestant Churches*, ed. and trans., Philip Schaff (New York: Harper and Brothers, 1877), 546.
69. "Articuli Arminiani," 547.
70. George Fox, *The Journal of George Fox*, ed. John L. Nickalls (Cambridge: Cambridge University Press, 1952), 8.

71. Fox, *Journal*, 35.

72. Fox, *Journal*, 400.

73. "The Westminster Confession of Faith," chap. 7, in *The Constitution of the Presbyterian Church (U.S.A.)*, part 1, *Book of Confessions* (Louisville: The Office of the General Assembly of the Presbyterian Church [U.S.A.], 1996), 6.037–6.042.

74. "Westminster Confession," chap. 8, 6.043–6.048.

75. Sor Juana Inés de la Cruz, "The Divine Narcissus," in *A Sor Juana Anthology*, trans. Alan S. Trueblood (Cambridge, MA: Harvard University Press, 1988), 163.

76. For further reflections on Sor Juana as an anticolonial theologian, see Michelle A. Gonzalez, "Sor Juana Inés de la Cruz," in *Empire and the Christian Tradition*, ed. Kwok Pui-lan, Don H. Compier, and Joerg Rieger (Minneapolis: Fortress Press, 2007), 229–42.

5

Christologies of Enlightenment and Renewal

The Reformation questioned authority. The ensuing centuries continued this trajectory, resulting in an age of Enlightenment that not only questioned authorities, but overthrew them. If the age of reform sought more appropriate authorities within the church or the life of faith, many voices in the age of Enlightenment found authority outside cathedral walls or the pages of Scripture. The charge to think for oneself, to rely on the mind that God has given, eventually led to the establishment of reason as a prime authority. Captured in Descartes's memorable dictum, *Cogito ergo sum* (I think, therefore I am), this dawning age questioned many previous interpretations of Jesus while recovering others from earlier times. Portraits that stressed Jesus as the cosmic ruler of the universe tended to fade in many interpretations, while a focus on Jesus as teacher (one of the most ancient images for Jesus) came to the fore. But this Jesus was a teacher of rational wisdom as well as religious truth.

Almost at the same time as this critical spirit of reason was sweeping across the West, a corresponding movement of personal renewal began to surface. Often dubbed as pietism, this movement sought to recover the basic devotional postures of Christian faith that had become submerged under layers of theological dispute. The pietists claimed to recover the simplicity of portraits of Jesus and the Christian life itself. Unless an image of Christ led to personal renewal, it was, so to speak, empty words. Pietism is often seen as a "counter" to Enlightenment, but many of the voices from this period in church history epitomize both movements. In many cases, the critical spirit of Enlightenment led directly to spiritual renewal. The portraits of Jesus that emerge from this period, then, are not simply a matter of contrasting "head" and "heart." Instead, they reveal the interconnections between them.

Yet, if the thrust of some Enlightenment thinkers is to interpret Jesus within the bounds of reason alone, by the end of the period, we encounter a Jesus who shatters the bonds of reason or any other construction that would contain him. The age of reason thus also reveals the ways in which reason falls short in interpreting the One whose disciples called teacher.

Blaise Pascal (1623–1662)

French scientist, mathematician, and theologian Blaise Pascal in many respects captures the dueling principles of the age of reason. Trained as a mathematician and physicist (perhaps best known for his formulation of "Pascal's Law" describing fluid pressure and mechanics), Pascal is a religious skeptic, confident in the powers of reason, until his conversion to

Catholicism in 1646, which occurred in dialogue with Jansenist monks who were caring for his ailing father. Pascal adopted much of the Jansenist outlook, including their strict interpretation of Augustine, the notion of irresistible grace, and human inability to turn to grace apart from grace. Pascal undergoes an even more dramatic "second conversion" in 1654, an experience he memorialized in words that he sewed into a garment that he carried for the rest of his life. His writings offered an acute diagnosis of the anxiety and loneliness of humanity when left only to the power of reason, a loneliness that can only be resolved in an encounter of faith. This encounter leads, inevitably, to a personal reckoning with Christ. The encounter does not so much leave reason behind, but it points to reason's limits. Pascal thus highlights both "head" and "heart" in the Christian journey and spends much of his remaining years trying to illustrate the harmony between faith and reason. His portrait of Jesus stresses both the personalism of each believer's encounter (and thus Pascal is sometimes heralded as a forerunner of existentialism) and the miracles of Jesus that are testament to his status as divine Son. Pascal's most influential theological work is a project that he never finished, an apology for Christian faith designed to invite skeptics into the riches of faith that focused more on a psychological analysis of the human dilemma in an age of reason than traditional proofs for God's existence or Christ's lordship. These reflections were posthumously dubbed the *Pensées* (thoughts), and have since become a classic of Christian devotional literature.

The *Pensées* does not epitomize the Enlightenment trend of portraying Jesus as teacher. Instead, it stresses the paradoxes of Jesus's life. Foremost among these paradoxes is the contrast between his glory as heralded Messiah and rejection as one despised. "Had ever man more brilliant fame? . . . Yet did ever man less enjoy his fame? . . . Three years he passes for impostor; priests and rulers reject Him; friends and kinsmen despise Him. At length, He dies, betrayed by one disciple, denied by another, and forsaken by all."[1] This focus on Christ's abject status is hardly new to Christology. As we have seen, it occupies significant space in both medieval and Reformation interpretations. But unlike these earlier emphases on Christ's misery and rejection, Pascal does not suggest these traits as something the disciple needs to imitate (as in Luther's theology of the cross or in Francis's exhortation to poverty), but rather as a mark of Christ's solidarity with us. Jesus is thus "everyman" in the sense that he takes on himself the despair and anxiety of each one of us, when left to the confines of reason alone. Jesus is the answer to each one of our questions, the resolution to the restlessness of life. This is what it means to proclaim his universality: "I contemplate Jesus Christ in all individuals and in ourselves: Jesus Christ as father in His Father, Jesus Christ as brother in His brethren, Jesus Christ as poor in the poor, Jesus Christ as rich in the rich, Jesus Christ as doctor and priest in the priests, Jesus Christ as sovran [sic] in princes, etc."[2] An encounter with Jesus is hence a homecoming. If modern anxiety renders us lost, Jesus shows us where we belong. This portrait of Jesus does not surrender reason; indeed, the trajectory of the *Pensées* offers ample arguments for why the human condition *needs* redemption. But Pascal's appeal also recognizes human limitation. If Descartes's dictum stresses "I think, therefore I am," Pascal might rephrase it as "I am Christ's, therefore I am." In this portrayal, reason and faith coincide, while personal encounter takes precedence over christological orthodoxy. In many respects, Pascal's work foreshadows later strains of pietism, but differs from them in its insistence on never leaving reason behind.

Hermann Reimarus (1694–1768)

If a figure captures the early confidence of the age of reason, it is certainly Reimarus, a professor of Hebrew in Hamburg who was trained in theology as well as biblical and classical languages. He gravitated toward rational accounts of Christian faith, testing most claims of the faith in light of reason. This led to a rather deistic account of creation: a distant, noninterventionist God and a rejection of miracles. But his most significant impact on subsequent theology was undoubtedly his portrayal of Jesus, an account that he probably thought was so controversial that he did not publish it during his lifetime. This interpretation, contained in *A Defense of Rational Worshipers of God*, was published posthumously in excerpts by Gotthold Lessing. Reimarus, in this work, rejects the historicity of the Gospels. According to Reimarus, the Gospels document the disappointment of his followers, who had hoped for a political Messiah, who then reinterpret Jesus as announcing a spiritual realm. But this Jesus is neither congruent with Jesus's own self-understanding and mission nor his followers' initial hopes. Out of the failure of Jesus's original mission and the disappointment of his disciples emerges a Christology that subsequent generations inherit. Reimarus thus makes one of the first attempts to find the historical Jesus among the pages of the Gospels through close, critical examination of its words and themes. The Jesus that the first generation of believers has bequeathed to us, in other words, is not completely reliable. It is up to us, using all of the powers of the human mind, textual examination, and the like, to discover who Jesus *really* is.

Reimarus's chief argument is that Jesus *changes* in light of a failed mission. The disciples and other early followers "hoped in Jesus as a *secular* savior of the nation of Israel up until his death, and after the failure of this hope, only after his death, did they build the system of a *spiritual* suffering savior for the whole human race. It also follows that their previous system of the goal, teaching, and actions of Jesus changed."[3] The Gospels, then, are not eyewitness accounts of the life of Jesus, but retrospective reinterpretations of that life as his followers come to grips with failure. Whereas nearly every previous interpretation of Jesus assumes a historical character to the Gospels, Reimarus treats the New Testament more as propaganda. Many of the details are historically false, but the "truth" of the narratives is available to later eyes. We might say that the Jesus movement was founded on an initial falsehood (an interpretation of Jesus that is not historically true), but that yields a spiritual posture that we might welcome as true. But we should never claim that Jesus actually said and did all of the things that are recorded in the Gospels. This interpretation of Jesus, for obvious reasons, rarely gained ground in the wider church. Even for later voices in the twentieth century, who argued for more symbolic readings of the Gospels, few would stake theological claims on an assumption of the historical falsehood of the church's stories about Jesus. One of the bedrocks of Christian faith—and by this I mean not only a narrowly conceived "orthodoxy"—is that the healing ministry, teaching, and crucifixion are reliable events in history (even if the details of that history are contested). Likewise, the resurrection, however difficult it might be to explain or decipher, is also an event that encounters persons in history. To claim that most of the data contained in the Gospels is more akin to historical falsehood than truth is, for most Christians, a step too far. Yet much of Reimarus's spirit remains alive in corners of the academy, such as the Jesus Seminar and ever-recurrent quests for the historical Jesus. The premium in this mode is to test the words of the Gospels, to see if they fit with other historical data we have about the first-century Mediterranean world. Does the Jesus of the Gospels, in other words, fit with what we know to be true about that time period? And if he doesn't fit, how might that be accounted for? This hermeneutic of suspicion, undoubtedly, is Reimarus's greatest legacy for the ongoing interpretation of Jesus. It treats the words of the Gospels not as museum pieces that cannot be analyzed or that must be accepted at face value. It might even allow contemporary interpretations to pay greater attention to those words on the page, to probe beneath them, to find out as much as we can, to question, and to assess. It allows us, in other words, to recognize that the writers of the Gospels also had their own interests; they were not simply neutral observers to history, but gave their own cast, reflected their own biases, in crafting a portrait of Jesus. Reimarus, in other words, allows us to recognize Mark's Jesus as well as Matthew's, Luke's, and John's.

Jonathan Edwards (1703–1758)

The most significant North American theologian of the colonial period, Jonathan Edwards came from a family of Congregationalist preachers and was educated at Yale, where he was both exposed to Enlightenment thought and recruited into disputes against Arminianism. After graduating from Yale, he teaches there briefly before becoming copastor with his grandfather at Northampton, Massachusetts, a large congregation that becomes important to the revivalist movement known as the Great Awakening. Edwards writes prolifically about this phenomenon, and though he criticizes some elements of it, he mainly defends the Awakening. In addition to being a renowned preacher, Edwards writes extensively on philosophy and classical Calvinist themes. His pastoral career concludes in Stockbridge, a frontier town, where he engages in missionary work with the Native population for eight years. Appointed as president of the College of New Jersey (now Princeton University), Edwards only serves in this post for three months before dying of smallpox. His Christology is influential both for its paradoxical imagination and its incorporation of the aesthetic.

On the one hand, Edwards reiterates many of the classic themes of his Reformed heritage. In a sermon on Revelation, Edwards juxtaposes Christ's humiliation and glory, which are revealed simultaneously. To understand Christ truly, we look to his final hours, during which he is subjected to the greatest ignominy: "Never was he in so great an exercise of his condescension, humility, meekness, and patience, as he was in these last sufferings; never was his divine glory and majesty covered with so thick and dark a veil." And yet at the same time, this act of yielding to suffering reveals "divine glory" fully and clearly.[4] God's glory takes the form of the suffering servant. In suffering, Christ is "delivered up to the power of his enemies," but by means of them he also "conquered and overthrew his enemies. Christ never so effectively bruised Satan's head, as when Satan bruised his heel."[5] Jesus is lion and lamb: the one who conquers sin, death and evil (as a lion) by submitting himself to them (as a lamb) and demonstrating their power, ultimately as empty.

These themes are common to many christological formulations, both within and beyond Reformed circles. But perhaps the most significant dimension of Edwards's interpretation of Christian faith is his incorporation of the aesthetic into the ethical demands of faith, which has consequences for how we understand Christ's beauty. In his classic *The Nature of True Virtue*, Edwards notes that true virtue, or the embodiment of the good, is "*benevolence to being in general* . . . which is immediately exercised in a general good will."[6] This disposition of the heart to being, moreover, comprises beauty and love: "If the essence of virtue, or beauty of mind, lies in love, or a disposition to love, it must primarily consist in something different both from complacence, which is a delight in beauty, and also from any benevolence that has the beauty of its object for its foundation."[7] True virtue, furthermore, consists in the love of God, the end and focus of our earthly loves. Seen in this wider framework, Jesus Christ is the embodiment of true virtue: the one in whom the aesthetic (beauty) and the ethical (the call to do the good) converge. His ministry, teaching, suffering, death, and resurrection show us both the path of the good life and the shape of a beautiful life. In him, even the event of the cross, which might at first glance appear as ugly, emerges as a beautiful event. Jesus is the beautiful One who frees us to love God again. The most enduring contribution of this orthodox Calvinist, tinged with a Puritan heritage suspicious of alluring beauty, is a way of appreciating Jesus as the embodiment of beauty.

John Wesley (1703–1791)

Born into an Anglican family in Epworth (father Samuel was a priest and mother Susanna was well-versed in biblical languages and classic theology), Wesley was educated at Oxford and ordained into the clergy. He travels to Georgia to serve as a missionary, a journey that proves pivotal. During a storm at sea, Wesley panics but is struck by the calm demeanor of some Moravian passengers. This experience leads him to explore Moravian piety more deeply, an exploration that continues after his return to England. On May 24, 1738, Wesley has a well-documented conversion experience in a chapel on Aldersgate Street, London. After hearing Luther's *Preface to Romans* being read, Wesley's heart is "strangely warmed" and he experiences assurance that Christ's death has taken away his sins and saved him from death. The Aldersgate experience rejuvenated Wesley's ministry, resulting in efforts to renew and reform practices in the Church of England, astonishing literary productivity, and an almost ceaseless itinerant preaching schedule.[8] Almost all of Wesley's theology emerges from his sermons, borne from his conviction that theology needs to bear fruit in the life of faith.

As a "practical" theologian, Wesley's focus on Jesus tends more toward the transformative impact of Christ's saving work than abstruse discussions of his person and/or nature. Throughout his sermons, he distances himself from more hard-line Calvinist positions. In one sermon, "The Lord Our Righteousness," Wesley distinguishes between "imputed" righteousness and "imparted" righteousness: On the one hand, we are justified by Christ's righteousness alone, which is given to us not according to our own merits: undeserved, this righteousness is *imputed* to us. Our claim to this righteousness is possible only through faith, which is also given to us. Faith, in other words, is not our work. But this is not the end of the story, for justification bears fruit, which Wesley calls "imparted righteousness," or "implanted righteousness." Wesley attends to such fruits throughout his preaching corpus, stressing the transformation of the person in light of Christ's grace, our renewal in the image of God, whereby "we believe, we love; we endeavor to walk in all the commandments of the Lord blameless."[9] This transformation is not because of merit, but solely because of Christ's righteousness. Nonetheless, the Christian life need not be characterized by a lifelong paradox, of being simultaneously justified and sinner. The far horizon of Christian hope, in light of Christ's transforming grace, is "perfection," in which the human person lives fully out of grace and not out of sin. This formulation proved to be one of the more controversial Wesleyan themes, but he believed that we effectively discount grace if we do not grant at least the possibility of the total transformation of the person, in light of Christ's redeeming work: "a restoration not only to the favour, but likewise to the image of God; implying not barely deliverance from sin but the being filled with the fullness of God."[10]

Wesley's emphasis on Christ's transformative work leads him to embrace one of the more ancient (and often neglected) images of Christ: the great Physician. In Wesley's mind, we are not merely reckoned as righteous, but slowly healed so that we actually become more righteous. Sin not only has spiritual and psychological consequences for Wesley but physical ones as well.[11] Our falling into sin is rightly considered dis-ease. Christ comes for nothing less than to cure this disease, a transformation in which the image of God is restored in us, freeing us in humility, love, freedom, and happiness.[12] This may be the most enduring and innovative aspects of Wesley's Christology. It is rightly seen as a holistic depiction of Christ. Considering how often the Gospels depict Jesus as healer, it is surprising that the theological tradition has often opted for forensic rather than physical images for describing Christ's saving work. Wesley's Christ, in other words, comes not merely to address a "spiritual" problem, but to redeem the whole person, body, soul, and spirit. In this sense, his Christology recovers the Gospel imagery of the earthy Jesus who blesses and feeds bodies.

Friedrich Schleiermacher (1768–1834)

Widely regarded as the father of modern theology, Schleiermacher came from a Calvinist family in Silesia, but was educated in a pietist, Moravian boarding school, a Moravian seminary, and eventually the Lutheran university in Halle. Ordained into the Reformed church in 1794, Schleiermacher was possessed of an ecumenical spirit and actively worked toward the unification of Reformed and Lutheran churches. Well-acquainted with the writings of the Enlightenment, Schleiermacher was dissatisfied with the ways in which these writings reduced religion to ethics or knowledge. He became attracted to the budding Romantic movement in the German-speaking world, and eventually developed an account of religion (most famously articulated in his *Speeches*) rooted in feeling. The chief religious impulse, for Schleiermacher, was the *feeling of absolute dependence*, an awareness of human limitation, intimation of infinity, and the budding consciousness of God. This understanding of feeling—different from mere emotion—proved enormously influential in subsequent theology, offering an alternative to Protestant scholastic dogmatism and Enlightenment-tinged rationalism. A renowned preacher and pastor, Schleiermacher also was instrumental in founding the University of Berlin, where he taught for twenty-five years. His Christology is distinctive in that it focuses on both the self-consciousness of Jesus and Christ's redemptive work.

Jesus, for Schleiermacher, stands at the center of Christian faith. Jesus's absolute, perfect consciousness of God is the pivot on which our redemption hinges. Schleiermacher does not prove that Jesus Christ is the Redeemer by appealing to his miracles, his healings, his resurrection, or his prophecy, but by an appeal to the ongoing life of the Redeemer in the believing community. Jesus Christ is the Redeemer because he continues to invite those who would follow him into a new way of being and living in the world—he changes us by giving us the awareness and consciousness that we lack. Schleiermacher thus appeals not only to what Christ has done, but to what he continues to do among us. Jesus is the One possessed of the perfect awareness of God, so that his life becomes a reflection or a window of God's work in relation to us. In Christ—whether in his earthly life or in his ongoing life in the community of faith—God's work becomes transparent to us. Jesus surrenders everything else other than perfect God-consciousness so that God can rightly be said to work through him. Schleiermacher thus reinterprets Chalcedon not through categories of "being" or "nature," but through activity and consciousness. Because Jesus of Nazareth is transparent to God's activity, he can be described as fully divine. "To ascribe to Christ an absolutely powerful God-consciousness, and to attribute to him an existence of God in him, are exactly the same thing."[13] Jesus's redeeming work is to impart this God-consciousness to us. As Keith Clements writes, "Through personal communion with Jesus, the inner life of the believer is re-created. Christ is truly the second, life-giving Adam."[14] This invitation to participate in Christ's consciousness denotes Schleiermacher's recovery of mysticism, a captivating vision that hearkens to earlier christological visions of deification as well as a pietist stress on devotion. Redemption in Christ represents the transformation of the person, where we are drawn into deeper communion with God: "We are also expected to reflect on the divine in mankind in general, not only in Christ, for the concept of the Holy Spirit is nothing else than that. The divine becomes located in human beings, among whom we ourselves are included."[15]

Schleiermacher's focus on the redemptive work of Christ does not mean that he neglects interpretation of Christ's person. But when Schleiermacher turns in this direction, he rejects any supernaturalism that places Jesus outside the normal course of human development. Indeed, he is among the first theologians to critically examine (and speculate about) Jesus's social and psychological growth. Schleiermacher rejects the suggestion that Jesus was born with perfect God-consciousness or with perfect awareness. Instead, he was born as a vulnerable baby like any other, and he developed—physically, intellectually, emotionally—in all the ways that the rest of us do. To claim anything else is to reject Jesus's humanity and embrace docetism. But Jesus's development was also unique. Whereas we are invariably stunted in our growth—we grow into sin and separation from God—Jesus developed without conflict. Jesus grew from "the condition of purest innocence to one of purely spiritual fulness of power."[16] Jesus thus grew into his ministry; as a person of his time, he reflected some of the dominant cultural and quasi-scientific assumptions of his day.[17] Jesus is sinless because he develops without conflict. What he does, then, is to complete human nature, showing us who we are meant to be all along, and invites us to become it in the gathered community of the church.

Schleiermacher's interpretation of Jesus is undoubtedly more subjective than it is objective. Subjective theories of the atonement after all are more compatible with mysticism and stress on participation. But unlike many other mystical readings of Jesus, Schleiermacher minimizes the cross and Jesus's suffering as objects of special devotion. For him, Jesus's suffering alone does not save. He considers it improper "to ascribe such a special reconciling value to His physical sufferings. . . . These sufferings in themselves have only the loosest connexion with His reaction against sin."[18] In Schleiermacher's view, the cross by itself does not save; rather, the cross is the result of Jesus's unrelenting identification with God. Jesus bears perfect God-consciousness, but sinful humanity rejects this consciousness (in others and for itself). Jesus's consciousness becomes the one thing that sin cannot bear, and hence we kill Jesus. The cross, then, points chiefly to *our* sin rather than to the way that Jesus redeems. What saves, in the end, is Jesus's gracious invitation to participate in the church, which is the witness to Jesus's God-consciousness. In the church is revealed the "continuous activity of His sinless perfection."[19] Jesus is not simply a teacher who shows us the way; he takes us there, he draws us near, and makes us his own. "What we celebrate [at Jesus's birth] is nothing other than ourselves as whole beings—that is, human nature, or whatever else you want to call it, viewed and known from the perspective of the divine."[20] To be a Christian, to be redeemed, is to become who we really are, to accept our dependence on God and God's grace. The strength of Schleiermacher's Christology is how it embraces God and the world in the same movement; redemption in Christ does not take us out of the ordinary, but embeds us within it. In Christ, we see that loving God and the world are not antithetical to one another, but bound up with one another. And it is Jesus Christ who shows us this, who frees us to be ourselves and love God *in* the world. If the often-cited weakness of his Christology is that it does not take sin with radical enough seriousness, Schleiermacher would probably retort that sin does not have the final word in the cosmos. Instead, it is Jesus's God-consciousness that is the hope of all, that promises to transform all.

G. W. F. Hegel (1770–1831)

Hegel was born in Stuttgart to a middle-class family. His mother was a devout Lutheran, and his father was a civil servant. He seems to have imbibed both his father's "worldliness" and his mother's piety.[21] His education included both classical and Romantic streams, culminating in a theological degree at Tübingen. Upon graduation, he does not take a parish, but becomes a tutor to a wealthy family in Bern, Switzerland. His first university appointment is at Jena, the university where he also earns his doctorate. This locale is also the site for his most famous work, *Phenomenology of Spirit*, parts of which were composed as Napoleon's troops were invading Jena. Called to the University of Berlin in 1818, he teaches there for the rest of his life and where he becomes Schleiermacher's colleague. The two do not have a close relationship and represent different strands of theology in the wake of the Enlightenment. Hegel's branch is more rooted in rational concepts than feeling.[22] Indeed, Hegel represents a strand of philosophical idealism that claims that the highest expression of Christian faith is that it can be "thought" rationally and coherently. Known for an extensive philosophy of religion, Hegel also developed a Christology that hinged on the knowability of God and incorporated tragedy and suffering into God's very being.

Unlike Schleiermacher, who regards the Trinity as a secondary claim of faith (and the consequence of religious consciousness), Hegel sees the Trinity as the first fact of Christian faith. The Trinity represents the spiraling Spirit of life that is God; God makes Godself known to creation in this ever-branching manifestation of divine self-disclosure. For Hegel, God is knowable as Spirit, and related to the world: Spirit is God who is the pulse of life itself, displaying energy, movement, life, differentiation, and reconciliation. God becomes known in relation to other subjects. "The making or creation of the world is God's self-manifesting, self-revealing. . . . What God creates God himself is."[23] God is always mediated through something other in creation; our consciousness of God, for

Hegel, is also the self-consciousness of absolute Spirit. Because God gives Godself as Spirit, we participate in the consciousness of God.

Hegel's Christology is pneumatological, as Jesus of Nazareth is the one filled by the Spirit, who proclaims the inbreaking of God's reign, who lives "only for the truth, only for its proclamation; his activity consists solely in completing the higher consciousness of humanity."[24] Jesus Christ is the God-man, who points to the ultimate reconciliation between God and humanity. We have become estranged from God, through sin, and Jesus offers healing: the divine oriented toward us, and our own orientation to God.

> Human beings can know themselves to be taken up into God only when God is not something alien to them, only when they are not merely an extrinsic accident on God's nature, but rather when they are taken up into God in accordance with their essence and freedom. The implicitly subsisting unity of divine and human nature must be revealed to humanity in an objective way; this is what happened through the incarnation of God.[25]

The movement to unite humanity with God, to overcome the gulf of estrangement, is neither smooth nor inexorable. Instead, as Jesus's cross demonstrates, the journey toward reconciliation is traced with suffering, tragedy, and scorn. Whereas Schleiermacher minimizes the cross in relation to redemption, Hegel maximizes it and radicalizes it, focusing on how it affects God's very life. Christ's death is on the one hand "the most complete proof of humanity, of absolute finitude; and in deed Christ has died the aggravated death of the evildoer. . . . In him, humanity was carried to its furthest point." But his death is also something more, expressed in stark language: "*God has died, God is dead*—this is the most frightful of all thoughts, that everything eternal and true *is not*, that negation itself is found in God."[26] Jesus's crucifixion reveals the depth of estrangement, the pain of negativity found on the path toward reconciliation, which is not erased, but incorporated in the life of God. The cross, in this regard, does not only happen to and affect Jesus—it affects God.

Death and negativity, however, are not the final word of the Christ event. Instead, that word is new life: "It is God who has put death to death, since he comes out of the state of death. . . . It is out of infinite love that God has made himself identical with what is alien to him in order to put it to death."[27] Nonetheless, even in the new life, death and negativity are not left behind, but contained as moments within that life: "The thought that God godself had died on earth—that alone expresses the feeling of this infinite grief; just as the thought that God is *resurrected* from the grave expresses its reconciliation. By God's life and death God is humbled, by God's resurrection humanity has become divine."[28] Just as Christ's death brings negativity and death into God's life, Christ's resurrection brings our life into God's. The strains of divinization are again here evident. The resurrection is not simply something that happened to Jesus; it recurrently happens *to us*.

Hegel's christological vision is assuredly speculative, perhaps even wildly so. It attempts to hold on to the historical events in the life of Jesus, particularly related to his crucifixion, while moving beyond history and considering the movements of Christology (incarnation, crucifixion, resurrection) as moments of the divine life. This makes the Jesus story a cosmic story. The pattern of Jesus's life is the pattern of how God creates, sustains, and redeems all of creation. And it is the pattern of how all life is taken up and subsumed in the life of God, Absolute Spirit. It is a vision that claims much (perhaps too much), but it is a compelling vision nonetheless. In an age like ours that is attuned to suffering, tragedy, and rupture, Hegel's Jesus brings such tragedy into God's very life, offering hope by redeeming it without forgetting it or leaving it behind.

Jarena Lee (1783–1864)

Born in Cape May, New Jersey, Lee was separated from her parents and became a domestic servant at the age of seven. In a compelling autobiography (the first to be published by an African American woman in the United States), Lee writes of numerous struggles—suicidal thoughts, a call to preach the gospel (resisted by men), and the loss of her husband—and how God's providential hand sustained her. Though many questioned her call to preach—including African Methodist Episcopal bishop Richard Allen—Allen and others eventually recognized her gifts, rendering her the first woman authorized to preach in the AME Church. Her Christology, as we can trace it, emerges mainly in her autobiography, revealing a personal Savior intimately concerned with the details of her life, One who comes to save women and men.

Lee writes tellingly of her struggles against sin and how Christ releases from bondage. Her writing here is vivid and embodied. In the midst of prayers of struggle against Satan, Lee recalls that she said, "'Lord, *sanctify* my soul for Christ's sake?' That very instant, as if lightning had darted through me, I sprang to my feet, and cried, 'The Lord has sanctified my soul!' There was none to hear this but the angels who stood around to witness my joy—and Satan, whose malice raged the more."[29] Jesus works on behalf of freedom, proclaiming release to the captives, granting new life that can be felt in the marrow of one's bones. Throughout her autobiography, Lee testifies to a gift of freedom experienced in the body as warmth, elation, and light. Salvation in Christ is not primarily cognitive; it bathes and blesses the body. One of the prime gifts of this newfound freedom is the ability to speak about it. Echoing her own call to preach, Lee writes: "My tongue was cut loose, the stammerer spoke freely; the love of God, and of his service, burned with a vehement flame within me; his name was glorified among the people."[30]

At a time when women's preaching was all but nonexistent, Lee's account of the Christ who gives birth to women's speech was even more radical. She asked pointed questions that disrupted established church practices about who is authorized to preach and speak. In response to those who would deny her own voice, Lee writes: "If the man may preach, because the Savior died for him, why not the woman, seeing he died for her also? Is he not a whole Savior, instead of a half one, as those who hold it wrong for a woman to preach, would seem to make it appear?"[31] Lee's portrait of Jesus, in a straightforward way, overturns patriarchal practices. Its critique of many earlier Christologies is that they have drawn mistaken conclusions from Jesus's male gender. What is most significant about Jesus is not his gender, but his humanity—a humanity that claims and blesses all bodies, giving freedom to dismantle strictures imposed by others. In subtle ways, Lee's depiction of Jesus foreshadows subsequent work in feminist and liberation theology. Jesus saves because Jesus sets us free, body and soul.

John Henry Newman (1801–1890)

Educated at Oxford, English cleric John Henry Newman was a patristics scholar who became a leading figure in the Oxford Movement within the Church of England, which sought to recover earlier church teachings and revive its liturgy. Though he is sometimes dubbed a "traditionalist," Newman's legacy is complex. Strongly influenced by the Enlightenment, Newman's writings probe the power and necessity of reason, while also outlining reason's limits. An advocate for the freedom of the church in relation to the state, Newman eventually converts to Catholicism in 1845 (and eventually becomes cardinal in 1879). In many ways he is as much a "modernist" as a "traditionalist," arguing as he does for the development of doctrine over time, and the importance of reason to the life of faith. His Christology is less remarkable for its content than it is how he accounts for the growth and transformation of Christology itself.

Newman claims that the earliest Christians had no need for Christology. "The first generations of the Church, needed no explicit declarations concerning His Sacred Person. Sight and hearing superseded the multitude of words; faith dispensed with the aid of lengthened Creeds and Confessions. There was silence. 'The Word was made flesh'; 'I believe in Jesus Christ his only Son our Lord'; sentences such as these conveyed everything, yet were officious in nothing."[32] Sight and sound, in this vision, take precedence over words. The portraits that subsequent generations have drawn of Jesus are necessary for us, but are derivative of the original generation's understanding of Christ. The words, Newman claims, became necessary because "the light of his advent faded and love waxed cold."[33] Disputes about Jesus's identity and work arose, and thus the first creeds were constructed: "We are obliged to speak more at length in the Creeds and in our teaching, to meet the perverse ingenuity of those who, when the Apostles were removed, could with impunity insult and misinterpret the letter of their writings."[34] Portraits of Jesus emerge, in short, because of our limitations, and differing tenors will continue to emerge in the face of new heresies that threaten the faith. This is how Newman accounts for the *development* of doctrine in the church. Christology does not descend de novo from heaven, as if doctrine were given to us on a plate. Rather, it emerges over time, in response to various crises in the church. And one should expect doctrinal development to continue. It is not fixed, but is responsive in every era to the exigencies of the time.

Even if the earliest creeds pale in comparison to seeing and hearing the Savior, their ongoing significance for the church are paramount. The earliest ecumenical creeds stand as signposts for all subsequent christological reflection, offering the "terms in which we are constrained to speak of our Lord and Savior, by the craftiness of His enemies and our own infirmity."[35] These creeds, in other words, mark the boundaries of orthodoxy, within which portraits of Jesus might emerge. Portraits of Christ that go beyond the walls of the early creeds are to be rejected; but multiple angles might be amplified within these walls. And thus Christologies and portraits of Jesus will continue to emerge, but must always be tested in relation to the earliest creeds. In light of this development, we must recognize two things: (1) Whatever portrait of Jesus we construct, it will always fall short of the first generation's reception of Jesus; 2) our portraits, creeds, and doctrines will eventually fade when we come face-to-face with the Savior. Newman's account of Christologies is thus steadfastly traditional (in its valorization of the early creeds), while also open to further development. And it displays an apophatic streak in that it recognizes the limits of *all* christological speech. In its recognition of growth and limits, Newman's portrait of Jesus remains significant for a modern period concerned with change over time.

Horace Bushnell (1802–1876)

Born in Connecticut, Horace Bushnell received his education at Yale and served Congregational churches, most significantly a long pastorate in Hartford. He is a bridge figure who mediates the transition from revivalism to emerging Protestant liberalism, reflects both Enlightenment and Romantic trajectories, and attempts to mediate disputes within Congregationalism between "orthodox" and "Unitarian" factions. In many respects, he is the founding figure of American liberal theology, perhaps most renowned for his work on Christian education, *Christian Nurture*, which argues against revivalists, and promotes the first years of a child's life as instrumental for subsequent faith development. Bushnell also develops a keen theory of religious language, which argues for its *figurative* significance. Religious language cannot be reduced to its literal sense; instead, all religious language conveys something of the individual's subjective experience of the holy. This is why religious faith invites an abundance of imagery and words for the same thing: atonement, sin, Trinity, redemption. These multiple images, words, and figures convey something of the "whole" that no one word or image can express on its own.

This theory of religious language bears fruit in Bushnell's Christology, which also argues for multiple images for Jesus. His manner of interpreting the divine and human in Christ is both distinctive and echoes Schleiermacher in its avoidance of language of person or essence. We do not call Jesus divine because there is some part of his biology that contains the stuff of divinity. Instead, Jesus is divine because Jesus expresses God's nature in his life, teaching, and obedience unto death. Jesus is divine, in this regard, because he shows us, concretely, God's activity in the world. This leads directly to Bushnell's understanding of the atonement, which recognizes that the suffering of an innocent Jesus for the sake of others' sins is morally questionable. This "objective" understanding of the atonement alone, in short, is insufficient. Nonetheless, we are not to dispense with objective understandings of the atonement. Instead, we need to recognize their incompleteness. Unless an "objective" understanding is complemented by a "subjective" account, our interpretation of what happens in Jesus's death is shortsighted. It is equally important to recognize what happens *in us* in the atonement. In the words of Claude Welch, Bushnell claimed that atonement needs to begin with "the subjective side, the assertion that it is men who need to be reconciled rather than God."[36] Jesus's death, then, is "not a sacrifice in any literal sense,"[37] but it points to the transformation and reconciliation that God accomplishes in us: a new community of the church that embodies reconciliation.

Bushnell's Christology is thus an example of what he calls "Christian comprehensiveness," which privileges not one form of christological language over another, but recognizes their complementarity. Objective language is the form of language used in worship, particularly in relation to the sacrament of communion, while the subjective language points to the human experience of redemption. If one calls Bushnell a pioneer of American liberal theology, it is not because he advocates jettisoning traditional language, but because he encourages the reclamation of traditional language by recognizing its multivalence and the limits of all language. What happens in Christ cannot be reduced to a few sentences of orthodox speech. The strength of this position is that it enables the church to hold on to ancient language while continuing to search for the meaning of these ancient words today. In this sense, each generation is invited—and even compelled—to claim and be claimed by the person of Christ anew.

Ludwig Feuerbach (1804–1872)

Born in Bavaria, Ludwig Feuerbach began his university studies in Heidelberg, but then transferred to Berlin, where he studied under the guidance of Hegel. Strongly influenced by his teacher, Feuerbach took a bold turn that has come to epitomize the "left wing" of Hegelianism. This wing strips away idealism to reveal the supposed material core of all philosophy and theology: concern with the human person and embodied material existence. His writing and teaching proved immediately controversial, resulting in his departure from academe. The heart of his "theology," if one can call it such, is that all statements about God are ultimately statements about the human. God-talk is simply the projection of our noblest impulses about ourselves. The end goal of Christian faith, in his most famous work, *The Essence of Christianity*, is to abandon the notion of an independent God apart from ourselves and to focus our attention on the betterment of the human condition. As Feuerbach writes, "The course of religious development [is] . . . that man abstracts more and more from God, and attributes more and more to himself."[38] His Christology is, not surprisingly, an atheistic one, but this does not mean that christological doctrine does not contain truth. Feuerbach argues for retaining christological language, but like all religious language, we ought to recognize its proper referent: not God, but the human.

Feuerbach retains language about the incarnation because it contains truth *about us*. The claim that God becomes human is the mystery of the incarnation. Feuerbach affirms this, albeit with a twist: "Man was already in God, was already God himself, before God became man, i.e., showed himself as man."[39] The truth of the incarnation is not some miraculous condescension of the divine into history; rather, it is the recognition that the human person—as we are—is deified, to be cherished and honored. When the church says that God offers the Son to the world in love, the real meaning of this language is that love is supreme. When 1 John claims that "God is love" (1 Jn 4:16), what is really meant is that love conquers God. "Who then is our Savior and redeemer? God or love? Love; for God as God has not saved us, but Love, which transcends the difference between the divine and human personality."[40] Love is the noble aim of humanity: what we strive for, what we value, what saves us from ourselves. In Feuerbach's view, Jesus represents the abstraction of all that we ought to hold dear in ourselves. Jesus, in this sense, is who we want to be. If he is, as the church claims, the incarnation of love, we ought to celebrate that love in ourselves.

The church's language for Jesus reveals the depths of our own longings. In positing a Redeemer, we reveal that we long to be set free from bondage—to arbitrary morality, to self-imposed limitations. The passion of Jesus represents the death of these bonds, but it also conveys the depth of our own feeling and passion—a feeling that is even willing to undergo death: "The passion of Christ is the highest confidence, the highest self-enjoyment, the highest consolation of feeling; for only in the blood of Christ is the thirst for a personal, that is, a human, sympathizing, tender God allayed."[41] Jesus is thus the "longing for a personal God" whom we find in ourselves; "the blending in one of feeling and imagination."[42] The church's depiction of a Savior other than us, when rightly considered, leads back to a humanity that hopes in itself. As we seek to understand the church's confession, we better understand ourselves, because in confessing Christ, we confess ourselves. In the end, Feuerbach's depiction of Jesus evaporates. What is left is each one of us staring at a mirror of ourselves.

Some have claimed that Feuerbach represents the logical end result of the "liberal" move that privileges human experience in deciphering various doctrines. I believe that charge is misguided. The question, in my view, is not whether—but to what extent—we privilege human experience. To claim that doctrine can avoid experience is dubious. Doctrines arose because of the human need to make sense of the "new life" and the "good news" that the first generations in the faith experienced in light of Christ's coming. There is no end-run around experience. The question, instead, is the referent of experience. To claim, as Feuerbach does, that the human is the locus of all theological claims is as unwarranted as it is to claim that my feeling of the wind takes precedence over the *reality* of the wind that causes my feeling. The question, in other words, is the relationship between experience and the inaugurator of that experience. Feuerbach privileges the former at the expense of the latter. As a result, there really is no Jesus left to depict. His Christology, in effect, leaves us rather alone in the world.

Søren Kierkegaard (1813–1855)

A native of Copenhagen who spent nearly his entire life within that city, Søren Kierkegaard studied theology and philosophy but did not serve in an academic or parish post. A small inheritance (and a failed engagement to the woman he claimed to love) allowed him to devote his rather short life to writing, often under pseudonyms. A vehement critic of some strands of the Enlightenment (especially the Hegelian wing), Kierkegaard also argues in many of his works that establishment Christianity has become almost irredeemably compromised. Bourgeois Christianity has removed the scandals of faith and confused faith with citizenship and polite society. Hardly a systematist, Kierkegaard writes more argumentatively and, at times, contradictory pieces. His use of literary pseudonyms allows him to experiment with theological positions. But beneath the complexity of these interchanges are some commonalities: Christian faith places a premium on *encounter* in faith (a trait that has led many to consider him a founding figure in existentialism) and is a scandal that cannot be smoothed over. Renowned for his depiction of various "stages" of life (aesthetic, ethical, and religious), Kierkegaard's portrayal of Jesus is, in some respects, a shock to the Enlightenment that had at times rendered Jesus a rationalist.

In one regard, Kierkegaard has a minimalist Christology. In one of his most famous works, *Philosophical Fragments*, he writes: "Even if [Jesus's] generation had not left anything behind except these words, 'We have believed that in such and such a year the god appeared in the humble form of a servant, lived and taught among us, and then died'—this is more than enough."[43] One of the mistakes that the Enlightenment has made is that it thinks it can make Jesus palatable by amplifying his teachings, showing their consistency with "modern" worldviews and the like. For Kierkegaard, only the bare-bones claim—that the God-man came, taught, suffered, and died—matters. Nearly everything else contributes not to the edification of clarification of faith, but to its betrayal.[44] What matters is the encounter of the believer with Christ in faith. All the rest, so to speak, are details. Nonetheless, as prolific as he is, Kierkegaard supplies some content to the One whom Christians call Savior.

Kierkegaard often employs the most ancient title for Jesus, the name—according to the Gospels at least—that his disciples called him: teacher. Jesus is the teacher who gives the "condition" and the "truth."[45] His teaching is not so much ethical precepts as it is an encounter with the living truth, and hence he is Savior, deliverer, and reconciler as well, delivering "the person who had imprisoned himself."[46] His teaching is for others to follow. Again, Kierkegaard is not explicit on the content. The teacher Jesus issues a command: follow me! In this regard the teaching is not to be dissected. It confronts us with its radical demand: to give up our previous life and supposed security, and cast our lives with the crucified Teacher.

This is the very thing that Enlightenment perceives as a scandal. This recognition, perhaps, is the one thing that the Enlightenment gets right: Jesus "is and wants to be the sign of offense and the object of faith; to judge him according to the results of his life is blasphemy."[47] Jesus is One who cannot be known through rational investigation. We don't get any closer to a "true" picture of him by a scientific investigation of the biblical text (à la Reimarus), the construction of a philosophy of religion on the basis of his teaching (à la Hegel), or an accurate depiction of his supposed religious self-consciousness (à la Schleiermacher). The "real" Jesus cannot be encountered or understood in most of the ways that the Enlightenment and pietism suggest. "One cannot *know* anything at all about *Christ*; he is the paradox, the object of faith, exists only for faith."[48] Kierkegaard's approach to Jesus, though it rejects some of the devotional posture of much pietism, does share this in common with pietism: the primacy of faith. The "real" Jesus, so to speak, is not an object to reason, but the person who encounters us in faith. Faith is the third "stage" of the journey: beyond aesthetics, beyond ethics, epitomized in Abraham's willingness to agree to God's abhorrent command to sacrifice Isaac.[49] Hence Kierkegaard's Jesus is less the embodiment of beauty or ethical teacher, and more the One who summons his followers in faith: Jesus "has no doctrine, no system; basically he knows nothing; there are a few aphorisms, some maxims, and a couple of parables, which he goes on repeating or revising."[50] This Jesus, in the end, is an offense: to tidy ethical teaching, to polite, bourgeois Christianity, to comfortable existence in the world. When he calls, he jolts us out of complacence and calls us to suffer.

Kierkegaard's retrieval of the suffering Christ, however, is different from medieval or Reformation portrayals, which often stressed *physical* suffering. It is a suffering borne, first, out of love: "His whole life is a story of suffering, and it is love that suffers, love that gives all and is itself destitute."[51] In making this claim, Kierkegaard is hardly novel. The reason for Christ's suffering, in most classical portrayals, has been for the sake of love. (Perhaps no one epitomizes this as much Julian of Norwich.) What is distinctive about Kierkegaard's portrayal is the stress on *psychological* suffering. "Christ's sufferings . . . have been much and often discussed. . . . But in all this, an entirely different kind of suffering seems to be forgotten, the suffering of inwardness, suffering of soul, or what might be called the secret of the sufferings that were inseparable from his life."[52] By effectively placing the primacy on Christ's inward sufferings, Kierkegaard privileges the interior life: The cross that Jesus invites his followers to take up is felt more in the psyche than the flesh. Perhaps in this way, Kierkegaard's Jesus represents not a total rejection of the Enlightenment, for the Enlightenment privileges psyche as well. Nonetheless, Kierkegaard's Jesus is radical for its time: It rejects the prevailing sensibility that Jesus's teaching can be ordered and classified. It rejects comfortable piety. In the end, it leaves us with One who simply calls to take up the cross and follow. If we accept this call, we should expect little more than suffering, scorn, and rejection in return. Kierkegaard's portrayal of Jesus is strongest in its rejection of various distortions or reductions: equating Jesus with his teaching; reducing his person to a pious phrase. Where it falls short, at least in this reader's eyes, is that it mainly strips away the baggage that has accumulated around Jesus, leaving us with an even more radical theology of the cross than Kierkegaard's own Lutheran heritage. The question left in this reader's mind is: Where in the midst of stripping away baggage and smashing idols is the abundance of the new life that Jesus gives? In Kierkegaard's Christology, it is easier to determine who Jesus *is not* and more difficult to discern who he *is*.

George Eliot (1819–1880)

George Eliot is the penname of Mary Ann Evans, one of the premier novelists of the nineteenth century. Born in Warwickshire, England, Evans was raised in a strict evangelical household but came into contact with Enlightenment-influenced Christianity at a later date, having learned German and gaining exposure to the works of Feuerbach and D. F. Strauss. She translated Feuerbach's *Essence of Christianity* into English and began writing novels, adopting the name of Eliot, in part because male authors had greater success than female writers at the time. Her remarkable series of novels explores the religious landscape of the nineteenth century, including Protestantism (*Adam Bede*), Catholicism (*Middlemarch*), and Judaism (*Daniel Deronda*). She is included in this christological survey not because she offers a doctrinally developed portrayal of

Jesus, but because of the deeply incarnational themes in many of her works. Eliot shows us how christological themes imbue a work of fiction and give expression to the question: Who is Christ for us today?[53]

At the heart of Eliot's vision is the conviction that God encounters humanity in the midst of the ordinary and commonplace. Reality itself conveys depth, holiness, and meaning. Religious faith orients us to this "mystery" beneath the "real." In Peter Hodgson's words, for Eliot "the objective of religion is to reorient human beings from self-centeredness to reality-centeredness, with 'reality' understood to include other persons, the larger human and natural community, and the ultimate mystery of things."[54] The God who encounters us in Jesus Christ does not lift us out of the ordinary, but grounds us within it. Eliot prioritizes religious impulse or feeling rather than doctrine. The point of Christ's coming is not to establish a fixed vocabulary for describing *how* God interacts with humanity, but to orient humanity to the holiness revealed in creatureliness. This is what the "God-man" conveys. Eliot's novels are thus filled with characters that—in various ways—introduce us to the way of Jesus Christ. Not strictly "Christ figures" or mere symbols, these characters instead convey something of what it means to *follow* Christ. One of these memorable characters is Dinah in *Adam Bede*, a Methodist preacher who speaks of—and embodies—God's redemptive presence in the midst of suffering. Through Dinah's speaking and action, the hearer is opened to the God who comes near in Jesus, revealed in God's solidarity with the oppressed, who suffers for the sake of love.

Eliot offers a Christology of representation in her novels. Jesus is the representative of God for us, showing us the shape of divine pathos and love, and we become representatives of Christ as we are caught up in the way of Jesus. Hers is also a Christology of participation: The point of Jesus's coming is not simply to transfer grace to undeserving sinners, but for us to become participants in God's ongoing love for the world, revealed in Jesus, continually present in the gathered community. Her novels are also noteworthy for the way in which they stress the redemptive role of community: in family, friendship, and the gathering of persons who become oriented to the depths of the real. Christology, in this sense, bleeds into ecclesiology, though the church is hardly confined to those gathered on Sunday morning.

Eliot's incarnational themes are important for at least two reasons: (1) In its attentiveness to multiple religious expressions, her Christology offers an introduction for engaging religious diversity, compelling us to ask: How is Christ present in traditions outside the walls the church and even outside Christianity itself? The redemptive transformation revealed in Jesus, for her, is hardly limited to orthodox channels. (2) Her stress on the ordinary and commonplace serves as a guard against any Christology that escapes responsibility for *this* earth, *this* place, and *these* people. The One who comes, comes not to take us out of our home, but to orient us within it. In an age when some evangelical preachers were encouraging a focus on the next life, this one-time evangelical turned attention to the *now*.

Adolf von Harnack (1851–1930)

Born in Dorpat (in present-day Estonia), Harnack was raised in a traditional Lutheran home and studied at the university in his hometown. A gifted scholar, his career takes him to several universities, culminating in the University of Berlin. His primary interest was historical, particularly the development of doctrine over time. His *History of Dogma* is still considered a classic, even if its conclusions were controversial at its time of writing (and ever since). Harnack's chief argument is that the essence of Christianity, contained in the teaching of Jesus, had become obscured over time, particularly through the introduction of Hellenistic philosophy. Part of the theologian's role was to recover the simplicity of this message through historical investigation, to steer Christian faith from teachings *about* Jesus (doctrine) to the teaching *of* Jesus. His interpretation of Jesus, in many respects, represents the culmination of the liberal trajectory, a portrait of Jesus stripped of supernaturalism, focused mainly on Jesus's simple, timeless message of freedom, relationship to God (and others), and love.

Harnack's Christology emerges through close reading of the Gospels, which he claims convey a distinct style of teaching. The Jesus who speaks on the pages of the New Testament is one whose teaching arises almost effortlessly. His person, as well as his message, is an invitation to hear and follow. "Everything seems to pour from him naturally, as though he could not do otherwise."[55] Harnack's portrayal of Jesus as teacher here bears some resemblance to Schleiermacher's, in its emphasis on placidity. This Jesus is no apocalyptic prophet, but a teacher of practical, liberating wisdom. "His whole life, all his thoughts and feelings, were absorbed in the relation to God, and yet he did not talk like an enthusiast and a fanatic. . . . He is possessed of a quiet, uniform, collected demeanor, with everything directed to one goal. He never uses any ecstatic language, and the tone of stirring prophecy is rare."[56] Jesus is single-minded in his mission to share good news with all who would hear, but he does so without frenzied urgency.

The content of Jesus's teaching is, at its core, simple. Harnack identifies three themes that constitute the essence of

Christianity: (1) the coming kingdom of God; (2) God the Father and the infinite value of the human soul; and (3) a call to higher righteousness and the commandment of love.[57] One of Harnack's favored metaphors in discussing Jesus's teaching is to distinguish between the "kernel" and the "husk." Much of what passes for doctrine—christological or otherwise—is "husk" that has accumulated around Jesus's pure and simple teaching. The contemporary follower of Jesus is right in stripping away this husk, in order to expose the kernel: what Christian faith is all about. This kernel, summarized in Harnack's three points above, is meant not only for Jesus's immediate audience, but for all audiences and all time, even if these teachings must be appropriated in new ways today. But Jesus's message is the only thing that sets us free from arbitrary authorities (ecclesial and political), from unwarranted self-interest, and from any idols we construct. Jesus's teaching about the coming reign of God is the entering of God into the human soul "and laying hold of it," the rule of God within us.[58] The teaching about the Fatherhood of God and the infinite value of the soul teaches us to cherish human individuality, given and blessed by God, so that we are dependent on God. Jesus's teaching about the love commandment binds us to others in community, to cherish each other, to love God and neighbor.

This predominant image of Jesus as teacher does not mean that Harnack dispenses with the traditional language of Jesus's divinity. Indeed, Harnack clings to the image of Jesus as God's Son, though he interprets it rather differently from others in the tradition. Jesus's divinity, or Sonship, is not a subject for metaphysical investigation. We need not determine what his divine nature comprises, as if it were a part of him alongside his humanity. Echoing and perhaps amplifying Schleiermacher, Harnack claims, “It is ‘knowledge of God’ that makes the sphere of the Divine Sonship. It is in this knowledge that he came to know the sacred Being who rules heaven and earth as Father, as *his* Father.”[59] In this read, Chalcedon and Nicaea are the accretions that cling to Jesus; they do not describe, at their core, who or what Jesus is: only his teaching does. The problem with much classical Christology, in Harnack’s eyes, is that it attributes too much to Jesus’s person and too little to his message. The Jesus we meet in the Gospels proclaims much about the kingdom of God and the commandment of love, and rather little about himself. His teaching is not self-referential, but God-referential. Or, as Harnack puts it, “*The Gospel, as Jesus proclaimed it, has to do with the Father only and not with the Son.*”[60] Jesus does not want followers who can describe who he is; he seeks followers who will embody the way of life that he teaches. He does not so much require belief as much as he wants people to follow the Way.

The appeal of Harnack’s Jesus is its stunning simplicity, its unwavering focus on the Fatherhood of God, the community of humankind, and the love that binds all together. Clearly, these are elements of Jesus’s teaching that are indispensable. Ignoring them would amount to a distortion of the good news. And it should be noted that this focus on Jesus’s teaching means that Christology need not be wed to a particular metaphysics, culture, or worldview. Nonetheless, the Jesus that emerges from Harnack’s rigorous historical investigation winds up looking rather much like a liberal Protestant, focused less on the cultic and more on timeless truth. In other words, Harnack’s Jesus might unwittingly resemble the calm citizen that liberal democracies crave. Whether this Jesus can resist the principalities and powers that run antithetical to the gospel is an open question. For some in the twentieth century, this Jesus had lost his prophetic edge.

Alfred Loisy (1857–1940)

Often referred to as a Catholic modernist, Alfred Loisy was born in Ambrières, France, and educated in Paris. Primarily a biblical scholar, Loisy was one of the first Roman Catholics to adopt historical-critical methods of investigation. His most significant work, *The Gospel and the Church*, is a direct response to Harnack. Whereas Harnack claimed that the original teaching of Jesus can be retrieved and distinguished from church doctrine, Loisy claimed that the essence of Jesus's teaching has been lost to history. What remains is the doctrine of the church, which is a legitimate outgrowth of Jesus's original teaching, even if it differs from it. Though intended as a way of showing how doctrine came to be (and how it should be upheld), these thoughts proved immediately controversial, resulting in Loisy's loss of his teaching post and eventual excommunication. The portrait of Jesus that emerges in this work pays more attention to Jesus's historical context than Harnack's, though it also emphasizes a timeless core found within church doctrine.

According to Loisy, it makes a difference *when* and *to whom* Jesus came. Unlike Harnack, who often minimizes Jesus's Jewish context, Loisy claims that we cannot know Jesus apart from it. "The Gospel, appearing in Judaea and unable to appear elsewhere, was bound to be conditioned by Judaism. Its Jewish exterior is the human body, whose Divine Soul is the spirit of Jesus. But take away the body, and the soul will vanish in air like the lightest breath."[61] Jesus is, first and foremost, Messiah: the hope of the Jewish people, the symbol for the coming of

God's reign, the embodiment of God's promises to Israel. He comes not only for Israel, but for the world as well. But to abstract Jesus from the promises God makes to Israel is to distort his incarnation. He comes to a particular people, and only as such can he be said to be for others. Loisy thus reintroduces an important theme that many Protestant liberals of the age overlooked: Jesus the Jew. Only in his particularity as a member of the house of Israel does Jesus offer any hope for the world.

Yet in his historical particularity, Jesus also embodies and proclaims a message that transcends history. Loisy claims that we cannot retrieve this "kernel," however, apart from the "husk" that is the church traditions that surround Jesus. For Loisy, this message is conveyed in a vision, carried on in the work of the church: Jesus's "dream was His project, the realization of perfect happiness in perfect justice, of immortality in holiness. This realization was already complete in Him, by His union with God, His faith in the Heavenly Father, the inner certainty of the eternal future guaranteed to humanity in His person and by His agency."[62] What is modernist about this interpretation of Jesus is its focus on Jesus's consciousness, devoid of supernaturalism. Jesus comes to a particular culture, but speaks to the whole world because his message is compelling, and it is carried on in the church that proclaims his name. Loisy thus sees continuity between Jesus and the church where some others sense a disconnect. Even if Jesus never intended to found the church, the fact remains that the church arose in his wake. And it is this body that is entrusted with carrying out the vision.

Pandita Ramabai (1858–1922)

Born in western India to a Hindu family, Pandita Ramabai had access to education in ways that were atypical for girls at the time. Travels to England brought her into closer contact with Christianity, particularly the Sisters of Wantage, and eventual conversion and baptism. Her return to India is marked by dramatic work in social reform, particularly concerning the status of women. In her autobiography, she writes of her own conversion, how it contrasted with her traditional upbringing, and how Jesus comes for all people, regardless of gender or social status.

In some regards, Ramabai presents her early life as a foil to the fullness of truth revealed in Jesus. The heart of Jesus's message is *free, unmerited grace.* Strongly influenced by pietism, this interpretation places priority on the gulf between the sinner and the freely given salvation offered by Christ. But in Ramabai's analysis, this is particularly freeing news for women in her context. The "false" idea promulgated in traditional Hinduism is that one *merits* future happiness. "This I could never hope for, since a woman, as a woman, has no hope of Moksha according to Hindu religion."[63] The Jesus who comes to save is also the Jesus who erases the boundaries between castes and genders, dismantling any human tradition that sets up distinctions between "haves" and "have-nots." She writes, "The Bible declares that Christ did not reserve this great salvation for a particular caste or sex."[64] Thus Jesus emerges, at least in her context, as a social revolutionary: declaring false anything that would prevent any person from accessing the promises of grace.

Ramabai represents another voice in the midst of pietism that anticipates liberation Christology. Jesus sets us free not merely spiritually, but also from the bonds of physical and psychological oppression. Jesus lifts up those who have been considered lesser by the powers that be. In colonial India, this was truly good news, inspiring social reform in the Way of Jesus.

Ernst Troeltsch (1865–1923)

Born in Bavaria to a Lutheran family, Ernst Troeltsch's work is representative of a strain within Protestant liberal theology known as the history of religions school, which emphasized the historically and culturally conditioned nature of each religion. His training was in theology, which he taught at various universities in Germany until he made the move to teach philosophy at Berlin. Modernity, according to Troeltsch, unleashes historical consciousness, which requires us to investigate all religious phenomena, dogmas, and practices according to modern historical-critical methods. Theology does not exist above such investigation. The Christian faith is *relative*, not absolute. Troeltsch's Christology thus places a premium on historical investigation, while also recognizing the limits of "discovering" the Jesus of history.

Troeltsch adopts the Christocentrism common to Protestant theologies in the wake of the Reformation. Jesus is the one figure with whom Christian faith stands or falls. And to get Jesus right, to distinguish the true Jesus from false interpretations, one must conduct rigorous historical investigation. But as soon as we commence such investigation, we encounter a question: "Today the *central* question is whether the apostolic community's belief in Christ and redemption can be traced back to the impact of Jesus and is consistent with his inner person; or whether their belief in a savior-god and his redemptive death was appropriated from some non-Christian mystery cult and grafted onto the more or less vague remembrances of a Jewish rabbi."[65] The question of the "real" historical Jesus, in other words, emerges at the beginning of the history of the Christian church. It is not merely a question for our time, but for *all* time. How much of the church's confession of Jesus as Christ is true to Jesus's own person and how much is a result of subsequent communities' own interests and issues?

Troeltsch answers this question by noting how thoroughly imbricated Jesus is with the believing community. His answer, in other words, doubts the assurance that some investigations of the historical Jesus would claim (such as Reimarus's). Communal interpretation *of* Jesus, over time, has so completely saturated his identity that there is no way to recover a "pure" historical Jesus who is unaffected by subsequent interpretation. This is not something to be lamented, but celebrated, because "we have no sources other than the testimony of the communities themselves."[66] This means that Jesus will always necessarily appear with multiple faces, each illuminating different aspects of his influence on the community (and that community's reception of him). "We cannot see him simply in terms of his appearance alone; it is only in the stream of his effects, in the light of a Paul, an Augustine, a Luther, that we fully understand him."[67] This is part of what Troeltsch means by the "relative" nature of Christian faith; the faith always comes mediated to us by a particular time, place, and context. Jesus, in this sense, is always relative to the age; new ages will emphasize different aspects of his character than ours, just as we highlight differing aspects of him than Luther, Calvin, or Augustine.

Troeltsch's Jesus, in short, bleeds over into community: a theme common to liberal theology from Schleiermacher to Harnack. In interpreting the *triplex munex*, the threefold offices of Jesus (Prophet, Priest, and King), Troeltsch indicates that his kingly role is most central, because it represents his "lordship over the community. . . . The point of Jesus' life was to create a community, and the community plays a decisive role in the goal of leading human beings to God."[68] The community gathered in Jesus's name, in no small part, might be described as an extension of the incarnation. Troeltsch's ecclesiology-Christology contains elements of mysticism, whereby the presence of the risen Christ is given to the believer through the community of faith.[69] Jesus saves because of this creation of a new community that continually mediates the offer of salvation to others. Salvation in Christ is also salvation for and with the community: "Redemption is always contemporary, proceeding from the faith in God that the community mediates to us."[70] There is no relationship to Jesus apart from this community.

By uplifting the role that community plays in mediating Christ's saving work, Troeltsch also critiques several interpretations of Jesus's death. He is most emphatic in rejecting an Anselmian view of the atonement, which would claim that Jesus's sacrificial death was necessary to satisfy the demands of divine justice. In addition to noting ethical objections to the suffering of an innocent victim, Troeltsch notes that "the most serious objection, finally, is the religious one: the whole construction of this doctrine of redemption presupposes a juristic idea of God, which, in addition to being a monstrous anthropomorphism, is also plagued by the internal contradiction of requiring God to make satisfaction to himself in the form of a redeeming death."[71] Even if such interpretation of Jesus became necessary at a certain point in Christian history, the notion of Christ's satisfaction is no longer pertinent today. Redemption comes, not through death, but in the new community gathered in Jesus's name. Troeltsch makes the following quip, to hammer his point home: Jesus "did not say, I shall gain salvation for you through my death, but only: 'The Kingdom of God is at hand.'"[72]

Troeltsch notes the difficulty in recovering a purely historical Jesus, unaffected by the claims of the communities that surround him. But in the end, this is not something to be lamented. Our access to Jesus is always mediated by community, and hence we need the witness of communities that have gathered before our time. One responsibility of the present generation is to make the claim—and be claimed by—Jesus ever anew. In doing so, the present generation may dispense with earlier interpretations of him, but only after careful listening, sifting, and consideration of the redemption that is offered in Christ, through the community. Troeltsch's Jesus thus makes the experience of redemption stunningly present, *now*. But at the same time, his approach invites the question: What happens in those cases when the community is not being faithful to redemption in Christ? Communities, to state the obvious, are tragically flawed; they sometimes follow idols of their own making. In Troeltsch's approach, what are the checks against communities that distort redemption and follow other idols: race, nation, or anything else? What happens to Jesus, in other words, when communities fall short?

Albert Schweitzer (1875–1965)

This survey of Enlightenment-influenced Christologies concludes with the writings of a theologian with perhaps the most interesting biography of all. Albert Schweitzer hailed from Alsace, France, and earned degrees in philosophy, theology, and medicine. Beyond these degrees, he was a virtuoso organist. He served as Lutheran pastor and organist in Strasbourg, in addition to teaching at the university. After publishing several distinguished academic works, Schweitzer founded a clinic and served as a medical missionary in French Equatorial Africa, work for which he eventually earned the Nobel Peace Prize in 1952. Schweitzer also became noted for a well-developed ethic that reverenced all life: animal, plant, and human. His most influential theological work is *The Quest of the Historical Jesus*, published in 1906, which problematized some of the previous "quests" to recover Jesus's historicity. Though he argues that many of these previous attempts wind up finding what the searcher wants to discover (hence, Harnack's Jesus looks remarkably like a polite, German bourgeois citizen) and that many aspects of Jesus's history are irretrievable, he also argues for an eschatological core to Jesus's message that continues to call the contemporary generation.

The hardest-hitting aspect of Schweitzer's portrayal of Jesus is that many previous "discoveries" of Jesus were more akin to the investigator looking into the mirror. We invariably find a Jesus who winds up looking like ourselves, no matter what kind of theological cloak or pious language we don. "The Jesus of Nazareth who came forward publicly as the Messiah, who preached the ethic of the kingdom of God, who founded the kingdom of heaven upon earth, and died to give his work its final consecration, never existed. He is a figure designed by rationalism, endowed with life by liberalism, and clothed by modern theology in a historical garb."[73] Modern theology—indeed, all theology—ought to recognize the influence of its own presuppositions and interests on the figure of Jesus. We cannot disentangle one from the other, and hence we ought to be modest in any attempt to describe the "historical" Jesus. There is much about him that simply cannot be known.

Schweitzer thus deflates many previous attempts to arrive at the core of Jesus's person.

Nevertheless, it is not the case that we can say *nothing* about Jesus's historical person and message. But the thing that we can say is the very thing most liberal attempts have ignored: Jesus's radical eschatological message. Schweitzer's Jesus is an eschatological prophet; his ministry and teaching are based on an eschatological worldview that is alien to our time. Liberal theology "could find no equivalent in themselves to the thoughts of Jesus, and were therefore incapable of translating his world-view from its late-Jewish form into their own forms of understanding."[74] This Jesus comes as a stranger to the modern world: his worldview is not our own. We think of progress and hope for a better day tomorrow; Jesus comes announcing the end of history and the coming of God's reign. And when this inbreaking of God's kingdom did not occur within his lifetime, Jesus gave up his life for the sake of it: he embodies in his death the coming of the kingdom. We cannot know Jesus unless we recognize him as a strange prophet in our midst.

If Jesus's eschatological horizon constitutes the core of his history, however, this does not mean we can only claim him as a wild-eyed harbinger of the end of days.[75] What is most significant about Jesus is not his historical message, but his spiritual influence: "Our relationship to Jesus is ultimately of a mystical kind. . . . We can achieve a relation to such a personality only when we become united with him in the knowledge of a shared aspiration . . . and when we rediscover ourselves through him."[76] Jesus is thus both a stranger and an intimate: His context is so radically different from our own that we cannot retrieve that context for our time. And yet we know something about him because of the ongoing work of his spirit who has inspired every age. Schweitzer's famous ending to his *Quest* captures this paradox:

> He comes to us as one unknown, without a name, as of old, by the lakeside, he came to those men who did not know who he was. He says the same words: "Follow me!," and sets us to those tasks which he must fulfil in our time. He commands. And to those who hearken him, whether wise or unwise, he will reveal himself in the peace, the labors, the conflicts, and the suffering that they may experience in his fellowship, and as an ineffable mystery, they will learn who he is.[77]

The One who will always be stranger to us is also One who calls us to seek him. But more important than seeking is to be caught up in the work that his Spirit has inspired. Schweitzer's Jesus is thus only discovered on the way.

Conclusion

The age of Enlightenment began with a confidence that Jesus might be discovered by being freed from the bonds of arbitrary authorities, whether ecclesial or otherwise. To think for oneself was also to be set on the path toward a more accurate depiction of Jesus. This age ended in the wreckage of the First World War, a bloodbath unlike any the world had ever seen, spurred in part because of the "progress" of mechanization made possible through reason and scientific investigation. At the end of this period, it is harder to have utter confidence in the powers of human reason. Instead, one became more attuned to reason's limits. Though Schweitzer's depiction of an apocalyptic Jesus was constructed before the dawn of World War I, it is easy to see how this Jesus might reflect this tumultuous context. Along the way from Pascal to Schweitzer, however, multiple voices argued not for the overthrowing of authority but for its critical recovery: in pietism, in interpretations (like Schleiermacher's and Troeltsch's) that emphasized the constructive role of community. What emerges at the end of this rich period of theological history is a more tempered view of authority in relation to Jesus. At the end of this period we discern that there is no access to Jesus apart from communal remembrance, that our interpretations and portrayals of him are influenced by those who have gone before us, and by the communities we call home. This does not mean that we accept our community's interpretation of Jesus at all costs, for there are many ways that communities can distort Jesus. But it does mean that the person that the church confesses as God's Son and the communities that have experienced redemption by his Spirit are forever linked.

Notes

1. Blaise Pascal, *Pensées*, trans. H. F. Stewart (New York: Pantheon, 1950), 321.
2. Pascal, *Pensées*, 319.
3. Hermann Samuel Reimarus, *The Goal of Jesus and His Disciples*, ed. George Wesley Buchanan (Leiden: Brill, 1970), 80 (emphasis added).
4. Jonathan Edwards, *The Excellency of Christ: A Sermon* (Waiheke Island: Floating Press, 2009), 35.
5. Edwards, *Excellency of Christ*, 42.
6. Jonathan Edwards, *The Nature of True Virtue* (Mansfield Centre, CT: Martino, 2015), 3.
7. Edwards, *Nature of True Virtue*, 7.
8. Wesley traveled an estimated 250,000 miles and preached between forty and fifty thousand sermons during his life. See Ariel Zambrano, "Wesley, John," in *The Westminster Dictionary of Theologians*, ed. Justo L. González, trans. Suzanne E. Hoeferkamp Segovia (Louisville: Westminster John Knox, 2006), 353.

9. John Wesley, *The Lord Our Righteousness*, in *John Wesley's Sermons: An Anthology*, ed. Albert C. Outler and Richard P. Heitzenrater (Nashville: Abingdon, 1991), 388.
10. John Wesley, *The End of Christ's Coming*, in Outler and Heitzenrater, *John Wesley's Sermons*, 449.
11. In one sermon, Wesley attributes the hardening of the arteries to the initial consumption of the forbidden fruit. See John Wesley, *The Image of God*, in Outler and Heitzenrater, *John Wesley's Sermons*, 17.
12. Wesley, *Image of God*, 19.
13. Friedrich Schleiermacher, *The Christian Faith*, ed. H. R. Mackintosh and J. S. Stewart (Edinburgh: T&T Clark, 1989), 387.
14. Keith W. Clements, "Main Themes in Schleiermacher's Theology," in *Friedrich Schleiermacher: Pioneer of Modern Theology*, ed. Keith W. Clements (Minneapolis: Fortress Press, 1991), 57.
15. Friedrich Schleiermacher, *The Life of Jesus*, ed. Jack C. Verheyden (Philadelphia: Fortress Press, 1975), 87.
16. Schleiermacher, *Christian Faith*, 383.
17. For example, Jesus would have probably accepted the idea that the sun revolves around the earth, but at the same time this lack of scientific knowledge in no way detracts from his perfect God-consciousness.
18. Schleiermacher, *Christian Faith*, 437.
19. Schleiermacher, *Christian Faith*, 425.
20. Friedrich Schleiermacher, *Christmas Eve: Dialogue on the Incarnation*, trans. Terrence N. Tice (San Francisco: EM Texts, 1990), 82.
21. See Peter C. Hodgson, introduction to *G. W. F. Hegel: Theologian of the Spirit*, ed. Peter C. Hodgson, Making of Modern Theology (Minneapolis: Fortress Press, 1997), 1.
22. Hegel's criticism of Schleiermacher's concept of feeling is very strong at times: "If religion in human beings is grounded solely on a feeling, such feeling has rightly no other characteristic than to be the *feeling of absolute dependence*; and a dog would then be the best Christian, for the dog carries this feeling most strongly within itself, and its life is spent primarily in it." G. W. F. Hegel, "Foreword to Hinrichs's *Religion*," in Hodgson, *Hegel*, 166. For Hegel, freedom, rather than dependence, is the chief religious impulse.

23. G. W. F. Hegel, *Lectures on the Philosophy of Religion*, one-volume ed., ed. Peter C. Hodgson (Berkeley: University of California Press, 1988), 129.
24. Hegel, *Lectures on the Philosophy of Religion*, 459.
25. Hegel, *Lectures on the Philosophy of Religion*, 456.
26. Hegel, *Lectures on the Philosophy of Religion*, 465. "The human, the finite, the fragile, the weak, the negative are themselves a moment of the divine, that they are within God himself, that finitude, negativity, otherness are not outside God and do not, as otherness, hinder unity with God. Otherness, the negative, is known to be a moment of the divine nature itself." Hegel, *Lectures on the Philosophy of Religion*, 468.
27. Hegel, *Lectures on the Philosophy of Religion*, 466.
28. Hegel, "The Resumption of the Whole into One," in Hodgson, *Hegel*, 89.
29. Jarena Lee, "A Female Preacher among the African Methodists," in *Afro-American Religious History: A Documentary Witness*, ed. Milton C. Sernett (Durham, NC: Duke University Press, 1985), 167–68.
30. Lee, "Female Preacher," 178.
31. Lee, "Female Preacher," 169.
32. John Henry Newman, "Sermon III: The Incarnation," in *Newman against the Liberals: 25 Classic Sermons by John Henry Newman*, ed. Michael Davies (New Rochelle, NY: Arlington House, 1978), 127.
33. Newman, "Sermon III," 127.
34. Newman, "Sermon III," 128.
35. Newman, "Sermon III," 137.
36. Claude Welch, *Protestant Thought in the Nineteenth Century*, vol. 1, *1799–1870* (New Haven, CT: Yale University Press, 1972), 267.
37. Horace Bushnell, *God in Christ: Three Discourses* (Hartford: Brown and Parsons, 1849), 234.
38. Ludwig Feuerbach, *The Essence of Christianity*, trans. George Eliot (New York: Harper & Row, 1957), 31.
39. Feuerbach, *Essence of Christianity*, 50.
40. Feuerbach, *The Essence of Christianity*, 53.
41. Feuerbach, *The Essence of Christianity*, 147.
42. Feuerbach, *The Essence of Christianity*, 148.
43. Søren Kierkegaard, *Philosophical Fragments / Johannes Climacus*, trans.

Howard V. Hong and Edna H. Hong (Princeton: Princeton University Press, 1985), 104.

44. "In truth, the eighteen hundred years have not contributed a jot to demonstrating the truth of Christianity; on the contrary, with steadily increasing power they have contributed to abolishing Christianity." Søren Kierkegaard, *Practice in Christianity*, trans. Howard V. Hong and Edna H. Hong (Princeton: Princeton University Press, 1991), 144.

45. Kierkegaard, *Fragments*, 15.

46. Kierkegaard, *Fragments*, 17.

47. Kierkegaard, *Practice*, 23.

48. Kierkegaard, *Practice*, 25.

49. See Kierkegaard, *Fear and Trembling/Repetition*, ed. Howard V. Hong and Edna H. Hong (Princeton: Princeton University Press, 1983).

50. Kierkegaard, *Practice*, 48.

51. Kierkegaard, *Fragments*, 33.

52. Kierkegaard, *Practice*, 137.

53. In the following interpretation of Eliot, I am deeply indebted to the work of Peter C. Hodgson, who first introduced me to her novels. See Hodgson, *The Mystery beneath the Real: Theology in the Fiction of George Eliot* (Minneapolis: Fortress Press, 2001).

54. Peter C. Hodgson, "Eliot, George," in *The Cambridge Dictionary of Christianity*, ed. Daniel Patte (Cambridge: Cambridge University Press, 2010), 363.

55. Adolf von Harnack, *What Is Christianity?*, trans. Thomas Bailey Saunders (Philadelphia: Fortress Press, 1986), 33.

56. Harnack, *What Is Christianity*, 35.

57. Harnack, *What Is Christianity*, 51.

58. Harnack, *What Is Christianity*, 56.

59. Harnack, *What Is Christianity*, 128.

60. Harnack, *What Is Christianity*, 144.

61. Alfred Firmin Loisy, *The Gospel and the Church*, ed. R. Joseph Hoffmann (Buffalo, NY: Prometheus, 1988), 115.

62. Loisy, *Gospel and the Church*, 115.

63. Pandita Ramabai, "A Testimony," in *In Her Words: Women's Writings in*

the History of Christian Thought, ed. Amy Oden (Nashville: Abingdon, 1994), 325.

64. Ramabai, "A Testimony," 325.
65. Ernst Troeltsch, *The Christian Faith*, trans. Garrett E. Paul (Minneapolis: Fortress Press, 1991), 87.
66. Troeltsch, *Christian Faith*, 94.
67. Troeltsch, *Christian Faith*, 98.
68. Troeltsch, *Christian Faith*, 100.
69. Troeltsch's threefold typology of religious communities—church, sect, and mysticism—understands mysticism as the most developed expression of the community.
70. Troeltsch, *Christian Faith*, 275.
71. Troeltsch, *Christian Faith*, 281.
72. Troeltsch, *Christian Faith*, 282.
73. Albert Schweitzer, *The Quest of the Historical Jesus*, ed. John Bowden (Minneapolis: Fortress Press, 2001), 478.
74. Schweitzer, *Quest*, 482.
75. Indeed, Schweitzer's own biography suggests he saw more to the life of Jesus. His entire career as a medical missionary, for example, is based on some kind of sense that the end is *not* near, that Christians—as they seek to follow Christ—are called to seek the betterment of *this* world and to reverence all life.
76. Schweitzer, *Quest*, 486.
77. Schweitzer, *Quest*, 487.

6

The Twentieth Century and Beyond

The first half of the twentieth century was marked by the scourge of two devastating wars that erupted in the heart of Christendom. One of the theological effects of this context was the whittling away of confidence that had been present in earlier centuries. What did it mean when the people of a nation that professed to follow Jesus wound up killing six million Jews? What did it mean to follow in Christ's way of peace when another predominantly Christian nation used nuclear weapons in the name of ending the Second World War? What did it mean to confess Jesus in an age wracked by war, an increasing divide between rich and poor (on both a national and global scale), and ecological devastation? The twentieth century laid bare enormous challenges to faith—not mainly because of reason, but because of ethical, political, and environmental crises. Who is Jesus, and how does one follow him on this increasingly imperiled planet we call home?

The portraits of Jesus that emerge in this astonishingly rich theological era are as varied as the communities that gave them birth. Amid the wonder of this diversity emerge at least a few common themes. First, these portraits tend to be less confident in their use of reason, their rejection of earlier authorities, or their theological import for all. They tend, even amid their enormous variations, to recognize that reason is not the final arbiter of an authentic depiction of Jesus. Hence, there is in many of these portrayals a "second naiveté"[1] in relation to tradition, a recovery of traditions after they have passed through the fires of critique. In the second half of the century, these interpretations of Jesus veer more toward the contextual than the universal. They recognize the inescapable connection between Jesus and the communities that bear his name. To confess Jesus is to confess him at a certain time and place, among certain neighbors. Part of this recognition involves interaction with other faith claims and other religious traditions. Many Christologies of this period, therefore, engage the wisdom of faiths other than Christianity. In doing so, they recognize that Jesus does not belong to Christianity alone.

Finally, one of the marks of this fascinating period is the expansion of voices depicting Jesus. The grip of Western culture on depictions of Jesus has now been broken. As Christianity begins its third millennium, a full two-thirds of Christians now live in the global South, reflecting many contexts for whom Platonism, Aristotelianism, and contemporary existentialism are rather remote. The most explosive growth of the Christian church (and hence, of pictures of Jesus) is now occurring outside Europe and North America. Accompanying this growth is the flourishing of depictions of Jesus that reflect on race, gender, culture, and sexuality. As Christianity faces its future, its portrayals of Jesus do not belong to one people alone.

Pierre Teilhard de Chardin (1881–1955)

The first theologian we encounter in this pivotal century was something of a polymath. Born in a rural region of central France, Pierre Teilhard de Chardin was drawn to the outdoors as a child, which led to his interest in biology. He enters the Jesuits in 1902 and focuses on the natural sciences. His first teaching post is in Cairo, where he begins to develop what is later to become his cosmic vision, a theological account of the world that takes evolutionary biology and geosciences seriously and posits a web of organic interconnection between all things. During the First World War, Teilhard serves as a stretcher-bearer, where he is exposed to the horrors of that conflict. After the war, he earns a doctorate in geology and departs for China, where he spends much of the rest of his life. There he is involved in numerous expeditions, including the excavation of "Peking Man," a pathbreaking event in paleontology. Throughout his life, he wrote theology, though most of these writings were not published until after his death. These theological writings are novel in their incorporation of cutting-edge science, and in many respects foreshadow later attempts in the twentieth century to engage science as a dialogue partner and the subsequent movement of process theology. His interpretation of Jesus veers in a cosmic direction, depicting Christ as leading creation toward its "Omega Point," or eschatological completion in the life of God.

Teilhard's Jesus is unabashedly cosmic. His Christology glosses over the Gospels, but it is not concerned primarily with Jesus as a historical figure or even Jesus's teachings. Instead,

Teilhard is occupied with the pattern of cosmic life that finds its focal point in Christ. This Christology is deeply sacramental, incarnational, and evolutionary. The incarnation of Jesus is the means by which God makes all matter holy. What happens in Jesus is what is destined to happen to all things. The focal point of our participation in this process is the Eucharist: "A single event has been developing in the world: the Incarnation, realized, in each individual, through the Eucharist."[2] God's coming in the flesh of Jesus Christ anticipates the fulfillment of all things in God and opens our eyes to the incarnation all around us. In other words, Teilhard does not restrict the incarnation to a first-century Jewish prophet. Instead, "Christ reveals himself in each reality around us, and shines like an ultimate determinant, like a centre, one might almost say like a universal element."[3] When we take part in the Lord's Supper, we become a part of what God is doing in the world, and we recognize our own participation in that process. Teilhard writes that the incarnation summons us to bring ourselves, in order to complete the work that God has begun: "With each one of our *works*, we labor . . . to build the Pleroma; that is to say, we bring to Christ a little fulfillment."[4] The work of Christ is thus not fully accomplished until the end of days. The incarnation of Jesus, in this regard, lures us into the future by showing us the pattern of a Christ-shaped life, the life that gives life to the world.

Teilhard is fond of neologisms, one of which is "christogenesis." By this term he means the Christ-led cosmic process of evolution, whereby the being of all creation is divinized as it finds its fulfillment in Christ, the Omega Point. Jesus is the Word in whom all things are created, the Crown of creation, who guides all things in the course of evolution, and the end of creation revealed at the eschaton. This cosmic Christ encompasses past, present, and future, and in doing so also encompasses us: "The Christian knows that his function is to divinize the world in Jesus Christ."[5] The path of christification, however, is neither seamless destiny nor unblemished progress. Even if Christ is luring all things, suffering and tragedy erupt on the scene. This is one of the ways in which Teilhard interprets the cross of Jesus. The crucifixion happened not just to Jesus; it happens to all in the nitty-gritty of life. What is more, life itself is possible because of death: whether we are talking about basic sustenance (creatures eating other creatures or plants) or the vast cycles of life on planet earth. Jesus doesn't erase death, but experiences it and brings it into the heart of God: "We must overcome death by finding God in it. . . . Christ has conquered death, not only by suppressing its evil effects, but by reversing its sting."[6]

But the cross also symbolizes something more. It is not merely the incorporation of suffering and death into life; it is not only the triumph over its evil effects; it is also a way into greater life. Teilhard reappropriates the medieval image of the cross as a ladder that allows us to ascend to God. The cross allows us to go "beyond the frontiers of the sensible world" and even break with it. We are not to "swoon in the shadow, but to climb in the light, of the Cross."[7] Teilhard's Jesus thus contains deep strands of mysticism: What happens to Jesus is an invitation for us to be formed by Christ.

Finally, Teilhard's Jesus is eschatological. The point of it all—incarnation, crucifixion, and resurrection—is for Christ to come again, to be realized in each fragment of creation. Teilhard interprets the apocalyptic imagery of the New Testament along these lines. "The kingdom of God is within us. When Christ appears in the clouds he will simply be manifesting a metamorphosis that has been slowly accomplished under his influence in the heart of the mass of mankind."[8] This eschatological focus is thus both intensely personal (Christ becomes real in each one of us) and vastly cosmic (Christ is present throughout creation).

The strength of Teilhard's Christology is how he places it within an evolutionary view of the cosmos. Whereas some traditionalists saw the dawning discoveries in biology, geology, and other sciences to be inimical to Christian faith, Teilhard offers one way of seeing consonance and convergence between science and theology. His Christology allows us to be thoroughly modern and thoroughly Christian at the same time. His approach also highlights the cosmic nature of Christ's work in ways that much theology since the Reformation had minimized. Indeed, he offers a corrective to overly personal or individualized visions of Christ that had emerged in the nineteenth century. At the same time, despite his insistence on the cross, it is more difficult to see how this portrayal of Christ adequately addresses the vast suffering of the modern world. The process of christogenesis seems inexorable. Does the ladder imagery, in the end, encourage Christ's followers to rise above and forget the suffering that lies below the cross?

Rudolf Bultmann (1884–1976)

Rudolf Bultmann was born in northern Germany, the son of a Lutheran pastor. The younger Bultmann studied under the influence of Protestant liberals, including Harnack. Having taught at various universities, he eventually takes a post at Marburg, where his work becomes widely discussed, at home and abroad. Though primarily a New Testament scholar, Bultmann has probably had a more enduring impact on subsequent theology than New Testament studies. His work is characterized by several themes: first, his project of "demythologization," which claims that the worldview of the New Testament writers and its three-tiered universe (heaven above the earth, hell below it) are foreign to modern readers. We do not understand the universe and ourselves along these lines. The contemporary interpreter, therefore, needs to probe behind the mythologies of the biblical writings to arrive at their meaning for us *today*. Along this way, Bultmann is keenly influenced by existentialism, particularly the work of Martin Heidegger. The "existential" message of the Christian faith is a message of freedom. Salvation in Christ frees us from the prison of self-justification and self-strength, to live in light of the future that God promises anew each day. Bultmann's Christology, therefore, is contemporaneous, in its emphasis on the now, and revisionist, as it reinterprets basic Christian beliefs (such as cross and resurrection) without resorting to mythology.

Bultmann's overriding image for Jesus is as a preacher, the One who proclaims the kingdom of God. This proclamation occupies the center of his ministry and symbolizes his ongoing legacy. But Bultmann discerns a difference between Jesus's own presuppositions about his preaching and the way it should now be received. Through close investigation of the Gospels, Bultmann claims that Jesus expected the end of the present age to happen soon. "Jesus expected . . . this . . . in the immediate future, and he said that the dawning of that age would already be perceived in the signs and wonders which he performed, especially in his casting out of demons. Jesus envisaged the inauguration of the Kingdom of God as a tremendous cosmic drama."[9] All of the imagery that saturates his preaching—the rending of the heavens, the cosmic triumph of the Son of Man, the tribulations that signal the dawning of a new age—Jesus expected as actual, cosmic events. The problem with receiving this message today is that modern persons do not inhabit this three-tiered universe. They do not expect the dramatic intervention of God's hand and live without resorting to the need to have God intervene. Furthermore, the events that Jesus expected to occur soon have, in fact, never occurred. This is why demythologization is necessary. What constituted the heart of Jesus's preaching about the kingdom of God? The cosmic spectacle or something else? Demythologization, as Bultmann practices it, is not the *elimination* of biblical mythology, but a way of *interpreting* mythology for our time. Using this method, Bultmann claims that the heart of Jesus's eschatological preaching is "that this world is temporal and transitory, yes, ultimately empty and unreal in the face of eternity."[10] Jesus's preaching emphasizes the contingency of our lives and their fragility in light of God's future.

When Jesus exhorts his audience to repent, he calls them to recognize this contingency, dependency, and to abandon all attempts to justify themselves. Instead of positing ourselves as self-made persons who are the masters of our destiny, we repent of this posture. The salvation that Christ brings is not a cosmic transaction that rebalances the scales of justice or vanquishes the powers of evil, symbolized in Satan. Instead, it is a salvation that frees us for the future that God holds. When we hear and accept the message of Jesus, we are changed: "The deeper meaning of the mythological preaching of Jesus [is] to be open to God's future which is really imminent for every one of us . . . to be prepared, because this future will be a judgment on all men who have bound themselves to this world and are not free, not open to God's future."[11] Christ's salvation frees us from ourselves to be radically for the future.

At every step of the way, Bultmann's interpretation of Jesus focuses on the change that his message brings in the present.

The atonement, in his eyes, is not an event that happened long ago, but a transformative moment for each individual who is seized by faith. In some respects this is a radically Lutheran reading of Jesus: it all stands or falls in the encounter of faith. Jesus, effectively, is nothing apart from the eyes of faith. And this Jesus, when encountered in faith, is totally present in the moment. The Jesus that makes a difference is not the historical figure of two thousand years ago, but the Jesus who meets us *now*. The influence of pietism is also strong here, emphasizing the new birth of the believer in Christ. Jesus, the eschatological preacher, offers a realized eschatology: "Jesus Christ is to be understood as the eschatological 'once for all.' As an eschatological event this 'once for all' is always present in the proclaimed word, not as a timeless truth, but as a happening here and now."[12] Jesus leaves us, in the end, not a teaching or a doctrine, but a person who changes us, who frees us in faith to find security only in God.[13]

One of the more intriguing aspects of this interpretation of Jesus is Bultmann's view of the resurrection. We make a mistake, Bultmann claims, if we understand Christ's resurrection chiefly as a miraculous event that happened to Jesus's body. To claim it as such is to resort to mythology and to relegate the meaning of resurrection to the past. The real miracle of the resurrection, instead, is what happens *to us*. The resurrection captures the awakening of faith in the first generation of disciples and in every generation hence. On Easter morning, the disciples who arrive at the empty tomb are seized by faith, accept the proclamation of Jesus, and are open to the new life that God gives. Resurrection, in this sense, happens anew every day, in each person changed by faith. To the eyes of faith, resurrection takes place every morning.

Bultmann offers a consistent interpretation of Jesus that is accessible to modern sensibilities. If much of the mythology of the New Testament has become a stumbling block for interpretation of Jesus, Bultmann's approach allows us to reclaim the existential core of Jesus's preaching: his call to repentance, conversion, and the urgency of change. This approach is also noteworthy in its diagnosis of the modern temptation toward self-sufficiency. Bultmann's Jesus leads those whom he calls back to the One he calls Father. But in doing so, Bultmann also focuses chiefly on the individual in his interpretation of Jesus. The Jesus that matters, in his reading, is the Jesus that changes persons, one at a time. It all stands or falls with the moment of faith. In the end, there is something rather private about Bultmann's Jesus: it leaves the individual alone in the encounter with God in Christ. As a result, the political and the cosmic slip away. We are left with a Jesus who has little to say about social arrangements and life beyond the individual. As a result, Bultmann's Jesus has surprisingly little to say about ethics or even the *life of the world*.

Karl Barth (1886–1968)

Often regarded as the most influential theologian of the twentieth century, Karl Barth was born in Basel, Switzerland. His father and both of his grandfathers were pastors. Barth's theological training was with preeminent German liberal theologians, including Harnack (though Barth never completed doctoral studies). When he was twenty-three, Barth became ordained in the Reformed church and took a series of pastorates that had a profound effect on his theology. Most significant among these was a pastorate in the small town of Safenwil, where Barth became disillusioned with his own liberal training. The theology of his teachers seemed remote from the concerns of his working-class parishioners. As World War I erupted, Barth also found that many of his teachers seemed unwilling to resist the growing nationalism in Germany. In a bombshell book published in 1919, Barth's commentary on Romans, he attacks "natural theology," characteristic of liberalism that seeks to ascend to God through anthropology. This method is doomed because it fails to recognize God's transcendent otherness. We do not know God by contemplating human experience, but only through the revelation of God in Christ, which jolts us out of complacency. This emphasis on revelation resulted in a rediscovery of theologies of the Reformation (especially Calvin), earning Barth the title of the founder of neo-orthodoxy. Barth's commentary attracted much attention, and led to several university appointments in Germany. As Nazism arose, Barth spoke out vociferously in opposition. His involvement in writing the Barmen Declaration and refusal to take a loyalty oath to Hitler resulted in his expulsion from the University of Bonn in 1935. After that, he accepts a post at Basel, where he teaches until retiring in 1962. His magnum opus, *Church Dogmatics*, was written there, a compendium of Christian doctrine written not chiefly as a tightly organized systematics, but as a piece of "occasional theology," which continually revisits, amplifies, and expands on the primary theme of God's revelation in Christ. Barth's Christology, therefore, is difficult to summarize, but recovers many Reformation themes, including the often-maligned topic of election. It also focuses on the Bible as the primary witness for understanding who Jesus is.

Like Bultmann, Barth focuses on Jesus's proclamation of the kingdom of God. Who Christ is is captured in what he proclaims. But unlike Bultmann, Barth does not interpret Jesus's proclamation in an individual, existentialist manner. His proclamation does not immediately give us the gift of new freedom, but discloses how far from God we are: "The new thing of Jesus is the invading kingdom of God revealed in its alienating antithesis to the world and all its orders."[14] Jesus's proclamation of the kingdom disrupts the status quo, revealing itself in alienating otherness. God's kingdom cannot be compared to any kingdom or orders we know in this world, however good we might think they are. This Jesus who proclaims cannot be appropriated by us for our own interest. When we hear Jesus's proclamation, we are judged, and all of our accomplishments are relativized.

This "otherness" of the kingdom is evidenced, Barth claims, if we look at Jesus's own posture vis-à-vis the political movements of his day. He distanced himself from the Zealots, for example, and rejected their plan of a militant overthrow of Roman imperial authority. Barth claims that Jesus "did not represent or defend or champion any programme—whether political, economic, moral, or religious, whether conservative or progressive. He was equally suspected and disliked by the representatives of all such programs, although he did not particularly attack any of them. Why his existence was so unsettling on every side was that He set all programs and principles in question."[15] Barth dubs this element of Jesus his "passive conservatism," not that Jesus was a conservative, but that he stood in question any human attempt to save itself. Jesus, in the end, directs us back to God, for he is the only one who bridges the massive gulf between us and God.

If Jesus embodies this form of "conservatism," however, he does not accept the status quo. As the revelation of God, Jesus judges the world and takes the side of the poor: "If we do not know Him as this poor man, as this (if we may risk the dangerous word) partisan of the poor, and finally as this revolutionary."[16] What is revolutionary about Jesus, however, is not his adoption of a particular political/economic program, but his rejection of the current state of affairs and his claim that only God can redeem it. Jesus criticizes all of us, and even our noblest attempts to better ourselves and better our world apart from God. The kingdom is the radical inbreaking of God and God's ways into the world—not parallel with our ways, but a departure from them. If we do not know Jesus as the proclaimer of this kingdom, we do not know him at all. And as proclaimer, Jesus judges us.

We misinterpret Christ if we see him only as a judge, convicting us of sin. In Barth's interpretation, Jesus also embraces us as partner. It is only through Christ that God draws near to us. In Christ "God's deliverance of man accomplished, God's gift to man present in fulness, God's claim and promise to man declared. In him God has joined Himself to man. And so man exists for his sake."[17] If the proclamation of the kingdom first reveals itself in alienating otherness, it is also the thing that welcomes us home, making us know that we belong to God. Later in Barth's career, he modifies some of his earlier stridency, claiming that God reveals Godself in Jesus not only in otherness but also in God's "humanity." "In Jesus Christ there is no isolation of man from God or of God from man. Rather, in Him we encounter the history, the dialogue, in which God and man meet together and are together, the reality of the covenant *mutually* contracted, preserved, and fulfilled by them."[18] To claim Christ as Emmanuel (God with us) is precisely this—that in Christ God wills for all time to be our partner. The incarnation, in the end, for Barth is not about a speculative, ontological theory of how divine and human natures can exist together in one person, but a relational promise: God chooses us as God's own, for eternal partnership.

Barth's interpretation of Jesus continually invokes the language of humiliation and exaltation. Jesus bridges the chasm between humanity and God brought on by humanity's sin. In Christ, God ventures "into the far country, and conceals his glory. . . . He is truly honored in this concealment."[19] Jesus reveals the condescension and voluntary self-humiliation of God on our behalf. We misunderstand this if we see it as cutting God down a few notches, because God's glory is revealed in lowliness, God's power in weakness. This is why the kingdom of God is fundamentally unlike anything that we can imagine; this is why Jesus is the herald of that kingdom—it reveals any order that we would create on our own as empty.

Barth's interpretation of Jesus's death recalls the heritage of the Reformation, but also reinterprets that language. The primary image for interpreting Jesus's death is that he is the Judge who is judged in our place. Barth asks, "Why did the Son of God become man, one of us, our brother, our fellow in the human situation? The answer is: in order to judge the world."[20] But in "judging" us, he takes our judgment as his own. "The son of God fulfilled the righteous judgment on us men by Himself taking our place as man and in our place undergoing the judgment under which we had passed."[21] Barth calls this a "strange judgment," a reversal of what we'd expect. "There on the cross of Golgotha, hangs the man who in His own name and person represented me, my name and person, with God; and who again in His own name and person represented God to me in my name and person."[22] This isn't simply a recovery of Anselm's theory of atonement, but a radicalization of it. Jesus represents us to God and represents God to us—not only on the cross, but also in his life, teaching, death, and resurrection. Furthermore, in

Christ we are both eternally rejected and elected. On the cross, Jesus experiences God's rejection because of human sin, but also God's election of him as God's beloved. Barth thereby frees the doctrine of election from a way of speaking about persons (who are either elect or reprobate) to a way of talking about Christ. Humanity takes part in election because of God's election of Christ. Election is first and foremost a christological and not an anthropological category.

Barth's Christology also underscores divine vulnerability. In Christ, God takes a risk: "For God it means inevitably a certain compromising of Himself that he should determine to enter this covenant. Where man stands to gain, God stands only to lose. . . . God does not merely give himself up to the risk and menace, but He exposes Himself to the actual onslaught and grasp of evil."[23] In Christ, God undergoes the depths to be *for* us and *with* us. If the beginning of Barth's Christology emphasizes the alienating otherness of the kingdom, the end uplifts the extent to which God wills in Christ to be in solidarity with us.

Barth's Christology is vast, and we have only scratched its surface. What is most noteworthy about it is its critical recovery and reinterpretation of the tradition. Whereas some of his teachers were quick to dismiss previous interpretations of Jesus as babble to the modern age, Barth makes these traditions surprisingly alive. Furthermore, his depiction of Jesus takes seriously the ruptures of the modern world, the tragedy and suffering of the era that has rendered God remote. Yet, by directing attention to Christ, one senses how these ruptures do not have the final word. The result is a Christology that combines the personal, the political, and the cosmic, recovering the Reformed emphasis on Christ as Prophet, Priest, and King.

Paul Tillich (1886–1965)

Son of a Lutheran pastor, Tillich spent his childhood in small towns in present-day Poland, then moved to Berlin at the age of fourteen. His theological training, like Barth's and Bultmann's, was saturated with Protestant liberalism. But unlike Barth, he remained committed to liberal principles, most famously in his "method of correlation," which relates the "questions" and suppositions of modern culture to "answers" present within Christian symbolism. Theology's primary task, therefore, is *apologetic*: making the faith coherent for the modern age. Tillich served as a chaplain in World War I, taught at various universities in Germany, and became increasingly politically involved. His commitment to Christian socialism and opposition to Nazism resulted in persecution and his eventual expulsion from Germany in 1933. He became an American citizen and continued a distinguished teaching career at Union Seminary, Harvard, and the University of Chicago. His masterpiece, *Systematic Theology*, is a gem of apologetic theology, drawing extensively on existentialism and psychology. Its central argument is that humanity experiences estrangement (from itself and God) and overcomes that estrangement in the person and work of Jesus Christ, who is transparent to God, the Ground of Being.

Unlike Barth, Tillich does not spend much time exegeting the Gospels in interpreting Jesus. Tillich's chief concern is not historical, but typological: how Jesus manifests himself as the Christ. First and foremost, Christ is a *symbol*. Indeed, for Tillich, all religious speech is symbolic, because it expresses our "ultimate concern." We become idolatrous if we lose sight of the symbolism of faith. In Tillich's eyes, symbols (1) point beyond themselves, (2) participate in the realities to which they point, and (3) open up dimensions that were closed to us.[24] Jesus is the symbol of God because he points beyond himself *to* God, because he surrenders his existence to be *for* God, and because he participates in the life *of* God. Tillich's other favored title for Christ is "the New Being." He is the New Being because he shows the way to overcome estrangement, bringing together what had previously been alienated (humanity's estrangement from itself and separation from God). Jesus "becomes completely transparent to the mystery he reveals."[25] How does Jesus become transparent to God's being and work? By sacrifice. Here, Tillich makes the distinction between the man "Jesus" and the symbol "Christ." "He is the Christ as the one who sacrifices what is merely 'Jesus' in him. The decisive trait in his picture is the continuous self-surrender of Jesus who is Jesus to Jesus who is the Christ."[26] Tillich thus interprets the classic language of the creeds not along metaphysical lines (à la human and divine "natures"), but in existential terms. Jesus is God's Son because of his self-surrender. Yet Jesus's self-surrender is something different from martyrdom: "He not only sacrifices his life, as many martyrs and many ordinary people have done, but he also sacrifices everything in him and of him which could bring people to him as an 'overwhelming personality' instead of bringing them to that in him which is greater than he and they."[27] In all that he does and is, Jesus points others to God, the Ground of Being.

Given this emphasis on sacrifice, it is no surprise that the cross plays a prominent role. Like his treatments of all theological topics, however, Tillich's stress is on symbolism. In many respects, Jesus's cross stands as the prime symbol, both of who Jesus is and of the dynamics of faith. Again, his interest is not historical but typological. The cross is not something that merely happens to Jesus, but is the expression of faith that incorporates doubt. The cross is what allows the church to resist idolatry. It is the no to any doctrinal, liturgical, or philosophical expression or gesture that claims absoluteness. Tillich dubs this the "Protestant principle," in which all of our expressions fall under divine judgment. Nothing we can say or claim about the Christian faith is absolute (including our expressions about Jesus). "The Cross is understood as the divine judgment over man's religious life, and even over Christianity."[28] Jesus's cross shows us the way of truth not because it is the only expression of truth, but because it contains within itself its own negation, its own relativization. "The criterion of the truth of faith, therefore, is that it implies an element of self-negation. That symbol is most adequate which expresses not only the ultimate but also its own lack of ultimacy. Christianity expresses itself in such a symbol in contrast to all other religions, namely, in the Cross of the Christ."[29] In Tillich's framework, Jesus puts Jesus under question, refusing to absolutize himself. This, and nothing less, is the way of the cross and the way to overcome estrangement between ourselves and God.

Resurrection, in this framework, plays a decidedly second fiddle. As Tillich interprets the risen Christ, he does not claim that resurrection validates the trajectory of Jesus's life. It is not God's judgment of yes on Jesus's ministry. Rather, the resurrection is a consequence of our faith. It is as much an anthropological expression (a statement about us) as a theological one (a statement about God in Christ). "It is the certainty of one's own victory over the death of existential estrangement which creates the certainty of the Resurrection of the Christ as event and symbol."[30] Jesus saves humanity, then, by making us new beings in Christ. Salvation comprises a threefold movement: as we *participate* in the New Being, as Christ lays hold of us (regeneration); as we are *accepted* by the New Being (justification); as we are *transformed* by the New Being (sanctification) in community.[31] Classical language thus finds new expression in Tillich's Christology by correlating the questions of the modern world (questions of our estrangement) with the answers of Christian symbols.

Tillich's apologetic read of Christology yields much. Insofar as it attempts to illuminate the significance of the Christ event to modern sensibilities, his work should be applauded. It is also significant that his Christology attends to the negative, to the limitations of any one expression. By noting that all Christologies are symbolic, and that all contain elements of self-negation, Tillich's approach prevents one-sided interpretations of Jesus that become closed off to all others. But at the same time, Tillich's approach to Jesus is so symbolic that the patterns of history seem to fall away. Where, in Tillich's read, is Jesus's ministry of healing and proclamation? Surely they are more than fodder for the symbols of faith.

H. Richard Niebuhr (1894–1962)

Born in a small town in eastern Missouri, H. Richard Niebuhr was the son of a Protestant minister and brother to the esteemed ethicist Reinhold Niebuhr. Educated at denominational schools (Elmhurst College and Eden Seminary), Niebuhr eventually earned the PhD from Yale. Having worked as a reporter and minister, he returns to Eden to teach, then becomes president of Elmhurst, eventually to assume a post at Yale, where he embarks on a long and influential teaching and writing career. Though he is most often noted as an ethicist who developed a compelling account of human responsibility, his explicit theology has in some senses recently been rediscovered. His classic *Christ and Culture* develops not only a typology of Christian ethical postures; it also begins with a clear Christology that focuses chiefly on the image of Jesus as the Son of God.

Niebuhr begins his interpretation of Christ by acknowledging the plurality of titles that have accumulated around Jesus. Scanning the tradition, several come to the fore: teacher, lawgiver, revelation, creator of a new community. Some communities privilege some of these titles over others, and this privileging gets reflected in the community's ethics; for example, those who perceive Jesus primarily as a lawgiver tend toward rigorous ethical requirements that are binding on the community. But for Niebuhr, all of these titles are necessary, since they illuminate differing aspects of the life and legacy of Jesus. Though Niebuhr eschews elevating one title over another, it is clear that Jesus as the embodiment of love is significant. This is a theme that many Protestant liberals had also embraced, though in Niebuhr's hands it takes a different configuration. Jesus does not simply elevate love as the chief virtue; he shows us that love of God, the love that comes from God, is what grounds life in God. "The virtue of love in Jesus' character and demand is the virtue of the *love of God and of the neighbor in God*, not the virtue of the love of love. . . . For Jesus there is no other finally love-worthy being, no other ultimate object of devotion, than God."[32] In the end, what makes Jesus who he is is the love of God, a love that displays a twofold movement. In Jesus, we see the Son of Man and the Son of God, "who loves God as man should love Him, and loves man as only God can love. . . . There seems then to be no other adequate way to describe Jesus as having the virtue of love than to say that his love was that of the Son of God. It was not love but God that filled his soul."[33] Niebuhr, like many others in the nineteenth and twentieth centuries, interprets the Chalcedonian definition not in terms of metaphysics, but in terms of Jesus's activity. In loving God and loving us as God loves, Jesus reveals himself to be God's Son.

Unlike some of his contemporaries (Bultmann and Barth), Niebuhr decenters the eschatological preaching of Jesus: "Many of [Jesus's] most radical statements are not closely connected at all with expectancy of the coming kingdom, but rather with realization of the present rule of God in the course of daily and natural events."[34] Jesus, in this view, does not direct our attention away from the nitty-gritty, in anticipation of a kingdom that will arrive from above; instead, he directs our attention downward, to this world, for this is the world that God creates and redeems. In showing us the love of God, Jesus also teaches us to love the world.

The name that captures Jesus's activity most adequately, then, is Son of God. Jesus is the One in history who is uniquely devoted to God and single-heartedly trusts in God.[35] This radically monotheistic vision means that Jesus cannot be said to "save" humanity on his own. His saving work only comes *from God*. In this sense, it is most accurate to say that God saves in Christ, not that Jesus saves. "The power and attraction Jesus Christ exercises over men never comes from him alone, but from him as the Son of the Father. It comes from him . . . as a man living to God and God living with men."[36] Niebuhr's Christology thus directs our attention not to Jesus, but to the living God. As such, it is probably the most "other-directed" Christology we have yet seen. This, in the end, is what is most compelling about Niebuhr's interpretation of Jesus. It avoids "Jesusolatry," the absolutizing of Jesus, in the name of preserving Jesus's focus on love of God and neighbor (or better said, the love of neighbor through God). Niebuhr's Christology reminds us that Jesus—as portrayed in the Gospels—claimed rather little about himself and much about God and others. One question worth asking, however, is whether in the process Niebuhr's Jesus disappears.

Karl Rahner (1904–1984)

One of the most prolific and seminal Catholic theologians of the twentieth century, Karl Rahner was born in Freiburg, Germany, and became a Jesuit novice in 1922. His extensive philosophical and theological studies included a stint at the University of Freiburg, where he took courses from Martin Heidegger. His first teaching post was at Innsbruck, a stint that was cut short when the Nazis closed the university. During World War II, Rahner taught at a pastoral institute and engaged in pastoral work in Vienna. Returning to Innsbruck to teach, Rahner wrote prolifically, mainly in essay form, though he also published several influential books, including, toward the end of his life, *Foundations of Christian Faith*, which represents his most systematic work. Rahner's approach to theology takes the classic formulas of the faith as givens: The task of the theologian is not to discern whether they are true, but to interpret them in ways that modern persons can understand (because the language of the classic formulas is often remote from contemporary speech). This approach is directly reflected in his Christology, which considers Chalcedon foundational, and develops a Christology along the lines of evolutionary biology, combining Christology from above and below.

Rahner grounds his Christology in an account of the human person in creation. This is how he commences Christology "from below." To be human, as Rahner understands it, is to be open to God's Spirit in the world. Who we are, at our core, are beings made for God, to be addressed by God, to be claimed by Mystery. Christ is the fulfillment of humanity because he makes the destiny of humanity complete. And what is more, he is the fulfillment of creation itself. For Rahner, Christ appears not chiefly as a divine *response* to sin, but as the culmination of who we were meant to be all along. The incarnation is not a disruption of creation, but its continuation: "creation and Incarnation [are] two moments and two phases of the *one* process of God's self-giving and self-expression."[37] Jesus is thus the intersection of Christology "from above" (the movement of God's self-expression to creation) and "from below" (the orientation of humanity to receive God's self-expression). As such, the God-man is not a riddle to be solved, but the convergence of God's creative intent, and our capacity (by grace) to receive God's self-communication. "The God-Man is the initial beginning and the definitive triumph of the movement of the world's self-transcendence into absolute closeness to the mystery of God."[38]

Even if the end of creation and humanity is to accept God's mystery, we are obstructed from receiving it because of sin. The necessity of the incarnation, then, is that Jesus provides both God's *offer* of self-communication and humanity's *acceptance* of it. Like many others in the modern period, Rahner avoids abstract metaphysical categories in interpreting Chalcedon. The divine and human natures are described in terms of the offer and acceptance of salvation. Jesus is the "absolute Savior," who is "the climax of God's self-communication to the world . . . *both* the absolute promise of God to spiritual creatures as a whole *and* the acceptance of this self-communication."[39] Rahner's account of salvation in Christ is thoroughly incarnational: it is the coming of the Savior in the flesh that saves. Jesus's death alone does not save, but is seen in light of the entire story of redemption in offering and receiving God's very self.

Indeed, for Rahner, Christ's resurrection takes precedence over the crucifixion. We can only understand his death in light of Easter. In Rahner's account, resurrection is not simply a miraculous event two thousand years in the past. Instead, it is the capstone of the movement of creation toward divine Mystery, symbolizing the eternal acceptance of Jesus by God. "*This* Jesus with his *concrete* claim and his history is experienced in the resurrection experience as of permanent validity and as accepted by God. . . . There is present with him a new and unsurpassable closeness of God which on its part will prevail victoriously and is inseparable from him."[40] In dying, Jesus gives himself over to the Mystery that is God; in rising from the dead, God eternally validates the trajectory of Jesus's being-for-God.

Perhaps Rahner's most significant and thought-provoking contribution to Christology is his account of the saving work of Christ in relation to other religious traditions. Rahner holds firm to Catholic dogma that Christ alone saves. But his account of this saving work is not restricted to the Roman Catholic Church, or even Christianity itself. Wherever and whenever persons become opened to divine Mystery, to the gift of holy presence, there Christ is at work; there people are being saved. Rahner makes a distinction between "explicit" Christianity, where persons use the language of the church to describe salvation, and "anonymous" Christianity, where persons do not have such language. But Christ is really at work to save the world regardless of how and when such language is employed. "Christ is present and operative in non-Christian believers and hence in non-Christian religions in and through his *Spirit*."[41] Though some have faulted Rahner for the "imperialistic" implications of this stance (Christians having a superior vocabulary for describing others' religious experience), his point is to give an account for the conviction that God is really at work in Christ to save the whole world: If Christianity belongs to Christ, Christ certainly doesn't belong to Christianity alone.

Rahner's Christology is deeply incarnational, philosophically sophisticated, and at times difficult to understand. But his approach to Jesus has been enormously influential, not only in Catholic theology. His approach senses the interconnection between creation and incarnation and the relentless desire for God to communicate God's very self to creation. Many have described his Christology as "orthodoxy in modern dress," which seems an apt description. Some have claimed that he relies too heavily on Heideggerian-influenced philosophy; others have sensed in his work a deeply Ignatian motif of "finding God in all things." I believe the latter is more accurate. If his account of "anonymous Christianity" may not account sufficiently for the differences between religious traditions, at least his account of Christ's saving work is not restricted to persons who explicitly profess Christian faith.

Hans Urs von Balthasar (1905–1988)

Sometimes viewed as a counterpoint to Rahner, in part because his theology was favored by Pope John Paul II and Benedict XVI, Hans Urs von Balthasar was born in Lucerne and received a classical Catholic education. His university studies included time in Zürich, Vienna, and Berlin, where he engaged in both philosophy and literature. In 1929, he became a member of the Jesuit order and engaged in a variety of enterprises, including editing a magazine and as a student chaplain. He had longstanding friendships with the mystic Adrienne von Speyr and with Karl Barth. The relationship with the former led to the founding of a religious order whose members would engage in their "secular" professions as well as the life of the community. After leaving the Jesuits in 1950, he devotes himself to a massive trilogy, often considered his masterpiece. Appointed by John Paul II to become cardinal, Balthasar dies a few days before assuming the office. His Christology displays both aesthetic and dramatic dimensions, most notably in his interpretation of Christ's self-giving, which is the pattern of Jesus's life and God's life for the world.

One of Balthasar's favored names for Jesus is the One "sent." He is the one who carries out the Father's mission, to bear the onslaught of the world's sin in order that the world might be redeemed through him. Jesus is unwavering in carrying out this mission, in full obedience to the will of the Father. Balthasar thus claims that the incarnation is not a "necessity" in order to redeem sin, but is carried out in freedom. Jesus's mission "is like the artist or scholar who is so possessed by his vocation that he only feels free, only feels totally himself, when he is able to pursue this task that is so much his own."[42] Jesus's mission extends to all humanity, so that we might be drawn into this vocation. In Balthasar's words, we "are not only negatively 'redeemed' but positively endowed with missions ('charisms') that make [us] persons of profile and quality within the prototypical mission of Jesus."[43] Jesus's mission, in other words, is for *us* to be included in his mission.

The cross plays a prominent role in this mission. And though it is an example of agony and forsakenness, not only human but also divine ("Jesus reveals how God is forsaken by sinners"[44]), the cross is also a locus of beauty. Aesthetics, in fact, plays a dominant role throughout Balthasar's theology. He offers a reading of Christian faith through the lenses of the classical virtues—truth, goodness, and beauty—but by beginning his trilogy with beauty, he counters much of the classical tradition (where aesthetics is often relegated to third place). To understand what beauty is, we look to the life and death of Jesus. This "drama" of the cross is also enacted in Trinitarian life. What is beautiful here is the eternity of self-giving, donation, and receiving. What happens on the cross is also what happens in God: "The Son's answer to the gift of Godhead . . . can only be eternal thanksgiving (*eucharistia*) to the Father, the Source—a thanksgiving as selfless and unreserved as the Father's original self-surrender."[45] What happens in God's life happens in the life of Jesus, and is enacted and remembered in the sacrament of the Eucharist. Thus Balthasar's Christology is also sacramental, in that the patterns of table make present the ongoing mission of Christ in the world. "We are justified in thinking backward from the Eucharist—the Son's ultimate self-giving—to the covenant that it makes possible, and from there again to the creation that gains its meaning from the covenant."[46]

The most revolutionary aspect of Balthasar's Christology is his extended reflection on Christ's descent into hell. This is a topic about which many theologians—especially in the twentieth century—have remained silent. Some have seen it as a remnant of a more primitive worldview. But for Balthasar, the descent takes center stage, since it represents the vast extent of the divine mission, and Jesus's unwavering obedience to it. In descending to hell, Jesus undergoes the depths of sin's onslaught, everything that stands in opposition to God and God's purposes, all the while remaining divine. It is the ultimate extent of Jesus's self-emptying (*kenosis*):

> This opposition between God, the creative origin (the "Father"), and the man who, faithful to the mission of the origin, ventures

> on into ultimate perdition (the "son"), this bond stretched to breaking point does not break because the same Spirit of absolute love (the "spirit") informs both the one who sends and the one sent. God causes God to go into abandonment by God while accompanying him on the way with his Spirit.[47]

In this descent into hell, there is no withholding, no slackening of mission, only the radical depths to which Jesus goes in order to fulfill his mission, even to the point of abandonment. In this sense, the descent offers the most poignant moment of the Jesus drama: the One who is Sent to all, no matter the cost.

Balthasar's portrait of Jesus is less philosophical than it is literary, most effective in riveting our attention to the drama revealed in Christ. In Jesus, we see the pattern of theo-drama for all creation. Indeed, this Christology might be most suggestive in the ways that it demonstrates how philosophy falls short in portraying the person and work of Christ. Nonetheless, his employment of dramatic imagery relies on categories (such as "hell") that some would question as adequate for our time. That being said, the drama that Balthasar describes is one that is hard to ignore.

Dietrich Bonhoeffer (1906–1945)

With one of the most compelling biographies of the past century, Dietrich Bonhoeffer is often described as a modern-day martyr. Born to a prominent Berlin family, Bonhoeffer was an accomplished musician whose turn to theological studies was something of a disappointment to his family. He studied with several of the giants of liberal theology and spent a pivotal year in the United States at Union Seminary (New York), where his exposure to the plight of African Americans awakened him to the persecution of Jews in his homeland. He returned to a lectureship at the University of Berlin, and became more politically outspoken when Hitler rose to power in 1933. Two years later, he became director of an underground seminary that was later closed by the Nazis. In ensuing years, he became increasingly involved in the resistance, eventually becoming involved in a plot to assassinate Hitler. This led to his arrest, imprisonment, and death in a concentration camp during the closing months of World War II. Bonhoeffer's theology emerges in the context of these varied struggles and crises. His Christology thus shifts over time, beginning with fairly orthodox sacramentalism, turning subsequently to an ethical "command" Jesus, and finally to a "religionless" Christology toward the end of his life.

Bonhoeffer's first foray into christological thinking comes through the lens of ecclesiology, in his doctoral dissertation, *Sanctorum Communio*. In it, he has a fairly orthodox, "high church" Lutheran understanding of the church as sacrament. But the church is also a human institution, subject to the whims, mistakes, and sin of humanity. Nonetheless, church is where Christ is encountered. "*The history of the church is the hidden center of world history*. . . . For the church is Christ existing as church-community. . . . *The body of Christ is a real presence in history, and at the same time the norm for its own history*."[48] Jesus, in this view, is the One who creates a new community, calls us to become members of it, his body, and is present whenever we gather in his name.

In a later work, composed while he is directing the underground seminary, Bonhoeffer turns to Christ as the One who places a radical call on his followers. In this work, he criticizes how the church has turned the gospel of Christ into "cheap grace" that requires no resistance to the status quo, no willingness to sacrifice. Jesus calls us to costly grace: "It is grace, because it calls us to follow *Jesus Christ*. It is costly, because it costs people their lives; it is grace, because it thereby makes them live. It is costly, because it condemns sin; it is grace, because it justifies the sinner."[49] In the shape of Jesus's life, we see the cost of discipleship, for he is the one who gives up his life. We see in Jesus the cost to God and to humanity, for it costs the life of God's Son. But only in giving up one's life, surrendering it to God, is Jesus's life gained, and also the life of the world. Jesus issues a difficult and binding call: To find life one has to lose it.

When Bonhoeffer is imprisoned, his Christology takes yet another turn. These reflections are hardly systematic, since they occur in letters written to friends. Nonetheless, we can trace some discernible lines within them. Foremost among them is that Jesus is the "man for others," one whose very existence is formed by the gift of himself to others. Jesus's life here becomes a pattern for our own: We find life not in isolation, but in being bound to others, in responsible action on behalf of others. We also find Christ in the midst of acts of solidarity with others. In this phase, Bonhoeffer becomes increasingly disillusioned with the "establishment" church, and perhaps even religion itself. "What is bothering me incessantly is the question what Christianity really is, or indeed who Christ really is, for us today. The time when people could be told everything by means of words, whether theological or pious, is over, and so is the time of inwardness and conscience—and that means the time of religion in general."[50] Bonhoeffer shies away from metaphysical interpretations of Jesus; instead, his read is existential. Jesus does not belong to the church, but to the world: "Christ is no longer an object of religion, but something quite different, really the Lord of the world."[51] We encounter Christ as he calls us to embrace that world.

To embrace the world, however, is not to view it through rose-tinted glasses. Bonhoeffer urges those who would follow Christ's call to consider history from the "underside," from those who are oppressed. There we meet the crucified and risen Christ. "The Christian, unlike the devotees of the redemption myths, has no last line of escape available from earthly tasks and difficulties into the eternal, but, like Christ himself ('My God, why hast thou forsaken me?'), he must drink the earthly cup to the dregs, and only in his doing so is the crucified and risen Lord with him, and he crucified and risen with Christ."[52] God reveals God's very self in Christ, not in triumph and glory, but in taking the cause of the lowly. Bonhoeffer claims that in Christ we witness "God's powerlessness and suffering; only the suffering God can help. . . . The God of the Bible . . . wins power and space in the world by his weakness."[53] In following Christ, we also participate in the suffering of God for the world. Bonhoeffer thus resurrects patripassianism, the claim that *God* suffers in Christ. But he does this primarily to underscore divine solidarity with the suffering of the world. Because, in Christ, God experiences suffering, nothing is remote from the saving grace of Christ.

In these letters composed months before his death, Bonhoeffer rearticulates Jesus as the One who calls. But it is not a call to religion. Faith in Christ, is primarily trust in the new life that one is given in him. We are to be "caught up in the messianic sufferings of God in Jesus Christ. . . . The 'religious act' is always something partial; 'faith' is something whole, involving the whole of one's life. Jesus calls men, not to a new religion, but to life."[54] Though he eschews this label, Bonhoeffer suggests a "secular" Jesus, whose chief concern is not right belief, but right action in a world gone astray.

Bonhoeffer's varied Christology shows signs of adaptation over time. It is hardly systematic, but it is ethically compelling, especially considering the scope of Bonhoeffer's life. Its strength is in recalling that Jesus's teaching and healing ministry was occupied with *others* and in calling his disciples *to others*. To follow Jesus, for Bonhoeffer, is to embark on a way of life, to be summoned by others, and to find Christ in the midst of that summons. If some of the traditional soteriological questions in this Christology are less clear (how does Christ save in this framework?), at least the emphasis on costly grace is consistent throughout.

Vatican II (1962–1965)

Convened by John XXIII in 1959, commencing its official sessions at St. Peter's in 1962, the Second Vatican Council was a watershed moment in the history of the church. More than two thousand bishops were in attendance, as well as nearly a hundred observers from other Christian communions. The volume of writings produced by the council was astonishing, especially in comparison to previous ecumenical councils. John XXIII convened the council announcing the need for a spirit of *aggiornamento*, or renewal, in the church. He was convinced that the church needed to open its windows, to become more attentive to the work of the Spirit blowing in the world. And if the church adopted a less defensive posture vis-à-vis the modern world, those who had become alienated from the church would eventually come home. The council thus had an evangelical spirit at its core, even as it stressed the need for dialogue. The bulk of the official documents that arose from the council centered on ecclesiology, and many important liturgical reforms resulted from the council (e.g., movement from the language of the Mass from Latin to the vernacular; communion in both kinds). The documents also pay particular attention to the role of the church in the modern world, encouragement in ecumenical efforts, and the need for dialogue with persons of other religions (especially in relation to Jews). The documents also reveal a Christocentric core: Christ is the head of the church, the crown of humanity, and the One who is at work reconciling the world to God's very self.

John XXIII's opening remarks to the council noted that "Christ is ever resplendent as the center of history and of life."[55] This conviction, in many respects, runs throughout the documents: The turn to the world and the turn to Christ are one and the same. The call of the church, as a "pilgrim people," a people on the way to ultimate consummation in Christ, is also a call to the neighbor. Yet in pointing to Christ the center, the Vatican II documents pay significant attention to the circumstances of Jesus's history, as portrayed in the Gospels. The One who is ruler of the cosmos is also a Poor One. This is an element often neglected in earlier strands of nineteenth- and twentieth-century theology. In some respects, the conciliar documents anticipate movements of liberation theology, which arose in Latin America after the council. *Lumen Gentium*, the Dogmatic Constitution on the Church, notes that the memory of the poor Christ is a call for the church to present solidarity and action: "Just as Christ carried out the work of redemption in poverty and oppression, so the Church is called to follow the same path if she is to communicate the fruits of salvation to men."[56] Jesus's material poverty is not simply a historical accident: It is intimately connected with the way God chooses to reveal Godself—through the lowly—and serves an example for the present mission of the church, to be for the poor. In like manner, *Gaudium et Spes*, the Pastoral Constitution on the Church in the Modern World, highlights Jesus's occupation: "Let Christians follow the example of Christ who worked as a craftsman."[57] If the great class divide in the ancient world was between the underprivileged, who worked with their hands, and the privileged, who did not, the example of Jesus shows that God comes for the sake of the worker. In this regard, the Christology of Vatican II also contains the explicit blessing of human activity and labor: By becoming incarnate in this poor worker, God in Christ elevates the dignity of all work.

A humanizing tenor is evident in much Vatican II Christology. Jesus comes to humanity to reveal what it means to be human, to take us where we are meant to be all along. "Whoever follows Christ the perfect man becomes himself more a man."[58] God reveals in Christ our human vocation to be made partners with God in the ongoing work of Christ: "For since Christ died for all . . . we must hold that the Holy Spirit offers to all the possibility of being made partners, in a way known to God, in the paschal mystery."[59] Jesus shows us the shape of a redeemed life, to be radically for God and for one another. Liberated from sin, we are set free to be in community: "This communitarian character is perfected and fulfilled in the work of Jesus Christ, for the Word made flesh willed to share in human fellowship."[60] This is hardly an overspiritualized vision of salvation; Christ directs us to this world, to our neighbor in need, to this life. In recalling the details of his life, we are taught to cherish our lives and the life of the world.

One additional mark of Vatican II Christology is how it holds together (and perhaps in tension) straightforward affirmations about salvation exclusively through Christ with the hope that all might be saved. Like its ecclesiological declarations, which assert a priority to the Roman Catholic Church, many christological pronouncements echo classic Christian exclusivism:

"The Church believes that Christ, who died and was raised for the sake of all, can show man the way and strengthen him through the Spirit in order to be worthy of his destiny; nor is there any name under heaven given among men by which they can be saved."[61] Christ alone saves; nonetheless, Christ is working to save humanity outside the channels of those who name him as Savior. The church belongs to Christ, not vice versa. In a strikingly inclusive statement, *Lumen Gentium* notes, "Those who, through no fault of their own, do not know the Gospel of Christ or his Church, but who nevertheless seek God with a sincere heart, and moved by grace, try in their actions to do his will as they know it through the dictates of their conscience—those too may achieve eternal salvation."[62] The net here is a wide one: it might include those who have rejected the church out of a false understanding of it (or the church's defective proclamation of the gospel), or those of other religious traditions who do not know the gospel. The Rahnerian strain here is evident, even if the claim of "anonymous Christianity" is not. Christ is at work in all persons of goodwill and not only within Christians.[63]

Vatican II Christology institutes some important moves in both Roman Catholic and wider circles. It does so not primarily by "innovating," but by resurfacing several elements from earlier portrayals of Jesus. By uplifting Jesus's poverty and trade, the documents turn attention to the specter of poverty on a global scale. By claiming that Jesus reveals who we are, the documents recall Jesus as the healer of humanity. And by intimating that salvation in Christ is not restricted to the pronouncements of the church, the documents give voice to a universal hope that is present in some of the earliest Christologies of all (such as Origen's). Figuring out how much the post–Vatican II church has lived into these documents is a topic of endless debate. But the fact remains that the documents stand as authority in a truly global church.

Raimon Panikkar (1918–2010)

In many respects, Raimon Panikkar embodies the pluralism of the global age. Son of a Hindu father from India and a Catholic mother from Spain, Panikkar was born in Barcelona and eventually earned doctorates in philosophy, chemistry, and theology. Ordained as a Jesuit in 1946, he traveled extensively and taught in India for a time before eventually settling in the United States, where he held a professorate at the University of California, Santa Barbara. His writings are voluminous, often covering cross-cultural and interfaith topics (primarily among Christianity, Buddhism, and Hinduism). At the heart of his writing is what he dubs a "cosmotheandric" vision, according to which reality displays three dimensions: the divine, the earthly, and the human. All things reveal this threefold structure, and in some respects this represents Panikkar's rearticulation of the Trinity. His Christology contains much of this vision, along with explicit interfaith concerns.[64]

At the heart of Panikkar's Christology is a reinterpretation of the Philippians Christ hymn. Jesus is the embodiment of self-emptying, which is the pattern for divine, human, and planetary life. This kenotic movement is first present in the life of God. The Father empties himself in begetting the Son. The Son, in turn, empties himself and creates the universe. And the Spirit unites Father and Son and represents the goal of creation itself: reunification with the divine.[65] Jesus's death on the cross is the prime example of this pattern of kenosis, a dying that gives rise to greater life. For Panikkar, this amounts to a death of the ego, a dying to self-sufficiency. We see in Jesus the pattern of self-emptying for the sake of life: "He was one with the Origin of the universe, although in fact he was not the Origin; he had come from the Source and he had to return to the Source."[66] Jesus "goes out" from the Father in order to return to him. This, in short, is also how Jesus "saves" humanity: by showing the pattern of real life. As Don Schweitzer notes, "For Panikkar, Jesus saves not by doing as much as by enlightening."[67] Jesus shows us the pattern present in all life, as we are opened to this pattern, we too might embody it in our lives. Dying to our egos, we might rise again.

It is easy to see the influence of both Hindu and Buddhist strains in this Christology. In some respects, Panikkar reads like an apologetic for Christian faith, articulated through Hindu or Buddhist lenses. But this does not mean that Panikkar adopts all Eastern categories uncritically. Indeed, there are some aspects to Christology that question Eastern concepts. One of them is the concept of a suffering deity, revealed in Christ: "Hinduism attempts to go beyond the great scandal of pain and suffering by denying the existence of this pain and this suffering. Then they see that in Christianity pain and suffering have entered into the very heart of this God who came down to earth."[68] Likewise, the Buddhist theme of "detachment" runs strongly throughout: Jesus returns to the Father by letting go. One way of understanding sin is by unwarranted attachment to things of creation. Jesus saves by showing us the way of detachment and by finding rest in God.

Some have accused Panikkar of ignoring the historicity of the crucifixion. His primary concern is not with the events surrounding the cross, but how they present a universal pattern for God's life and for ours. Yet if we consider Panikkar's intent, to promote dialogue and mutual understanding between traditions, then this critique seems less significant. And it might suggest how his approach avoids relegation of the cross to the distant past. Nonetheless, there is something highly speculative to Panikkar's Christology: As much as he attends to one historical pattern (kenosis), his vision of salvation in Christ eventually takes us out of history itself.

Jürgen Moltmann (1926–)

Few contemporary theologians have had as wide an impact as Jürgen Moltmann. Born in northern Germany, Moltmann was drafted as a teenager in the waning months of World War II and spent the concluding months of that conflict in British prisoner-of-war camps. Emerging from this cataclysm—and being confronted with the horror of Nazi atrocities—Moltmann became a Christian and eventually studied theology during the heyday of neo-orthodoxy, earning a doctorate in 1952. Moltmann's first widely read book, *Theology of Hope*, recovers an eschatological orientation to Christian theology with an eye toward social transformation. His *Crucified God* proved even more influential, with its argument that the crucifixion is a Trinitarian event. A prolific writer, Moltmann's work has also engaged the ecological crisis and the yawning gulf of wealth between the Northern and Southern Hemispheres. His Christology is most significant in how it articulates Jesus's crucifixion and resurrection.

Moltmann centers his study of Jesus on the cross, recovering elements of Luther's approach, but revolutionizing it by considering the cross as the defining event in the life of *God*. Jesus's cry of dereliction, as recorded by Matthew and Mark, captures the essence of the crucifixion: forsakenness. But for Moltmann, it is not only Jesus's forsakenness that matters: "In the forsakenness of the Son the Father also forsakes himself. In the surrender of the Son the Father also surrenders himself. . . . To understand what happened between Jesus and his God and Father on the cross, it is necessary to talk in Trinitarian terms. The Son suffers dying, the Father suffers the death of the Son."[69] Jesus on the cross reveals the very heart of God—a God who suffers with humanity for the sake of humanity. Moltmann thus resuscitates the stance of patripassianism—the idea of divine suffering—in light of the cataclysms of the twentieth century. In the shadow of Auschwitz, in the wake of horrific wars, theologians such as Moltmann began to question theological stances that kept God at a distance from suffering. The God of redemption, Moltmann claims, is never removed from the pain of the world, but incorporates it into divine life, bears it, and offers possibilities of healing in response. To be sure, Moltmann is not claiming that God suffers in the same way that humanity does or that Jesus does. What God suffers is in experiencing the death of God's children, both Jesus and all children in the world.

The cross reveals this heart of God even more clearly than Jesus's birth or teaching. To understand who Jesus is, we look first to the end of his life on Golgotha. When we do, we see that what happened on that hill is not only an event within history, but the defining event in the history of God.

> The concrete "history of God" in the death of Jesus on the cross on Golgotha therefore contains within itself all the depths and abysses of human history and therefore can be understood as the history of history. All human history, however much it may be determined by guilt and death, is taken up into this "history of God," i.e. into the Trinity, and integrated into the future of the "history of God." There is no suffering which in this history of God is not God's suffering; no death which has not been God's death in the history on Golgotha.[70]

In addition to the echoes of Luther here, one can also sense the influence of Hegel. Moltmann, in no uncertain terms, considers the crucifixion to reveal the unfolding of God's action in history, and God's incorporation of world history into God's life. Moltmann's portrait of Jesus thus leads to a speculative doctrine of God. In a scientific age when much God-talk can seem problematic, Moltmann senses in the cross of Jesus ways of speaking about God that make sense to a world in agony.

As much as Moltmann's depiction of Jesus centers on the cross, his Christology does not leave Jesus or humanity hanging there. The cross is resolved in resurrection, which is the eschatological validation of the life of Jesus—and all human life—fulfilled in God. But unlike the crucifixion, which is an event within history, Christ's resurrection cannot be reduced to history. The resurrection cannot be classified alongside other events in history. Instead, Jesus's resurrection is *proleptic*: It looks forward and anticipates the resurrection of all. Moltmann claims that there are "no analogies" for resurrection in history. "'Raising of the dead' is an expression which looks expectantly towards the future proof of God's creative power over the non-existent."[71] And while Jesus's resurrection points to God's validation of the life of Jesus, the promise of God's presence incarnate in that life, we misunderstand the resurrection if we only see it as glorifying Jesus. For Moltmann, Christ's resurrection is as much a *future* event as it is contained in the past. "It points beyond itself, and even beyond Jesus, to the coming revelation of the glory of God."[72] In this sense, Moltmann's portrayal of Jesus is other-referential. Christ's resurrection, in this reading, has already happened *and* is always on the way. We are drawn into the future as we participate in the new life that Christ gives today.

Moltmann's Christology recovers themes that had become submerged in other portraits of Jesus. Especially attentive to the suffering of Jesus, it offers a lens for confronting the cataclysms of the past century while refusing to give those horrors the last word in history. By speculatively considering the crucifixion as an event in the life of God, Moltmann also counters a functional deism that often creeps into modern discussions. Moltmann's writings, to be sure, are voluminous, and the survey above only captures the basics of his christological vision. Nonetheless, one question is worth asking: How do Jesus's teaching and healing ministry fit into the cruciform pattern of his life?

Gustavo Gutiérrez (1928–)

Born in Lima, Peru, to a working-class family, Gustavo Gutiérrez experienced multiple health issues as a child but became a gifted student, eventually studying at universities in Peru, Belgium, and France. His doctorate in theology was earned at the University of Lyon, where he studied under the influence of modernists such as Yves Congar and Henri de Lubac. After these studies, he returns to Peru and pursues pastoral work in the barrios of Lima. There he experiences some tension between his theological training and the oppressive economic and political realities of the poor in his native land. He works closely with "base communities," groups of Christians who study the Bible and the Christian life in the context of political/economic oppression. This leads to his authorship of the first major book in the movement of liberation theology, *A Theology of Liberation*, published in 1971. The movement asserts a "preferential option for the poor," which emphasizes the well-being (physical, economic, political) of those on the underside of history. God grants the poor special favor, and the poor also have access to the gospel because of their condition. In the subsequent decades, this theological movement has had enormous influence, and though some of its exponents have incurred censure or silencing from the Vatican, Gutiérrez never has. Currently professor at Notre Dame, he continues an active speaking and writing career. His Christology emphasizes the liberating role of Jesus and offers a holistic understanding of salvation in him.

Two images lie at the heart of Gutiérrez's liberation theology: (1) the exodus, which symbolizes the journey out of slavery into freedom and wholeness; and (2) Jesus, who is the Liberator of all humanity. Jesus is the paradigmatic figure of liberation: "The liberating action of Christ—made human in this history and not in a history marginal to real human life—is at the heart of the historical current of humanity; the struggle for a just society is in its own right very much a part of salvation history."[73] Jesus is Liberator because he is the proclaimer of the kingdom: the coming reign of God that promises justice and wholeness to all. We see what that kingdom looks like when we look to Jesus. In welcoming the outcast, in healing the sick, in proclaiming good news to the poor, in dining with sinners, Jesus embodies the kingdom. His actions are political and economic, though they cannot be reduced to these categories. The mistake of some Christologies is that they have ignored the political and economic aspects of the gospel and rendered them "spiritual." But Jesus comes to address the whole person, not just one aspect of our humanity or one faction of persons: "Without liberating historical events, there would be no growth of the Kingdom. . . . In Christ, the all-comprehensiveness of the liberating process reaches its fullest sense."[74] Jesus embodies God's new reign and invites us to be participants in it as it becomes real in history.

Salvation in Christ, in this reading, is intensely this-worldly, though it is not reduced to the terrestrial. Gutiérrez views his work as a corrective: "Salvation is not something otherworldly, in regard to which the present life is merely a test."[75] This seems to be a direct counter to the Marxist charge that religion is the opiate of the masses: By teaching Christians to acquiesce to the status quo, the church promises the ultimate reward in the sweet by and by. For Gutiérrez, by contrast, the hope of salvation in Christ is also hope for *this* life, *this* world. Salvation in Christ is restoration to life in its fullness: with others, in all dimensions of life. There is no complete sense of salvation without attention to the physical, economic, and political dimensions of life.

In this sense, salvation in Christ is the culmination of God's creative work. Jesus unveils for us the dawning of the new creation, where all will partake in life's fullness. While Jesus inaugurates that new day, he also summons us to take part in it. There is no passivity here. Salvation is not merely given to us; we are not justified simply because of Christ's alien righteousness. Instead, we are called to labor on behalf of the new creation. Christ's work, in no uncertain terms, is supplemented by our work. "To work, to transform this world, is to become a man and to build the human community; it is also to save."[76] This latter emphasis has led some to charge Gutiérrez with Pelagianism, that salvation ultimately is something that we earn because of our own efforts. But if we keep the context of Gutiérrez's theological work in mind—the grinding poverty of Lima's barrios—then this charge is answered. The point is not to earn salvation, but to correct distortions of Jesus's person and work that have rendered them otherworldly. The greatest strength of Gutiérrez's portrait of Jesus is how it emphasizes Christ's transformative work. In this vision, the kingdom is not a lollipop presented at the end of life, but a newness in the midst of life that remembers Jesus's own proclamation for the poor. Jesus is good news for the whole person and the whole people of God.

Sallie McFague (1933–)

Born in Massachusetts and educated at Yale under the guidance of H. Richard Niebuhr, Sallie McFague earned her PhD in theology in 1964, at a time when very few women were teaching or pursuing research in American theological education. An Anglican, McFague spent most of her teaching career at Vanderbilt Divinity School, where she also served as dean. Her theological work is multifaceted. It focuses on the nature of religious language, stressing *metaphor* as a primary means of speech. It also is deeply committed to feminist principles and the liberating nature of Christian faith for women. Especially in her most recent work, McFague is one of the pioneers of ecological theology, the question of how Christian theology has both been implicated in the current ecological crisis, and how Christian faith might be brought to bear in ways that promote the healing of creation. This ecological turn became most prominent in *The Body of God*, published in 1993, which contains her most explicit Christology. In McFague's portrayal, Jesus comes for the sake not of humanity, but of all creation.

In this work, McFague's main argument is that we need to *relativize* our understanding of the incarnation in relation to Jesus and to *maximize* it in relation to the cosmos. Christian theology, she argues, has become not just Christocentric, but Jesus-centric. We have turned our eye so closely to Jesus that we have become unable to glimpse the presence of God throughout creation. "Everything that is is the sacrament of God, but here and there we find that presence erupting in special ways. Jesus is one such place for Christians, but there are other paradigmatic persons and events."[77] In this regard, her Christology places Jesus within the story of the cosmos. When we follow this lead, McFague claims that we become more attentive to the oppressed in our midst, including the earth, which is under threat. McFague's portrayal of Jesus takes cues from liberation theology, while widening that theology's focus to include the more-than-human world. And yet this move is not merely necessary in light of the women followers. Theologically, Ruether claims, Jesus's contemporary ecological crisis; McFague also argues that it is actually more faithful to ancient traditions, particularly Christian sacramentalism, which have consistently claimed God's presence *throughout* creation.

Even as Christology takes a cosmic turn, the life of Jesus still matters. We turn to Jesus first to see the shape of God's activity in, with, and under the world. Jesus, in this regard, is the shape of God's body for the world. We look first at Jesus and then that glance moves outward; Jesus unfolds into the world. "*The story of Jesus suggests that the shape of God's body includes all, especially the needy and outcast*. . . . The distinctive characteristic of Christian embodiment is its focus on oppressed, vulnerable suffering *bodies*, those who are in pain due to the indifference or greed of the more powerful."[78] The echoes of liberation theology and Moltmann are apparent here: Jesus Christ is the vulnerable One for all vulnerable ones on the planet—including the vulnerable planet itself. Nature, in this reading, is the "new poor." And when we consider the ministry of Jesus—how he gathers sinners together, dines with prostitutes, heals lepers, and proclaims good news to the poor—our eyes are turned to all who are vulnerable. To follow Jesus is to become a part of a movement that heals the body, where the hungry are fed, the sick healed, the enslaved go free.

McFague locates her theology within the lengthy history of Christian sacramentalism, which suggests that nature is charged with the grandeur of God.[79] The physicality of the world is a conduit of God's presence and God's intention, such that God can be encountered throughout creation. Nevertheless, we look to specific places—the ministry of Jesus of Nazareth, the bread and wine of the Lord's Supper—to gain clarity about the *shape* of that presence. McFague is thus not offering an undifferentiated nature spirituality, but a version of Christian sacramentalism that is grounded in the claims the church makes about Jesus Christ. Her work offers a cosmic Christ that links the Christian scandal of particularity—the incarnation of Jesus of Nazareth—with God's presence in all of creation.

One example of this linkage is her interpretation of the resurrection. We make a mistake, she claims, if we see resurrection as only a miracle that happened to Jesus. Something happened to Jesus, but the resurrection is more comprehensive than an event of the first century. Instead, Jesus's resurrection is paradigmatic for the life God gives to the world: "That life, not death, is the last word; that against all evidence to the contrary, all our efforts on behalf of the well-being of our planet and especially of its most vulnerable creatures, including human ones, will not be defeated. It is the belief that the source and power of the universe is on the side of life and its fulfillment."[80]

In even more recent work, McFague has taken up the theme of Christ's kenosis as paradigmatic for the life of the world. On a planet threatened by climate change, in an economic system that fosters extraction and exploitation of "natural resources," Jesus's example of self-giving and self-emptying offers a way to a sustainable future. The point of Jesus's life was not a one-time sacrifice for the sake of all, but to show us a way of simplicity and restraint: to live so that others might live.[81] Like her earlier work on incarnation, the emphasis is on the *model* of Christ. Salvation in Christ is not some act taken on our behalf, but a pattern revealed in the life of Jesus that points to the pattern of abundant life in the world.

McFague's Christology is rich and multifaceted. At its heart is the conviction that attention to the particulars of Jesus (incarnation, a ministry for the poor, a pattern of self-emptying love) yields a model for sustainable life on a threatened planet. The shifts in this Christology are multiple: away from atonement toward incarnational solidarity; away from justification toward sacramentalism; away from human-centered visions of salvation toward creation-centered ones. Along the way, some of the patterns of the past are abandoned, but others are recovered. However one assesses these moves, one cannot ignore McFague's challenge that often the church's Christology is too small. In her portrayal, Jesus is good news for the earth and all creatures.

Mercy Amba Oduyoye (1934–)

One of the most influential contemporary African theologians, Mercy Amba Oduyoye was born in Ghana, where she earned her bachelor's degree at the University of Ghana. She received further theological training in Cambridge, which included a master's degree. A Methodist ecumenist, Oduyoye currently teaches at Trinity Theological Seminary in Accra, Ghana. Her work interweaves multiple concerns: feminist, liberation, and postcolonial theory. Committed to the full inclusion of women in the church, Oduyoye's Christology is also noteworthy in how it draws on African traditional religions, incorporating the vocabulary and themes of those traditions into a portrait of Jesus germane to African contexts.

Oduyoye has done much work to survey the varied portrayals of Jesus in Africa. Prominent among them are images of Jesus as warrior and liberator. These two images "give us hope for space in which to be truly human. The Liberator will set us free through the process of redemption."[82] On a continent still bearing the wounds of colonial exploitation and now experiencing the depredations of neocolonialism in the form of multinational corporations extracting resources from the land, Jesus comes as one to overturn systems of domination and to uplift the poor. Oduyoye's account, however, differs from Latin American liberation theology in its incorporation of indigenous terms: Jesus the liberator is also the ancestor, *Okyeame*, who "stands between humanity and God as the spokesperson"; he is the royal leader, *Osagyefo*, "the one who saves the battle, the victorious warrior."[83] Much of Oduyoye's portrayal of Jesus involves inculturation: Jesus, the incarnate Son of God, also becomes incarnate in the African context. He takes African culture as his own, blessing and claiming it. Jesus does not come as a Westernized stranger, but as an intimate, known as ancestor, leader, and warrior. In this sense, Oduyoye's Jesus documents the growth of Christian faith in the wake of missionary efforts. If Christianity was introduced to the African context by European missionaries, the Christianity that took root in Africa is indigenous, incorporating elements of African traditions as it gives voices to Jesus, the Word made flesh.

In addition to emphasizing African elements in her portrait of Jesus, Oduyoye attends to women's experiences. One of the more significant examples of this is how she interprets blood and the life of Jesus. Countless interpretations of Jesus throughout the centuries have focused on blood and the agony of the cross; few, however, have made the connection to the role that blood plays in women's fertility and the way that blood often functions to marginalize women. In a work coauthored with Elizabeth Amoah, she writes, "This Christ is the liberator from the burden of disease and the ostracism of a society riddled with blood-taboos and theories of inauspiciousness arising out of women's blood. Christ liberated women by being born of Mary, demanding that the woman bent double with gynecological disorders should stand up straight."[84] Jesus is good news for women because he redeems their blood: what had been previously seen as tainted is now healed. Salvation in Christ recognizes that blood is healing, blood is life.

Another image that Oduyoye uplifts is Jesus as husband. She cites a hymn common in some African contexts: "I am married to Jesus, Satan leave me alone. My husband is coming to take me away into everlasting love."[85] This nuptial image conveys intimacy between Christ and the believer. In some regards, this is a reappropriation of medieval monastic interpretations of Jesus, keen with eroticism. Jesus is the resolution of the heart's desire and the One who kindles desire's flame. Communion with Christ is a marriage of passion, enveloping body and soul. The flip side of this interpretation of Jesus is that he also functions, in some traditional African contexts, as mother. Though this image is often not explicit, it underscores the prominence of the mother in traditional societies. Oduyoye connects this mothering role of Jesus to his relationships with women, as recorded in the Gospels. "Jesus of Nazareth, by the counter-cultural relations he established with women, has become for us the Christ, the anointed one who liberates, the companion friend, teacher, and true 'Child of Woman.'"[86] Jesus, in this context, functions as mother in that he nurtures us as children of God, drawing out the best in us, providing for our security.

Oduyoye's Christology interweaves several themes: Gospel depictions of Jesus, traditional African imagery, erotic mysticism, liberation and feminist theology. The result is a portrait of Jesus that employs images seldom found in Western Christologies, with special reference to the cause of women's flourishing. If the rapid growth of Christianity in Africa over the past century is any indication, then this composite portrait of Jesus has been very appealing. What is particularly compelling about Oduyoye's Christology is the way that Jesus responds directly to the pain of women's marginalization by redeeming blood, by liberating women to full personhood and participation in the life of the community.

Rosemary Radford Ruether (1936–)

One of the pioneers of feminist theology in the United States, Rosemary Radford Ruether is a lay Catholic theologian whose work has influenced subsequent generations. Born in Minnesota to a Catholic-Episcopal family, Ruether's theological education was at Claremont, one of the centers of progressive Christian thought in the country. A prolific author of more than thirty books, Ruether's distinguished teaching career includes a long-term post at Garrett-Evangelical Theological Seminary. Her writings reveal strong commitments to feminism, women's ordination, the recovery of suppressed strands of Christian tradition, and ecology. Christologically, she made her most lasting contributions by posing provocative questions of inherited traditions. Through these critical questions, she offers the germ of an alternative Christology in her magnum opus, *Sexism and God-Talk.*

In this book, she begins her christological exploration with the following question: Can a male savior save women? The question has particular resonance in her Roman Catholic context, since the maleness of Christ constitutes the chief theological reason why women cannot be ordained to the priesthood. Because Jesus's maleness has been used to exclude women from aspects of the church's life, women have the right to pose the question of salvation in Christ this boldly. Ruether begins to explore the answer to this question through a genealogy of interpretations of Jesus. Her chief claim is that the church's vision of Jesus has become infected with patriarchy and the valorization of power. Early on in the tradition, the proclamation of Jesus as Messiah became wedded to notions of imperial power, resulting in a vision that proclaimed Christ as Lord *over* others. Over time, it became increasingly difficult to distinguish the lordship of Christ from that of earthly kings: "Christology becomes the apex of a system of control over all those who in one way or another are 'other' than this new Christian order."[87] The male Christ became the excuse for perpetuating male domination, and the dominion of Western empires. Ruether explores some alternative Christologies in the tradition—such as androgynous and spirit Christologies—but finds them deficient as well, because they either (1) claim that the female gender is something to be overcome in Christ, or (2) perpetuate stereotyped gender roles.

Ruether develops her alternative Christology through a recovery of neglected themes within the tradition, particularly elements of the Synoptic Gospels' portrayals of Jesus. Central to her reevaluation of Jesus is his proclamation of the kingdom of God. Like many others in the twentieth century, Ruether finds here a key to interpretation. This kingdom is neither "nationalistic nor other-worldly,"[88] but is decidedly this-worldly. When Jesus proclaims the kingdom, he denounces the present state of affairs and promises a new order that is becoming real in his presence. It is not a promise for the distant future, but one that is realized *now*. Jesus shows us the shape of this kingdom through his radical reversal of the worship of power: "By adapting the word *servant* (slave) . . . Jesus drastically reverses the social references of divine redemptive activity, identifying redemption with the lowest persons in society (slaves) rather than the highest (kings)."[89] Jesus comes to proclaim and embody an inversion of the current order: Salvation is found in the lowly who are uplifted. Right relation is not found in power over others, but in power-with and mutual empowerment. Salvation in Christ looks like the creation of a new community where all are welcomed, where the mighty relinquish their power, and the powerless are lifted up. Jesus's true power lies in his self-emptying of the trappings of power, and in doing so he shows us the shape of new life.

This retelling of the Jesus story results in a Christology that Ruether claims is compatible with feminism. In order to do so, one has to strip away the accumulated masculine "mythology about Jesus as Messiah or divine *Logos*."[90] Ruether's Christology is thus deconstructive, in its disconnecting of patriarchal imagery from Jesus, and reconstructive, in its recovery of the Synoptic Jesus. Jesus emerges as a feminist, perhaps even the archetypal feminist, because he is resolutely committed to the flourishing of women, as evidenced in his gathering of women followers. Theologically, Ruether claims, Jesus's maleness has "no ultimate significance," thus eviscerating christological arguments against women's ordination. He is the liberator of all humanity, not because he is male, but because "he has renounced this system of domination and seeks to embody in his person the new humanity of service and mutual empowerment."[91]

Ruether, like Gutiérrez, focuses on Jesus's creation of new community as liberator. But by adding the urgency of gender, she offers a portrait of Jesus that strikes new chords in the tradition. Jesus, in this view, is the champion of women's liberation par excellence, and he accomplishes this by relinquishing patriarchy. Jesus saves because he overturns systems of domination and exploitation, showing that they are ultimately empty. In a church and in a society where women's full personhood has routinely been ignored, this portrait of Jesus is surely good news. If Ruether's Christology neglects some of the cosmic nature of salvation, it is because the struggle for gender justice is still being waged.

Elizabeth Johnson (1941–)

Perhaps the most influential feminist Catholic theologian in the United States, Elizabeth Johnson was raised in an Irish Catholic family in Brooklyn, joined the Sisters of Saint Joseph, and eventually became the first woman to earn a doctorate in theology at Catholic University of America. After teaching at the elementary and high school levels, Johnson eventually takes a post at Fordham University, where she currently works. Her theological work is meticulous in its recovery of underdeveloped themes in the tradition, and principled in its commitment to women's flourishing. Her watershed book, *She Who Is*, offers a spin on Irenaeus's dictum *Gloria Dei vivens homo* (the glory of God is the person fully alive): *Gloria Dei vivens mulier* (the glory of God is all women, fully alive). This book also offers a rearticulation of Christology by considering Jesus the incarnation of Sophia, divine Wisdom.

Like Ruether, Johnson exposes the links between Christology and ecclesial practices that marginalize women. Patriarchal Christology has bequeathed a problematic legacy, rendering Jesus's maleness normative for humanity as a whole, resulting in the view of "an affinity between maleness and divinity."[92] In rejecting patriarchal interpretations of Jesus, however, Johnson does not jettison tradition. Instead, she probes it more deeply, lifting up the image of Sophia (God's wisdom) as a christological touchstone. This biblical image—found in sources such as Proverbs—is analogous to the divine Word. But in the biblical record, Sophia is routinely depicted as female and referred to as God's colaborer in the ongoing work of creation (Proverbs 8). Jesus of Nazareth, in Johnson's reading, is Wisdom incarnate.[93] Wisdom comes in the flesh, let loose in the world for the sake of the world's flourishing.

In recovering this often-neglected strand of tradition, Johnson also restates the significance of Jesus's cross and resurrection. Like many twentieth-century theologians, Johnson rejects Anselmian readings of the atonement that understand the cross as necessary in the scheme of divine justice. Instead, the cross is a deeply tragic symbol, pointing to the scar of violence within creation: "Jesus' death was an act of violence brought about by threatened human men, as sin, and therefore against the will of a gracious God."[94] The cross, in short, is an affront to God's purposes rather than its fulfillment. It reveals the depth of human sin rather than the depths of divine love. Nonetheless, Jesus freely submits to the death brought about by a sinful humanity, in solidarity with all who suffer violence in a broken world. "The victory of shalom is won not by the sword of a warrior god but by the awesome power of compassionate love, in and through solidarity with all those who suffer."[95] On the cross, Jesus chooses the side of all history's victims, particularly women who bear the brunt of religious violence.[96] In becoming crucified, Jesus chooses another way: "The crucified Jesus embodies the exact opposite of the patriarchal ideal of the powerful man, and shows the steep price to be paid in the struggle for liberation."[97] The cross, in this sense, also represents the death of patriarchy, the hope for a way beyond it.

Jesus's resurrection, according to Johnson, is God's vindication of this alternative way, which is ultimately the way of salvation and flourishing. Johnson avoids military imagery that often accompanies resurrection hope: the strife is over, the battle won. Instead, she considers the resurrection as the resolute hope of the alternative way. "Faith in the resurrection affirms that God has the last word for this executed victim of state injustice and that word, blessedly, is life."[98] Recalling some of the detail of the Gospel of John, Johnson's reading of resurrection doesn't move beyond the wounds of the cross. They remain in the remembered injustice of a state execution, the death of an innocent man at the hands of a government that worshiped power. If Jesus's resurrection shows that those governments are ultimately empty, it also recalls that the voices of their victims still call us. The martyrs remain, and their voices contribute to the new life that Christ gives.

Especially in Johnson's depiction of resurrection, one can hear the chorus of the saints. Jesus, the incarnate Wisdom, comes for the sake of all creation's flourishing, but in doing so calls us to attend to the voices of those who suffer—both in the present and in history. This may be her greatest christological contribution: seeing in Jesus the path to deeper relation to the communion of the saints.[99] In doing so, she also sows the seeds of an ecological theology, in which the glory of God is *creation* fully alive. Jesus, in this regard, opens his followers to a much wider world.

James Cone (1947–2018)

Regarded by most as the "father" of black theology of liberation, James Cone was born in Arkansas and reared in the African Methodist Episcopal Church. Theological studies took him to Garrett-Evangelical Theological Seminary and an eventual PhD at Northwestern University. His theological training was steeped in the currents of neo-orthodoxy, particularly Barth, though he also imbibed the writings of Tillich and the Niebuhrs. A distinguished professor of systematic theology at Union Theological Seminary, New York, until his death in 2018, Cone's theological breakthrough came as he confronted the near absence of engaging race—and the struggle for black liberation—as a theological category. White theology, regardless of its liberal or conservative bent, operated on a presumed universal plane, ignoring the particularities of race, class, and culture. This move, which rendered mainstream theology blind to the crisis of racism in America, amounted to a betrayal of the particularity of Christian faith: that God enters into history, covenanting with Israel, leading that people out of slavery into freedom, becoming incarnate in a marginalized Jew in the first century. Only by attending to this particularity can Christian faith address the sin of racism that infects society. In several noteworthy books, Cone develops the image of the black Christ as a constructive alternative to Christologies that ignore race and racial violence.

Much is captured in Cone's claim that Jesus Christ is black. On the one hand, it is a claim about race and the ways in which white theologies have distorted Jesus's race. As a person of Middle Eastern descent, Jesus of Nazareth did not look like the portraits that adorn most European and North American congregations. His "race," in other words, is other than white. But Cone's claim of a black Christ is also about more than race. It symbolizes Jesus's social condition as a person on the underside of history, and it demonstrates that the incarnation of Jesus is to demonstrate God's solidarity with all who are oppressed. The black Christ is not simply a category of race; it is rather a symbol for what humanity has made of race, class, and culture. "Christ is black, therefore, not because of some cultural or psychological need of black people, but because and only because Christ *really* enters into our world where the poor, the despised, and black are, disclosing that he is with them, enduring their humiliation and pain and transforming oppressed slaves into liberated servants. Indeed, if Christ is not *truly* black, then the historical Jesus lied."[100] Cone connects the blackness of Jesus to his Jewishness, as a member of a group of people oppressed in history.[101] The claim that he is black is not only for the black churches, but for the church at large. Indeed, for Cone, we understand Christ's significance for all only through the lens of his black particularity: "The validity of any Christological title in any period of history is not decided by its universality but by this: whether in the particularity of its time it points to God's universal will to liberate particular oppressed people from inhumanity. This is exactly what blackness does in the contemporary social existence of America."[102]

The cross plays particular significance in Cone's understanding of Christ: It reveals "God's suffering solidarity with the victims of the world. Jesus' cross is God's election of the poor by taking their pain and suffering upon the divine person."[103] Here Cone echoes other twentieth-century theologians such as Moltmann and Bonhoeffer who consider the cross as God's incorporation of the agony of the human condition into God's very life. Only by incorporating it into God's life can it be redeemed; and it reminds us that there is no place where God is absent. Cone reimagines substitutionary atonement, not in terms of an innocent human victim taking the place of sinful humanity, but God's willingness to substitute God's self for us: "The cross of Jesus is God invading the human situation as the Elected One who takes Israel's place as the Suffering Servant and thus reveals the divine willingness to suffer in order that humanity might be fully liberated."[104] In rising from the dead, Jesus reveals the purpose of the cross: to set oppressed humanity free.

In *The Cross and the Lynching Tree*, Cone connects the cross to the specter of racial violence in America, most notably in white lynchings of African Americans throughout history. Cone castigates white American theology for neglecting the obvious connection, for ignoring the cross in its midst. In missing this connection, white theology has distorted its depiction of Jesus. Cone writes powerfully: "*Every time a white mob lynched a black person, they lynched Jesus.* The lynching tree is the cross in America. When American Christians realize that they can meet Jesus only in the crucified bodies in our midst, they will encounter the real scandal of the cross."[105] Cone juxtaposes cross and lynching tree not in a facile way, so that cross erases the terror of lynching. Rather, he poses the lynching tree as a challenge: how it forces us to acknowledge the ongoing terror posed to black bodies (including mass incarceration) and the depths of sin. If Americans fail to make the connection between cross and lynching tree, they risk rendering the cross an empty symbol or abstraction. Confronted with the lynchings of past and present, we come face-to-face with ongoing terror, even as the cross reminds us that there is hope upon hope because Jesus himself hung on a tree.

Cone's Christology is riveting and convicting. It critiques much of the Western tradition for ignoring the racial overtones of its purportedly neutral descriptions of Jesus. It calls attention to the oppressed and arrestingly summons us to see the connections between cross and lynching tree. And yet what Cone offers is not only a reconstructed theology of the cross. His portrayal of Jesus is also deeply incarnational, as it reflects on the person, status, and culture of Jesus; and, it is thoroughly a Christology of resurrection as it indicates that death does not have the final word.

Jacquelyn Grant (1948–)

One of the leading figures in womanist theology, Jacquelyn Grant was born in South Carolina and attended a Catholic elementary school before graduating from a public high school. Her undergraduate studies were at the historically black Bennett College. After seminary, she pursued doctoral work at Union Theological Seminary, New York, under the supervision of James Cone. There she became the first African American woman to earn the PhD in systematic theology. Her teaching career has been chiefly at the Interdenominational Theological Center in Atlanta. Undoubtedly, her most influential publication is *White Women's Christ and Black Women's Jesus: Feminist Christology and Womanist Response*, which offers a sustained critique of feminist approaches to Jesus and a constructive alternative that draws on the narratives of black women in America. Her womanist approach to interpreting Jesus criticizes feminist theologies for inattention to race and black theology for inattention to gender. The result is a Christology that in some respects echoes Oduyoye, with particular resonance to the experiences of American women of color.

In her interpretation of Jesus, Grant probably pays more attention to "ordinary" theology than anyone else in this historical survey. Her sources for constructing a portrait of Jesus are as much the narratives of slave women on the American continent as they are the classics of the theological canon. In this process, she uncovers neglected classics within the tradition. Jesus is reflected in the lives of those who call him by name, and most of these people do not have theological degrees. Hers is a Christology of the people and of the church. The ordinary piety of these believers matters in our understanding of who Jesus is. As she surveys the tapestry of African American belief, she notes, "In the experiences of Black people, Jesus was 'all things.' Chief among these however, was the belief in Jesus as the divine co-sufferer, who empowers them in situations of oppression."[106] Black experience in America is inseparable from the reality and legacy of slavery. In confessing Jesus as Lord, African American women throughout history have called him One who embraces their condition. Grant cites slave narratives where there is explicit identification between women's suffering and the suffering of Jesus:

> Come to we, dear Massa Jesus. De sun, he hot too much, de road am dat long and boggy (sandy) and we ain't got no buggy for send and fetch Ooner. But Massa, you 'member how you walked dat hard walk up Calvary and ain't weary but tink about we all dat way. We know you ain't weary for to come to we. We pick out de torns, de prickles, de brier, de backslidin' and de quarrel and de sin out of you path so dey shan't hurt Ooner pierce feet no more.[107]

In testimonies such as this, not only the sufferings of women become the sufferings of Christ (and vice versa), but oppressed women also become comforters to the Comforter. These women make a way for Jesus, who is the Way. This interweaving of Jesus and those who would follow him is striking: The women who remove the thorns and briers from Jesus's feet add to the work of Jesus. Jesus, in other words, needs others to make his work complete. Those who follow Jesus are not simply passive recipients of his saving work; they are summoned to become coworkers with him.

Grant extends the scope of the incarnation. The Christian scandal of particularity, Jesus Christ, takes root in lives other than his own. "God becomes concrete not only in the man Jesus, for he was crucified, but in the lives of those who will accept the challenges of the risen Savior the Christ. . . . This Christ, found in the experiences of Black women, is a Black woman."[108] As One who gathers laborers in the ongoing work of reconciliation, who is present with marginalized women as cosufferer and empowerer, Jesus takes shape in the bodies of black women.

Grant's language of identity is strong: by claiming that Christ *is* a black woman, she offers a corrective to Christologies that view black women as theologically "other." When Christology has been used to marginalize black women on the basis of gender and race, such a corrective is sorely needed. By recognizing incarnation in black female bodies, moreover, Grant considers the humanity of Jesus, rather than his gender, to be of ultimate significance. In coming to his particular form in first-century Israel, he comes to *all* persons throughout history. Only in and through the particular is there any hope for all creation. What is most enduring about Grant's approach to the story of Jesus is this: As we form an understanding of who Jesus is, we also need to pay attention to the arc of our lives. Jesus's story gives life as it attends to the particularity of our own unique stories.

Catherine Keller (1953–)

One of the leading American constructive theologians, Catherine Keller received her bachelor's degree at the University of Heidelberg (Germany), before her theological studies in the United States. Her PhD work at Claremont was under the guidance of John Cobb, one of the most significant process theologians of the last century. Process theology questions understandings of God that absolutize God's unchanging nature and monarchial power. The God of the Scriptures, process theologians claim, is not unmoved, unchanging, and absolute in power, but shows vulnerability, responsiveness, and even adaptation as God interacts with creation. Through a sophisticated system of philosophical analysis, process theology constructs an alternative to classical theism. Keller's work is influenced by this strand of modern theology, but is also conversant with feminist, ecological, and poststructuralist thought. The result is a multilayered, narrative approach to understanding Jesus, evident in her most systematic work, *On the Mystery*.

As she interprets Jesus, Keller names a distinct problem in history of doctrine: The classical creeds tend to abstract the Christ of faith from the life of Jesus. "The creeds all emphasize a supernatural origin, then cut right from his birth to his death and resurrection. They lack all mention of his living and speaking and loving, of his preaching, wisdom, healing, and prophecy."[109] She claims that Christ has become the shibboleth of Christian faith, the slogan that we must parrot correctly in order to stay within the fold of the faithful. In its most distorted form, this shibboleth is that we confess Christ as our personal Lord and Savior. The intricacy and multivalence of Jesus gets boiled down to a phrase (whether in a creed or a personal testimony) that must be accepted in order for us to be considered Christ's legitimate followers. In an aside, Keller remarks that it is doubtful whether Jesus himself would have passed the test of proper confession.

In response to these reductions of Jesus, Keller returns—in some respects—to the source: the Gospels, which depict Jesus's life and ministry. To understand who Jesus is, we look to his teachings, healings, and table fellowship. In these words and gestures, Jesus reveals the *basilea*, often translated as the "kingdom." Keller, however, avoids the patriarchal overtones of the typical English translation by retaining the Greek transliteration. In her interpretation of Jesus, the *basilea* is political, but never exhausted by political. "The *basilea* is not a political programme. But neither does it leave politics alone—especially when a contemporary empire draws upon Christ for legitimation."[110] Approximated, perhaps, in the language of "commonwealth," Jesus's actions focus on the common good of all under God. Jesus points to the *basilea* in his preaching, anticipates it in his parables, and embodies it in his healing. The *basilea* is something he claims has arrived already *and* is waiting yet to come: something that is present in his person *and* beyond him.

We see the *basilea* most distinctly in Jesus's parables that "deliberately and simultaneously . . . conceal what is revealed and reveal what it concealed."[111] Jesus's parables illustrate, but they don't erase mystery and questions about the *basilea*. And perhaps most importantly, Jesus does not tell parables about himself; they are about *others*: laborers in field, mustard seeds, creation, relationships. Jesus's telling of parables gives an indication of his purpose for coming and what salvation looks like: not so much to gather all people to himself, but to connect people to each other. "Jesus was simply not interested in people's relation to God in abstraction from their relation to others."[112] Jesus comes to connect and to show us new life through connection. The parables, which often focus on the vulnerable, such as laborers in the field, are firmly planted in this world. Salvation is to be freed for one another, especially those on the margins: "It is not just that *Jesus* is inseparable from the most vulnerable members of our own species: it is that he is teaching that inseparability as our *own* ultimate condition."[113] We are who we are in and through others.

In questioning some of the abstractions of the classical creeds, Keller also retains and reinterprets some of their elements. One of these retained elements is her interpretation of Jesus's uniqueness. To claim Jesus as unique is to claim "only this person, as far as we know, has so *realized* the divine lure as to become 'at one' with it. That intimate union or 'sonship' is not a metaphysical given but an event of becoming, itself symbolized by Jesus' baptism."[114] But in most renderings of Christ's uniqueness, he *alone* is God's Son. This is precisely where Keller asks questions again: The point of salvation, she argues, is not to keep us at a distance from God, but so that we too might become sons and daughters of God. "But to all who received him, who believed in his name, he gave power to become children of God" (John 1:12). Here Keller recalls one of the earliest understandings of salvation in the tradition. Salvation is not the mere balancing of the scales of justice, not only the cosmic defeat of evil, not only rekindling our hearts to love. Salvation, in its fullest sense, is glorification and divinization, whereby we become, by grace, a partaker in God's very life. This theme, echoed throughout history in mystics and martyrs, gains fresh perspective in Keller's imaginative reappropriation of Jesus's parables. One need not adopt neo-process thought to reclaim this important insight: Jesus comes to heal, reconnect, and transform, so that all might participate in the fullness that is God's life for the world.

Amos Yong (1965–)

One of the most prolific contemporary theologians on any continent, Yong was born in Malaysia to ethnic Chinese parents and immigrated to the United States as a child. Raised in the holiness tradition, Yong earned his bachelor's degree at Bethany College of the Assemblies of God and his PhD at Boston University. He is a leading Pentecostal theologian whose writings reveal an astonishing array of interests: interreligious dialogue, disability studies, hermeneutics, race, missiology, and political theology. He approaches each of these themes employing the loci of classical theology, with particular emphasis on the work of the Spirit. Indeed, as a renewal theologian, one of his chief aims is for the wider church (and not simply holiness traditions) to uplift the work of the Spirit in its thought and practice. His interpretation of Jesus consistently emphasizes Jesus as inspired by the Spirit, who accomplishes salvation and invites us to be participants in his work.

Yong's interpretation of Jesus is marked by close readings of the New Testament. In this sense, his Christology gets "back to the sources." As he reads Scripture, the Gospel of Luke emerges as particularly significant, since it emphasizes the role of the Spirit throughout Jesus's ministry. We see in this Gospel that Jesus is incarnate of the Spirit and that his entire life is Spirit-empowered.[115] From beginning to end, the Gospels connect Jesus to the Spirit: salvation in Christ, then, is also the work of the Spirit. Yong employs the traditional categories for interpreting Christ's saving work. He pays particular attention to Jesus's death. In a subtle critique of Anselmian visions of the atonement, which tend to isolate the cross from the life of Jesus and construe it as a demand imposed for the sake of divine justice, Yong claims that the cross represents Jesus's submission "to the consequences of sin" and destruction of "sin's power of death precisely through his perfected suffering and resurrection from the dead."[116] The cross, in this reading, is not something that God imposes on Jesus, but signifies the sin that Jesus overcomes through his sinless life. The sinless One submits himself to the cross not because God demands it, but in order to overcome the power of sin. Furthermore, Yong claims that Jesus's death does not glorify or consecrate violence as the means by which redemption is accomplished. Rather, the cross, in the end, evacuates violence of its power: God does not endorse violence, but chooses to work even through the violence that the world imposes: "While violence was clearly a part of the passion of Christ, it is more accurate to say that God uses and exposes its mechanisms rather than sanctions them." God redeems "the world despite the violence of evil people. Thus the sacrificial death of Christ, with whom God identifies, reveals a God of peace who submits to the violence of sinners in order to redeem the world from its spiral of violence."[117] The atonement, though it employs violence, ultimately leads to nonviolence. For the way of Jesus is the way of peace.

Though the cross might symbolize the depths and heights of Jesus's work, for Yong it is the entire trajectory of Christ's life that is salvific. Jesus's life "of humiliation and exaltation . . . overcomes the powers of sin, death, and the devil, and reopens the pathway to eternal life in the presence of God."[118] We cannot isolate a single moment of Jesus's life as what "saves," just as we cannot separate the life of Christ from the ongoing presence of the Spirit in his life. Jesus becomes, then, not simply the one who enacts salvation on our behalf; he is rather both the object and model for our faith. "People are thus to believe in him and emulate him."[119] To know Jesus, for Yong, is also to follow him. The portrait of Jesus and the portrait of the believer are in this sense forever interwoven.

Yong's most systematic treatment of Christ's person and work concludes with a threefold analysis of salvation in Christ, thus reclaiming a slogan of Philipp Melanchthon's that to know Christ is to know Christ's benefits.[120] First, Jesus's "sinless life breaks the power of sin and its attendant guilt on human hearts." Second, "Christ's miraculous ministry cures human bodies wracked by sin, heals human souls oppressed by sin, and reconciles human communities ravaged by sin." Third, "Christ's 'substitutionary atoning death, bodily resurrection, triumphant ascension, and abiding intercession' are the culmination and extension of his sinless life and miraculous ministry, not to be separated from the latter."[121] Life, ministry, death, resurrection, and ascension are interconnected, all one arc of the Spirit at work to draw all flesh near. To isolate one of these moments is to truncate the fullness of salvation offered in Christ through the Spirit. Ultimately, this salvation is the work of reconciliation: to bring together what has become estranged. In an intriguing exegesis of the Zacchaeus story (a pericope only found in Luke), Yong writes that Zacchaeus's "reconciliation to the God of Jesus included reconciliation with others, including his enemies (assuming he had them), and not merely interpersonally but also socially, politically, and economically, indicating that these are not extraneous to the gospel."[122] Jesus comes so that all might participate in the fullness of life in the Spirit.

Yong's Christology is steadfastly pneumato-centric. By connecting the Spirit to the entire trajectory of Jesus's work, he underscores the notion that salvation is not merely forensic, but involves the life of the believer in the life of the Triune God. And by considering salvation to embrace the body (both the body politic and individual bodies), Yong's account of salvation is holistic. This might be one of the gifts that Pentecostal theology bequeaths to the wider church, to recover the early sense of salvation as *sōtēria* (healing and wholeness), encompassing body and soul. Otherwise the Word doesn't really become flesh and dwell among us.

Conclusion

Twentieth-century portraits of Jesus are astonishingly diverse. How does one do justice to the array of Christologies presented in this chapter, especially when we could have easily included twice as many theologians? There probably is no way to do them all justice. And yet amid this diversity some common themes emerge: First is the recognition that Christ does not belong to any particular culture. The twentieth century began to live into the reality of Christianity's non-Western character. If the gospel began as "foolishness to Gentiles" (1 Cor 1:23), as Christianity enters its third millennium, a full two-thirds of Christians now live in the global South. Both of these recognitions of Christianity's origin and current status suggest that no one philosophy, worldview, or culture can claim Christ as its own. Instead, all cultures belong to Christ, and we should expect Jesus's portrait to take on different hues in differing contexts.

Second, many of the portraits of Jesus offered in this pivotal century point to the need to interpret the violence of the cross. In a century of cataclysmic slaughter, one is left asking, How is God in Christ present amid such violence? Many of the theologians we have encountered in this chapter remind us that the life of Jesus was no stranger to violence, and that even God is affected by it. As God seeks to make all things new, it is important that we attend to the violence inflicted on Christ, and the ways in which that violence (economic, political, military, and otherwise) is still present today.

Finally, the varied portraits of Christ also point to the multidimensionality of salvation in Christ. Christ's work, for most theologians of this century, is rarely boiled down to a single image. Instead, to consider Jesus rightly, we consider him as Prince of Peace, Liberator, Forgiver, Healer, Suffering Servant, Lamb of God, Ancestor, and Friend. Salvation in Christ involves the whole person: economic, political, physical, and spiritual. "I came that they may have life, and have it abundantly" (John 10:10). In order to signify this life, Jesus will always have many names.

Notes

1. Though he does not use this exact phrase, second naiveté is usually connected to the work of Paul Ricouer, who argues that contemporary interpretation moves beyond first readings, where one accepts previously established interpretations on the basis of authority, to a critique of those authorities, and finally, to a second naiveté that allows us to approach the religious text afresh. See Ricoeur, *From Text to Action: Essays in Hermeneutics II* (Evanston, IL: Northwestern University Press, 1991), 89–101.
2. Pierre Teilhard de Chardin, *The Divine Milieu* (New York: Harper & Row, 1968), 124.
3. Chardin, *Divine Milieu*, 125.
4. Chardin, *Divine Milieu*, 62.
5. Chardin, *Divine Milieu*, 72.

6. Chardin, *Divine Milieu*, 82.
7. Chardin, *Divine Milieu*, 103–4.
8. Chardin, *Divine Milieu*, 128.
9. Rudolf Bultmann, *Jesus Christ and Mythology* (New York: Charles Scribner's Sons, 1958), 12–13.
10. Bultmann, *Jesus Christ and Mythology*, 23.
11. Bultmann, *Jesus Christ and Mythology*, 31–32.
12. Bultmann, *Jesus Christ and Mythology*, 82.
13. Bultmann, *Jesus Christ and Mythology*, 40.
14. Karl Barth, *Church Dogmatics*, vol. IV/2, *The Doctrine of Reconciliation*, ed. Geoffrey W. Bromiley and T. F. Torrance (Edinburgh: T&T Clark, 1958), 177.
15. Barth, *Doctrine of Reconciliation*, IV/2:171–72.
16. Barth, *Doctrine of Reconciliation*, IV/2:180.
17. Karl Barth, *Church Dogmatics*, vol. II/2, *The Doctrine of God*, ed. Geoffrey W. Bromiley and T. F. Torrance (Edinburgh: T&T Clark, 1957), 94.
18. Karl Barth, *The Humanity of God*, trans. John Newton Thomas (Louisville: John Knox Press, 1960), 46.
19. Karl Barth, *Church Dogmatics*, vol. IV/1, *The Doctrine of Reconciliation*, ed. Bromiley and Torrance (London: T & T Clark International, 1956), 188.
20. Barth, *Doctrine of Reconciliation*, IV/1:222.
21. Barth, *Doctrine of Reconciliation*, IV/1:222.
22. Barth, *Doctrine of God*, II/2:750.
23. Barth, *Doctrine of God*, II/2:162–64.
24. Paul Tillich, *Dynamics of Faith* (New York: Harper & Row, 1957), 41–42.
25. Paul Tillich, *Systematic Theology* (Chicago: University of Chicago Press, 1951–1957), 1:133.
26. Tillich, *Systematic Theology*, 1:134.
27. Tillich, *Systematic Theology*, 1:136.
28. Tillich, *Dynamics*, 29.
29. Tillich, *Dynamics*, 97.
30. Tillich, *Systematic Theology*, 2:155.
31. Tillich, *Systematic Theology*, 2:176–79.

32. H. Richard Niebuhr, *Christ and Culture*, 2nd ed. (San Francisco: HarperSanFrancisco, 2001), 16.
33. Niebuhr, *Christ and Culture*, 19.
34. Niebuhr, *Christ and Culture*, 22.
35. Niebuhr, *Christ and Culture*, 27. Echoing this, one of Niebuhr's later works traces this "radical monotheism" in relation to culture. H. Richard Niebuhr, *Radical Monotheism and Western Culture* (New York: Harper, 1960).
36. Niebuhr, *Christ and Culture*, 29.
37. Karl Rahner, *Foundations of Christian Faith: An Introduction to the Idea of Christianity*, trans. William V. Dych (New York: Crossroad, 1978), 197.
38. Rahner, *Foundations*, 181. "The goal of the world is God's self-communication to it." Rahner, *Foundations*, 192.
39. Rahner, *Foundations*, 195.
40. Rahner, *Foundations*, 279.
41. Rahner, *Foundations*, 316.
42. Hans Urs von Balthasar, *Theo-drama*, vol. 3, *The Dramatis Personae: The Person in Christ*, trans. Graham Harrison (San Francisco: Ignatius, 1992), 225.
43. Balthasar, *Dramatis Personae*, 231.
44. Balthasar, *Dramatis Personae*, 225.
45. Hans Urs von Balthasar, *Theo-drama*, vol. 4, *The Action*, trans. Graham Harrison (San Francisco: Ignatius, 1994), 324.
46. Balthasar, *The Action*, 330.
47. Hans Urs von Balthasar, *Elucidations*, trans. John Riches (London: SPCK, 1975), 51.
48. Dietrich Bonhoeffer, *Sanctorum Communio: A Theological Study of the Sociology of the Church*, ed. Clifford J. Green, Dietrich Bonhoeffer Works 1 (Minneapolis: Fortress Press, 1998), 211.
49. Dietrich Bonhoeffer, *Discipleship*, ed. Geffrey B. Kelly and John D. Godsey, Dietrich Bonhoeffer Works 4 (Minneapolis: Fortress Press, 2001), 45.
50. Dietrich Bonhoeffer, *Letters and Papers from Prison*, ed. Eberhard Bethge, enlarged ed. (New York: Macmillan, 1971), 279.
51. Bonhoeffer, *Letters*, 281.

52. Bonhoeffer, *Letters*, 337.
53. Bonhoeffer, *Letters*, 361.
54. Bonhoeffer, *Letters*, 362.
55. John XXIII, quoted in Paul McPartlan, "Vatican II," in *The Cambridge Dictionary of Christian Theology*, ed. Ian A. McFarland et al. (Cambridge: Cambridge University Press, 2011), 528.
56. *Lumen Gentium*, in *Vatican Council II: The Conciliar and Post Conciliar Documents*, ed. Austin Flannery (Northport, NY: Costello, 1992), 357–58.
57. *Gaudium et Spes*, in Flannery, *Vatican Council II*, 943.
58. *Gaudium et Spes*, 941.
59. *Gaudium et Spes*, 924.
60. *Gaudium et Spes*, 932.
61. *Gaudium et Spes*, 911.
62. *Lumen Gentium*, 367.
63. *Gaudium et Spes*, 924.
64. An excellent survey of Panikkar's Christology is found in Don Schweitzer, *Contemporary Christologies* (Minneapolis: Fortress Press, 2010), 100–107. I am indebted to Schweitzer for his identification of salient themes in Panikkar's vast corpus of writings.
65. See Panikkar, *The Trinity and the Religious Experience of Man* (New York: Orbis Books, 1973), 46–64.
66. Raymond Panikkar, *Christophany: The Fullness of Man* (Maryknoll, NY: Orbis Books, 2004), 135.
67. Schweitzer, *Contemporary Christologies*, 104.
68. Raymond Panikkar, "Confrontation between Hinduism and Christianity," *New Blackfriars* 50, no. 584 (January 1969): 200. In addition to the suffering God, Panikkar claims that Christology also shows Hindus the divinity of humanity and the humanity of divinity.
69. Jürgen Moltmann, *The Crucified God*, trans. R. A. Wilson and John Bowden (New York: Harper & Row, 1974), 243.
70. Moltmann, *Crucified God*, 246. For Moltmann, the Son "is in fact taken up into the inner life of God, if in the cross of Christ he experiences the love of God for the godless, the enemies, in so far as the history of Christ is the inner life of God himself." *Crucified God*, 249.

71. Jürgen Moltmann, *Theology of Hope*, trans. James W. Leitch (New York: Harper & Row, 1967), 197.
72. Moltmann, *Theology of Hope*, 201.
73. Gustavo Gutiérrez, *A Theology of Liberation*, trans. Sister Caridad Inda and John Eagleson, rev. ed. (Maryknoll, NY: Orbis, 1988), 97.
74. Gutiérrez, *A Theology of Liberation*, 104.
75. Gutiérrez, *A Theology of Liberation*, 85.
76. Gutiérrez, *A Theology of Liberation*, 91.
77. Sallie McFague, *The Body of God: An Ecological Theology* (Minneapolis: Fortress Press, 1993), 162.
78. McFague, *Body of God*, 164.
79. McFague is fond of quoting "God's Grandeur," a poem by Gerard Manley Hopkins.
80. McFague, *Body of God*, 191.
81. See Sallie McFague, "Kenotic Theology," in *Blessed Are the Consumers: Climate Change and the Practice of Restraint* (Minneapolis: Fortress Press, 2013).
82. Mercy Amba Oduyoye, *Hearing and Knowing: Theological Reflections on Christianity in Africa* (Maryknoll, NY: Orbis, 1986), 102.
83. Mercy Amba Oduyoye, "Jesus Christ," in *The Cambridge Companion to Feminist Theology*, ed. Susan Frank Parsons (Cambridge: Cambridge University Press, 2002), 152.
84. Mercy Amba Oduyoye and Elizabeth Amoah, "The Christ for African Women," in *With Passion and Compassion: Third World Women Doing Theology*, ed. Virginia Fabella and Mercy Amba Oduyoye (Maryknoll, NY: Orbis, 1988), 43.
85. Oduyoye, "Jesus Christ," 164.
86. Oduyoye, "Jesus Christ," 166.
87. Rosemary Radford Ruether, *Sexism and God-Talk: Toward a Feminist Theology* (Boston: Beacon, 1983), 125.
88. Ruether, *Sexism and God-Talk*, 120.
89. Ruether, *Sexism and God-Talk*, 121.
90. Ruether, *Sexism and God-Talk*, 135.
91. Ruether, *Sexism and God-Talk*, 137.

92. Elizabeth Johnson, *She Who Is: The Mystery of God in Feminist Theological Discourse* (New York: Crossroad, 1992), 152.

93. "Jesus the Christ is the Wisdom of God in a concrete, historical gestalt." Johnson, *She Who Is*, 167.

94. Johnson, *She Who Is*, 158.

95. Johnson, *She Who Is*, 159.

96. The final chapter of *She Who Is* includes a litany of remembrance of women who were tortured and killed for the "cause" of the faith. Johnson, *She Who Is*, 262.

97. Johnson, *She Who Is*, 161.

98. Johnson, *She Who Is*, 163.

99. It is no coincidence that a subsequent book explored ecclesiology as the communion of the saints: Elizabeth Johnson, *Friends of God and Prophets* (New York: Continuum, 1998).

100. James Cone, *God of the Oppressed*, rev. ed. (Maryknoll, NY: Orbis, 1997), 125–26.

101. Cone, *God of the Oppressed*, 123.

102. Cone, *God of the Oppressed*, 125.

103. James Cone, "Black Theology in American Religion," *Journal of the American Academy of Religion* 53 (December 1985): 769.

104. Cone, *God of the Oppressed*, 124.

105. James Cone, *The Cross and the Lynching Tree* (Maryknoll, NY: Orbis, 2011), 158.

106. Jacquelyn Grant, *White Women's Christ and Black Women's Jesus* (Atlanta: Scholars Press, 1989), 212.

107. Grant, *White Women's Christ*, 213.

108. Grant, *White Women's Christ*, 220.

109. Catherine Keller, *On the Mystery: Discerning God in Process* (Minneapolis: Fortress Press, 2008), 136.

110. Keller, *On the Mystery*, 135.

111. Keller, *On the Mystery*, 137.

112. Keller, *On the Mystery*, 143.

113. Keller, *On the Mystery*, 144.

114. Keller, *On the Mystery*, 151.

115. Amos Yong, *Renewing Christian Theology: Systematics for a Global Christianity* (Waco, TX: Baylor University Press, 2014), 239.
116. Yong, *Renewing Christian Theology*, 244.
117. Yong, *Renewing Christian Theology*, 252.
118. Yong, *Renewing Christian Theology*, 245.
119. Yong, *Renewing Christian Theology*, 245.
120. Yong writes, in his analysis of the New Testament witness, that "Christ's person is inextricably tied in and with his work; in fact, who Christ is in himself is less vital than who he is *as us* and what he has done *for us*." Yong, *Renewing Christian Theology*, 238.
121. Yong, *Renewing Christian Theology*, 247–49.
122. Yong, *Renewing Christian Theology*, 227.

7

The Many Faces of Jesus: Reflections on the Future of Christology

Surveying two thousand years of the interpretation of Jesus is daunting and bewildering. In many respects, this book has only scratched the surface of Christology. I could have easily included four times the number of voices that I have examined. At best, this book has provided a few of the prominent highlights in the history of interpreting Jesus, exploring voices that still have an impact today. But it is obvious from this survey that the voices that are interpreting Jesus are constantly expanding. If that is the case, Christology surely has a future and it is likely a bright one. As the Christian church turns toward its third millennium, the ongoing work of interpreting Jesus for our time will surely continue. As the church embarks on that work, it will rely on those who have gone before, even as it looks toward including new voices in the conversation about Jesus. How might we draw on the collective past while searching for fresh ways to interpret the Word made flesh? I conclude with five remarks on things that "matter" as we seek to understand Jesus today and into tomorrow.

Culture Matters

The Jesus movement began as a renewing spirit within the faith of Israel. The first followers of Jesus, in the main, were Jews and Jesus himself was a Jew. Jesus Christ came to a particular culture and "was sent only to the lost sheep of the house of Israel" (Matt 15:24). The incarnation came to a specific culture, and when the church's interpretation of Jesus forgets Jewish culture (as it does when it espouses Christian supersessionism), it distorts the Jesus of the Gospels. However the church interprets Jesus, it interprets him falsely if it removes him wholly from the faith of Israel. There must always be some relationship between the church's confession of Christ and the faith that Jesus called his own.

At the same time that Jesus must bear some relationship to Jewish faith and culture, it is also clear that Jesus is not limited to *any* culture. Indeed, as the course of this book has shown, Jesus crops up in a wide variety of cultures that have also adopted him as their own (or perhaps better said, cultures that Christ has adopted as his own). The future of the church's Christology is therefore multicultural. We should expect and embrace the fact that religious iconography, theology, and biblical interpretation will take on the hues of the world's varied cultures. Jesus has many cultural faces, and this fact is not merely sociological. Indeed, it is borne out in the church's incarnational theology: As Word becomes flesh, Jesus comes to culture, taking and blessing it as his very own. If Jesus comes to a particular culture in the first century, he also comes to the world and to every culture. Every culture seeks to express him in its own vocabulary and idiom. In doing so, each culture recognizes its need for other expressions of Jesus. As H. Richard Niebuhr wrote, "Every man looking upon the same Jesus Christ in faith will make his statement of what Christ is to him; but he will not confound his relative statement with the absolute Christ."[1] It is therefore important not only that cultures and groups arrive at *their own* confessions of Jesus, but that they look to the witness of others as well. To interpret Jesus rightly, we need to look to cultures other than our own.

Bodies Matter

Word becomes flesh and dwells among us (John 1:14). Christ's incarnation means that bodies matter to our lives and to the life of God. Some seasons in the church's history have veered toward Gnosticism, toward the idea that bodies are a burden eventually to be destroyed. But orthodox Christology has always claimed something different: that somehow, some way, in Jesus, God blesses and claims the human body as God's very own. Jesus comes to heal bodies broken by sin, disease, and hunger. Salvation in Christ is not simply a matter of the soul, but involves the whole person, renewed in the image of God. The root word for salvation, *sōtēr*, connotes healing and deliverance. Jesus spends much of his ministry healing and feeding bodies. A full interpretation of Jesus will entail the recognition that all bodies are blessed by God: male and female, temporarily abled and disabled, young and old, Eastern and Western and all points in between. In coming to flesh, Jesus embraces all flesh as his own. Christology in the future must continue to attend to the body: how the body aches and how it is healed;

how our bodies long and desire; how we touch and connect; how we perceive beauty in all bodies. This will require a reexamination of the aesthetics of Christian faith, grounded in an apprehension of Jesus, the beauty of God.

Others Matter

In the Gospels, particularly the Synoptics, Jesus spends far more time talking about others than about himself. His actions—touching, blessing, healing, feeding, proclaiming, and forgiving—are other-directed. In his words and gestures, Jesus points to others and to the living God. Interpretations of Jesus, then, ought to avoid excessive self-reference. Jesus did not come to save himself; neither did he come to save folks like ourselves. Instead, Jesus stood at the threshold of the Jewish-gentile world, in the company of persons of varied backgrounds and cultures. As a person from Galilee, Jesus lived on the borders. His ministry centered on Galilee, and his followers are told to head to Galilee to meet the risen Christ (Mark 16:7), where he has already gone ahead of them. Jesus's life is one of encounter, and he invites us as his followers to encounter others as well. The church's confession of Jesus as the Christ ought to not leave us alone or with others like us, but introduce us to a wider world. The way of Jesus is not one of self-justification, or of the demonstration of the superiority of one form of faith over another. Rather, it is a way that leads into the company of others. One test of Christology for the future is the degree to which it invites openness to the others in our midst.

Violence Matters

Throughout the ages, the most prominent image for Jesus (and of the entire Christian movement) has been the cross. This symbol reminds us that a horrific execution stands at the center of Christian confession. Violence surrounds the interpretation of Jesus, just as it surrounds and ends Jesus's life. The church's interpretation of this violence has ebbed and flowed throughout the centuries: at times it has glorified it; at others it has minimized it. But, in the end, there is no escape from the violence that surrounds Jesus, just as there is no way to escape the violence that has infected human life since the dawn of time. The question is not whether to accept or ignore such violence; the question is how to interpret it and how to keep it in the front of Christian imagination. We interpret Jesus best when, like some in the medieval period and like contemporary liberation theologians, we consider the violence of the cross to be not a penalty or a demand imposed by God on an innocent victim, but when we see in it God's radical act of solidarity with those who endure the violence of a sin-sick world. It is the curse of the world's violence that sends Jesus to the cross, not the decree of a distant God. As we stand at the foot of the cross, our hearts are turned to all who suffer, to all who are in pain, to all who are oppressed. As our hearts are turned there, we are empowered by grace to work against violence. Because God in Christ suffers on the cross, moreover, there is nothing we can undergo, no place we can inhabit, where God is not already present *with us*. The cross points to God's radical act in Jesus, Immanuel (God with us), never to be apart from us. And because God is with us, there is always hope. The cross, in the end, empties violence of its power: God submits to it, and ultimately reveals it as empty. Our interpretations of Jesus, then, must continually bear in mind that the One who submits to the world's violence is also the Prince of Peace.

Life Matters

As prominent as the cross is in interpretations of Jesus, it does not have the final word. After Good Friday is Easter: God's vindication of the life of Jesus and the life of all creation. Christian confession of Jesus is also a confession of resurrection: that somehow, in some way, God brings new life out of loss, a new thing out of God-forsakenness. Jesus comes for the sake of life in abundance (John 10:10). Some of the earliest interpretations of Jesus (such as Irenaeus's) emphasized that Jesus came to renew not only human life but also the life of the earth. In an age of ecological devastation, this conviction is all the more important. How is the confession of Jesus as the Christ good news not just for humanity, but for the life of the world? It is such when those who confess Christ are spurred to take part in the healing inaugurated in Jesus's ministry: healing relationships, healing families, healing nations, healing the earth. Perhaps the most significant test of an interpretation of Jesus is whether it is life-affirming. In a world that witnesses unspeakable acts of death on a near-daily basis, whether in the form of vanishing polar ice or senseless mass killings in schools and houses of worship, to confess Christ as Lord of life is also to resist the forces that would destroy life. The interpretation of Jesus ought to lead to renewed life, wherever we find ourselves on this increasingly imperiled planet that we call home.

Notes

1. H. Richard Niebuhr, *Christ and Culture*, 2nd ed. (San Francisco: HarperSanFrancisco, 2001), 238.